The Invention of Sicily

The Invention of Sicily

A Mediterranean History

Jamie Mackay

VERSO

London • New York

First published by Verso 2021
© Jamie Mackay 2021

1 3 5 7 9 10 8 6 4 2

Verso
UK: 6 Meard Street, London W1F 0EG
US: 20 Jay Street, Suite 1010, Brooklyn, NY 11201
versobooks.com

Verso is the imprint of New Left Books

ISBN-13: 978-1-78663-773-4
ISBN-13: 978-1-78663-776-5 (US EBK)
ISBN-13: 978-1-78663-775-8 (UK EBK)

British Library Cataloguing in Publication Data
A catalogue record for this book is available from the British Library

Library of Congress Cataloging-in-Publication Data

Names: Mackay, Jamie Alexander Calum, 1990– author.
Title: The invention of Sicily : [a Mediterranean history] / Jamie Mackay.
Description: London ; New York : Verso, 2021. | Includes bibliographical
  references and index. | Summary: 'In this riveting, rich history, Jamie
  Mackay peels away the layers of this most mysterious of islands. It is a
  story with its origins in ancient legend that has reinvented itself
  across centuries: in conquest and resistance. Inseparable from these
  political and social developments is the nation's cultural patrimony' –
  Provided by publisher.
Identifiers: LCCN 2021017521 (print) | LCCN 2021017522 (ebook) | ISBN
  9781786637734 (hardback) | ISBN 9781786637765 (US ebk) | ISBN
  9781786637758 (UK ebk)
Subjects: LCSH: Sicily (Italy) – History.
Classification: LCC DG866 .M317 2021 (print) | LCC DG866 (ebook) | DDC
  945.8 – dc23
LC record available at https://lccn.loc.gov/2021017521
LC ebook record available at https://lccn.loc.gov/2021017522

Typeset in Fournier by MJ & N Gavan, Truro, Cornwall
Printed and bound by CPI Group (UK) Ltd, Croydon CR0 4YY

Contents

PART II: The Hypocrisies of Nationalism

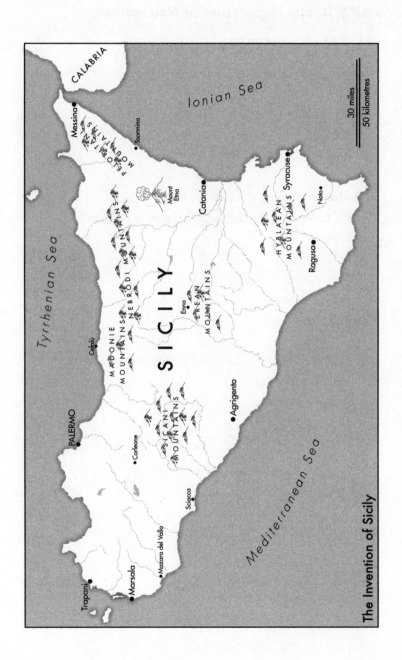

The Invention of Sicily

Introduction
The Limits of the West

The atlases say that Sicily is an island, and that might well be true. Yet one has some doubts, especially when you think that an island usually corresponds to a homogenous blob of race and customs. Here everything is mixed, changing, contradictory, just as one finds in the most diverse, pluralistic of continents.

Gesualdo Bufalino, novelist

I've always held that Sicily represents many problems, and many contradictions, that are not just Italian, but are also European in scope ... to some extent this island serves as a metaphor for the entire world.

Leonardo Sciascia, novelist and essayist

Sicily is one of the world's most important borderlands. Situated at the very centre of the Mediterranean, equidistant from Rome and Tripoli, closer to Tunis than Naples, the island marks the frontier between southern Europe and North Africa. For centuries people have viewed this volcanic landmass as a point of division between 'civilised' and 'barbarian' peoples, Christianity and Islam, and most tentatively and destructively of all, between

white and black races. Sicily has been surrounded by almost constant conflict. Ever since the third century BC, when the consuls
of the Roman Republic demarked the island as the frontline of
the Punic Wars, it has come to separate the Western world from
what lies beyond. In the medieval period, Catholic orders used
Sicily as a base from which to launch crusades against Muslims
in Jerusalem and, in later centuries, against the Ottomans. In the
twentieth century, Mussolini imagined the island as the centre
of his Mediterranean empire and, after WWII, the Americans
built NATO airfields and submarine bases along the south coast
to protect their interests in the Middle East. Today, right-wing
populists continue to perpetuate this divisive logic by presenting Sicily as the site of an 'invasion' by refugees, who they claim
pose a threat to a European way of life.

Borders, though, are rarely as definite as they appear on maps.
The longer you spend living around them, the less sense these
kinds of simplistic divisions make. Frontiers are places where
identities take on absurdly definite forms, in barbed wire fences
and vigilante patrols. At the same time, they're places where
boundaries between different cultures break down. Sicilian history is white, Christian and Western, certainly, but it has also
been, and still is, black, Arab and Muslim among other things.
Such ambiguities are present everywhere, but they are particularly visible on the shores of the Mediterranean. This is what
makes the region so exciting. It's also what makes it difficult and,
for some, uncomfortable. In a recent book, the author Kapka
Kassabova describes the frontier between Bulgaria, Greece and
Turkey rather poetically as a place where the divisions 'between
self and other, intention and action, dreaming and waking' dis-
solve.[1] The same might well be said of Sicily. Greek temples
blend with Norman castles, Spanish-baroque villas and English

gardens. The island itself is a kind of mirage which only becomes visible at the intersections of these complex cultural exchanges; precisely where the divisions between historical eras, identities and nations are at their most obscure. For the uninitiated this can be disorienting. During a visit to Sicily in 1910, Sigmund Freud took a carriage from Palermo, the capital, to Agrigento on the south coast. When he reached Syracuse, the island's most important ancient city, he was impressed by the art and architecture. Yet something disturbed him about this exotic, stiflingly hot place. Sicily, he reflected, was a benchmark of Western civilisation, but at the same time it was also wild and somehow dangerous. It was both inside and outside Europe. Shortly after returning to Vienna, the psychoanalyst was struck by an intense bout of paranoia and began to doubt his professional vocation. Later in life he came to view Sicily as a place where the unconscious and conscious minds become muddled: a limit point of the Ego itself.

Of course, Sicilians do not experience their homeland in such neurotic, fragmented terms. For the islanders themselves, life is and has always been characterised by the almost constant exchange of people and ideas across and beyond the Mediterranean. The enduring implications of this became clear to me in 2014 when I found myself talking with Leoluca Orlando, the mayor of Palermo, at a public event. I'd just moved to the city, and at the time I was looking to better understand how new migrants from Asia and Africa were integrating into the local community. Orlando insisted that to even begin to answer that question, and make some sense of the larger issue of how Sicily relates to the West, it would not be enough to think in terms of decades alone. Instead, he insisted, one has to engage seriously with the 'cosmopolitan roots' of the island's history, with a flow

of people that began in the ancient world and which, despite
various interruptions, has always had an impact on Sicilian identity. I was immediately struck by the mayor's use of the word
'cosmopolitan'. In the English-speaking world, this word often
serves as a euphemism for neoliberal globalisation. It's a concept
that a certain privileged elite, who have the resources to travel
for leisure, not to mention the right passport, use to voice their
frustrations with any form of localised, territorialised politics
that might seek to limit their power. When I suggested this to
Orlando, he retorted that this was just one rather hollow meaning
of the term. For most Sicilians, he continued, cosmopolitanism is
an *a priori* assumption, an unconscious, pre-political recognition
that all societies have a responsibility to humanity as a whole. Or,
as he rather boldly put it:

> Being Palermitan is not about blood, or heritage or even where you
> were born. It's about the simple choice of living in this city. This
> place has always been a kind of mosaic, a melting pot. We recognise
> difference not as something to be overcome, but as a value in itself.
> We find our unity not by clinging to what makes us exceptional, but
> when we mobilise among ourselves to defend universal human rights.

Of course Orlando does not speak for all Sicilians. Still, the
mayor is far from alone. He has served five terms in his position,
and enjoys considerable support among residents of Palermo
to this day. Since our meeting in 2014, I've come to learn that
hundreds of thousands of islanders, of different nationalities
and religions, have put forward their own versions of Orlando's
argument over the centuries, with myriad inflections. Sicilians
of all ages and social classes have contributed to this impressive humanistic vision, from the ancient philosophers who once

passed back and forth between Syracuse and the Library of Alexandria, to the fishermen who continue to rescue those in trouble at sea regardless of where they've come from. Somehow, though, scholars continue to overlook this aspect of the island's identity. While historians often describe Sicily as being 'multicultural', they usually do so as shorthand to describe a string of colonisations by Greeks, Romans, Byzantines, Arabs, Normans, French and Spanish, among other peoples. This is valid to a certain extent. There's a danger, though, that such a narrative ends up presenting the Sicilians themselves as passive victims of these global powers. Of course, anyone who has spent any time on the island will know that this is absolutely not the case. This book will therefore tell a different story: Sicily's history as an autonomous community rather than just a parenthesis to that of its better-known imperial masters. This is a story about kings and queens, wars and plagues and economic crises. What interests me most, though, are the deeper cultural processes through which Sicilians have constructed their own identity. By drawing on myths and legends, poems and paintings, recipes and protest slogans, I want to show how generations of islanders, from Greek tyrants and Roman slaves to medieval monarchs, bandits, socialist collectives and anti-mafia activists, have resisted outside oppressors to fight for their freedom.

In order to limit what could have been a sprawling tome, I've split the book into two sections. In part one, I cover a vast historical time frame, from the eighth century BC to the early modern period. This is by no means an exhaustive account. My goal here is simply to provide an overview of the diverse, polyglot, multi-ethnic, multicultural population that characterised Sicily's ancient and medieval history, and to offer a few suggestions about how this has impacted on the islanders' identity. In part two, I look in closer detail at Sicily's 'modern' history, from 1693 to the present day. As nationalism began to spread across continental Europe, numerous powers, from the Habsburg and Bourbon monarchies, to Italian liberals and fascists, sought to define the island by appeal to simplistic monocultural narratives. While they each succeeded to some degree, none fully achieved their goals. It's often said that Sicilians have rejected the idea of the modern state, and there is certainly some truth to this. In the final chapter, however, I argue that this scepticism is not only reactionary, it's also inextricably linked to the islanders' efforts to challenge the religious, nationalist and capitalist dogmas that have been imposed on them from afar. For this reason, it's surely worth considering seriously, and not, as is sometimes the case, simply rejected out of hand.

By the end of the book I hope the reader will have a better sense of the broad shape of Sicily's history, of how impressive and sometimes surprising its peoples' achievements were and how dramatic its recent decline has been. I do have another goal though. Since starting this project I've spent a considerable amount of time in Sicily reporting on the refugee crisis. This is, and remains, one of the key issues that will determine the island's future. In my conclusion I therefore return to the twenty-first century to outline what Sicily's history can tell us about this phenomenon. I've written elsewhere about the appalling conditions these individuals face, in asylum centres, in squats, waiting for work and residency permits or, in the worst cases, deportation. Here, though, I want to take the opportunity to highlight how migrants are also helping the island face up to some of its most difficult and long-standing problems, from poverty to organised crime and environmental devastation. This is a hugely important local story, but given the island's unique global history it inevitably raises issues that affect all of us. To really understand the possible implications for contemporary politics, however, there's no choice but to follow Orlando's advice and return to a time long before the island became a frontier, when Sicily was not just a European periphery but a meeting point for civilisations from across the ancient world.

PART I: Utopian Fragments

1
The Liquid Continent
(800 BC–826 AD)

The Colonies of Magna Graecia, Hellenistic Culture, Roman-Byzantine Occupations

After the fall of Troy, some of the Trojans escaped from the Achaeans, came in ships to Sicily, and settled next to the Sicanians ... There were also Phoenicians living all round Sicily, who had occupied promontories upon the seacoasts and the islets.

Thucydides, account of the Greek migrations
across Southern Italy, fifth century BC

Of all foreign nations Sicily was the first who joined herself to the friend-ship and alliance of the Roman people. She was the first to be called a province; and the provinces are a great ornament to the empire ... [It was here] our ancestors made their first strides to dominion over Africa.

Cicero, from his speech 'Against Verres', 70 BC

At the dawn of the eighth century BC the Mediterranean was just beginning to recover from a long period of social decline.

For centuries, since around 1200 BC, communities across the region that had once been centres of Bronze Age civilisation had been struggling against disease, natural disasters and piracy, which together decimated their populations. By 780 BC, however, many of the territories adjacent to the sea were beginning to recover. This was a time of reawakening. In the east, the Neo-Assyrian empire was beginning to expand its territory from Persia towards Egypt. To the west, the Etruscans were settling in the hills around Rome. Perhaps the most dramatic transformation, though, took place in the Greek-speaking city-states of the Aegean. For thousands of years peoples like the Minoans of Crete had played an important role in developing tools and early trade. But it wasn't until the eighth century that the most famous *poleis*, like Athens, Sparta and Corinth, began to develop from collections of villages into single, unified urban centres. New forms of culture emerged in tandem with this consolidation. In 776–72 BC, the first recorded Olympiad took place in the city of Elis, marking a new-found unity among the residents of these cities as well as a new calendar. Around the same time, Homer composed the *Iliad* and *Odyssey*, which are generally recognised as the founding works of Western literature. These dates are frustratingly vague, but together they represent the birth of a new kind of 'classical' world which, for our purposes here, marks the beginning of Sicily's own ancient history.

Scholars sometimes describe Sicily as being 'colonised' by Greece. It's important from the offset to distinguish this statement from the modern implications of that word. Starting from around 750 BC people from the Aegean cities did indeed settle on the island in large numbers. This immigration, though, was not so much a planned mission of territorial expansion – in an imperial model – as a spontaneous movement of peoples.

The Greek cities themselves were wealthy but politically volatile. Most were governed as autocracies, and, as such, rivalries among dynasties were fiercely fought, and wars were frequent. The urban areas were overcrowded and under-resourced, and on the islands, where fertile land was limited, famine was rife. As a result, hundreds of farmers, tradespeople, soldiers and priests decided to set out across the Mediterranean in search of fortune elsewhere. The majority headed towards Southern Italy, where they established small settlements across the Gulf of Taranto, in modern-day Puglia, in Calabria and eventually Naples on the Tyrrhenian coast. From the beginning, though, Sicily was one of the most coveted destinations. Its rich volcanic soil made it a good place to farm, and it also offered abundant supplies of alum, sulphur and salt, the last of which was highly valued in the Mediterranean market. Homer dedicated several verses to celebrating Sicily's natural advantages, describing it as a 'wooded isle' with 'innumerable goats' and 'well-watered meadows' where 'vines would never fail'.[1] Initially, the Greek presence on Sicily was limited to small conurbations and trading posts, but in 735 BC Thucles of Euboea founded Naxos, the first large-scale colony on the island, near modern-day Messina. This marked the beginning of a sustained programme of city building, which, over the centuries, attracted thousands of immigrants to the island.

The Greeks were the largest group to populate ancient Sicily, but they were not the island's only inhabitants. As early as the ninth century BC, long before Thucles and his followers were establishing themselves, the Phoenicians, a seafaring people from Tyre in modern-day Lebanon, had set up trading posts on the island's west coast, just across the water from what is now Tunisia. By the time the Greek presence was developing in a serious way, their own cities, the most important of which was named Motya, were already thriving thanks to a strong trade in silver, tin and luxury purple dyes. Sicily was also home to numerous smaller groups that historians sometimes call 'indigenous' peoples: namely the Sicanians, Sicels and Elymians. Some ancient Greek historians described these tribes as if they were primitive savages. In fact, they were well-organised agricultural societies, capable of producing metal weapons and other tools. Unfortunately, we know almost nothing about their values, culture or religion, though there is some evidence to suggest that they lived in large groups. The Roman Temple of Diana, for example, which is still accessible to visitors in the popular seaside resort of Cefalù in the north of Sicily, has Sicanian foundations, which, if nothing else, demonstrates that the island's inhabitants had developed sufficient scientific literacy to build monuments. Vast tombs in the south, like the rocky necropolis at Pantalica, likewise suggest that the island had a sizeable population dating back to the thirteenth century BC.[2] It's unlikely, though, that the arriving migrants were particularly concerned with these older pre-classical constructions. Their priority was to understand their immediate cohabitants, and it was indeed their encounters with these peoples that prompted them to give the island one of its first recorded names: Sikania.

At a glance, settlement building in Sicily seems to have developed along quite strict territorial lines. The Greeks occupied the island's south-east, while the Phoenicians established themselves in the north and west. In reality these divisions are crude at best and serve in some respects to obscure a great blurring of beliefs and cultural practices. In Lentini, one of the richest inland Greek colonies, the Sicel population integrated so closely with the migrants that they too must have played some role in the development of so-called 'Greek culture' in the centuries to come. Across the island, the Phoenician alphabet provided a means for the native people to express their cultures in a new manner, and this, ultimately, had an influence on the development of the Greek letter system. There were tensions of course. The Elymians were particularly persistent in challenging the military and economic expansion of the new migrants. Their main city, Segesta, was almost constantly at war with the Greek city of Selinunte until well into the fourth century BC. Yet even in this case, there is ample evidence that the cultures continued to weave in and out of one another. Segesta is still home to one of the island's best-preserved Greek-style theatres, as well as an impressive Doric temple thought to have been constructed by an Athenian architect. If war was common in ancient Sicily, this was largely a question of economic and political jostling, and did not necessarily preclude cooperation, dialogue and trade.

Sicily's ancient inhabitants were remarkably diverse in terms of their ethnicities, customs and political beliefs. This was by no means a 'white' culture. Nevertheless, starting in the seventh century, the islanders gradually began to develop some unified characteristics, particularly in the sphere of religion. Over hundreds of years all of the communities began to venerate what we now usually refer to as 'Greek' mythological figures.[3] It was Sicily that Daedalus and Icarus were trying to reach when they planned their escape from imprisonment in Crete using flying machines. We could, in this sense, interpret Icarus's own perishing, by 'flying too close to the sun', as a warning on the part of Aegean Greeks to any prospective emigrants thinking of embarking on the dangerous journey towards Sicily. The island was also home to Polyphemus, the Cyclops, who some historians have read as a symbol of the apparently 'blind' Sicels, Sicanians and Elymians. While some of the colonisers did feel a sense of superiority over the native islanders, the fact is that the vast majority of Sicilians, regardless of their ethnicity, would have turned to 'Greek' myths to name and explain the natural phenomena around them. The Strait of Messina – the main crossing between Sicily and Italy – was known as the home of the sea monsters Scylla and Charybdis; embodiments, one imagines, of the whirlpools and jagged rocks that cause difficulties for ships to this day. Similarly, the Aeolian islands, with their gusty breezes, were the domain to the kind and hospitable demigod, Aeolus, 'the keeper of winds'.

Several of the early myths about Sicily are concerned with refugees. Perhaps the best example is the tale of Arethusa, a naiad who is said to have fled to the island to escape the unwelcome advances of the river god Alpheios. According to this story, Artemis, the goddess of hunting, transformed the nymph into a fast-flowing stream, which is said to have surfaced in south-east Sicily, and as such provided an escape from the violence she faced in her homeland. Unfortunately for Arethusa, Alpheios was so determined to possess his beloved that he followed her to the island, and, surfacing in the same stream, forced himself on her. Other female deities, like Astarte, an African goddess of war and 'sacred prostitution', fought back against the patriarchal norms of classical culture. For the Sicanian and Phoenician population that worshipped her in the island's west, Astarte was not an object to be pursued, but a figure of dominant sexuality who combined the life-giving imagery usually associated with female gods, with notions of self-defence and conquest. The cult of Astarte gradually declined as Greek religion spread across the island, and the local population eventually repurposed her temple in Erice, a hill-town above the western port of Trapani, as a shrine to the love god Aphrodite, and later the Madonna. The fact that her temple existed at all, though, is an important and often overlooked indicator of how African traditions helped feed Sicily's mythological imagination.

Of all the Greek deities it was Persephone, the goddess of grain, who came to be most closely associated with Sicily. Some local cults considered the fertile fields around Enna, in the centre of the island, as the location where Hades abducted the young girl and confined her to the underworld to serve as his queen. In the Sicilian version of the story Demeter, the goddess of agriculture and Persephone's mother, rendered the island barren in protest against Zeus, her father, who had failed to intervene against her kidnapper. In an attempt to restore fertility to the land, and to pacify Demeter, Zeus ordered Hades to release Persephone. Below ground, though, circumstances had changed. During her time in the underworld, Persephone went on a hunger strike against her captor. Famished, she eventually gave in and consumed food from the world of the dead. This acceptance of hospitality, Hades argued, allowed him at least some 'legitimate' possession of the girl. Zeus and Hades debated the point, and finally reached a compromise. For half the year Persephone would be allowed back to the surface of the earth, to see her mother. The rest of the time she would be required to spend at Hades's side in the underworld. For Sicilians, Persephone's annual ascension to the world of the living, and reunion with Demeter, came to represent spring, her return to the underworld, and Hades's embrace, winter. To this day, some Sicilian farmers speak of two seasons rather than four in accordance with this ancient conception of nature.

One final tale about Sicily gives a rather different insight into the way ancient peoples made sense of their geographical surroundings. Mount Etna, the volcano to the island's east, was and still is Sicily's most magical place. Some local cults considered its snowy peak a pillar of heaven, the site of the fire god Hephaestus's divine smithy where he would forge weapons for the Olympians. The Greeks, though, were particularly afraid of what lay underground: Etna was also known as the domain of Typhon, one of ancient mythology's most terrifying monsters. There are countless chronicles of this grotesque figure. Hesiod offers a particularly extensive description in his *Theogony*, in which, in addition to a dragon-like appearance, he describes the beast as having a hundred fire-breathing snake heads, a strange, grotesque assortment of wings, claws and tails, and fire in the place of eyelashes.[4] Later poets describe him as having multiple arms and an array of features, including those of wolves, bears and lions, and specify that he can be recognised by his terrible roar which is comprised of howls, screams and barks.[5] In most versions, Typhon is the father of all monsters, and, together with his lover Echidna, is responsible for spawning a whole range of other creatures including the Chimera, Cerberus and the Sphinx. In addition to his grotesque physical appearance, Typhon was, above all else, an outlaw, a revolutionary and an enemy of the gods. The mythological tradition maintains that he attempted to overthrow Zeus in one of the most significant coups among the Olympians. When the attempt failed, the chief deity banished him to Sicily, imprisoning him there beneath the volcano where, in anguish, he would 'belch forth holiest springs of unapproachable fire'.[6]

The story of Typhon captures the dual character that Sicily held in the ancient Greek imagination. On the one hand the settlers saw it as a rich and fertile place. On the other, it was dangerous and unpredictable. While it offered sanctuary, it was also associated with exile, banishment and imprisonment. Some historians have read Typhon as a symbol of the anxiety mainland

Greek poets may have felt when confronted with stories about the mysterious new colonies. Whatever the truth of the matter, this sense of the island being both blessed and cursed is a fundamental premise of what will later become 'Sicilian culture'. As we shall see throughout this book, the idea of the island as a particularly polarised place – characterised by extreme contrasts of bounty and scarcity, pleasure and pain, beauty and ugliness – will obsess writers, artists and intellectuals for centuries to come. Sticking to the immediate context of Greek mythology, however, it remains more fruitful to understand the island in terms of its fundamental strangeness. Sicily was Greek, yet it was somehow Other; a land of migrants and mystery. It was a *tabula rasa*, where the tensions and contradictions of the Peloponnese world could be contained, but also let loose.

As elsewhere in the Mediterranean, it was the expansion of cities that enabled the spread of mythology across Sicily. Throughout the classical period, Syracuse stood above all others. Today, this sprawling traffic-choked conurbation on the eastern edge of the island looks rather worse for wear. In the fifth century BC, however, it was one of the most important cultural centres in the world; a rival to Athens in terms of its wealth and influence. Natural conditions played a major role in its early success. When Corinthian settlers founded the city in 733 BC they chose an ideal site. The urban area was unique among Sicilian settlements in that it was comprised of both a long stretch of coast and a small island just a few metres off the shore, known as Ortygia, which was blessed with a fresh water supply.[7] This island-within-an-island served as a natural fortress, but it also provided the city with two protected harbours, one of which was used for trade, the other as a dock for what would, over time, become a sizeable navy. In the context of the initial scramble to find territory, these were significant advantages and helped set the city apart from other, less well-positioned, settlements.

Syracuse's rise began in earnest in 485 BC when the city's aristocratic rulers conceded power to a renowned mercenary captain. Like most Greek city-states at the time, Syracuse was controlled by noble families, called the *gamori*, who passed power down through hereditary means. In the first decades of the fifth century BC, however, this ruling class was consumed by an inter-factional conflict which resulted in several of the most important historic families being banished. Eager to win back their positions of influence, a group of these exiled nobles turned to Gelon, a common-born warrior, for assistance. Gelon was a skilled horse-man who had amassed a large army made up of volunteers from small Greek towns and Sicel villages. Thanks in part to this large-scale public support, he had obtained control of much of Sicily's southernmost coast. The rebel *gamori* proposed him a deal. They would facilitate his rise to power in Syracuse, on the sole proviso that he would reinstate them into key administrative positions. Gelon agreed, and marched his army to the city, expecting a long-term siege. Faced with such a large military presence at the gates, however, the incumbent nobles quickly surrendered. The mercenary captain was therefore free to proceed, virtually unopposed, towards Ortygia, where he took power as the city's first tyrant.[8]

Under Gelon's rule Syracuse automatically took possession of all the Greek-speaking settlements along Sicily's south-east coast that had pledged allegiance to the warrior. This in itself was a significant gain for the city. In the months to come, however, the tyrant continued to embark on a number of small military campaigns during which he took control of other towns and villages further north, around Etna. By 480 BC Syracuse was more than just a city; it was a small-scale colonial state in its own right. Elsewhere on the island, neighbouring powers were understandably concerned by this development. That year Carthage, a Phoenician colony in what is now Tunisia, sent a large army comprised of troops from western Sicily, Sardinia and Corsica, to block Gelon's ascension. They met the Greek forces at Himera, a town just outside what is now Palermo, but were unable to break through Syracuse's well-trained lines of cavalry, archers and warriors. When Gelon's navy arrived, outflanking the Phoenician boats, the aggressors were forced to retreat back towards the North African coast. The victory was a triumph for the defending Greek forces and it had long-term consequences. For decades following their failed offensive the Carthaginians were forced to pay huge reparations and, as a result, their grip over the west of the island began to slowly decline.

Back in Syracuse the spoils of war provided the funds for a cultural revolution. Gelon had secured his city's status largely thanks to his skills on the battlefield. Between 478 and 467 BC, however, his brother Hieron I led Syracuse to global importance. While he was forced to engage in occasional conflicts with Carthaginian forces, Hieron was a peacetime ruler, less concerned with jostling conflicts than building a city that would reflect Greek ideals about what a civilised *polis* should look like. During his reign, Hieron developed Syracuse along the lines of an archetypal Aegean city, ordering the construction of squares, bath houses and Doric-style temples dedicated to Apollo, Zeus and Athena among other deities. Art and sport, charioteering and horse-racing in particular, were a key part of his vision. One of the most important initiatives that Hieron introduced was a pan-Mediterranean poetry competition that attracted performers including Pindar, Bacchylides and quite possibly the exiled Xenophanes, to the city.[9] The event was an important contribution to civic life in its own right. Just as importantly, though, it sent a message to the Aegean rulers that the Syracusan elite was as sophisticated, and forward-thinking, as that on the mainland.

One can get some idea of the kind of place ancient Syracuse was by looking at the city's theatre, which is still home to one of Italy's most celebrated dramatic festivals. The huge semicircular edifice visible today actually dates to the second century BC. Nevertheless, the construction that Hieron I established was significant enough to attract the attention of some of the most important figures in the fifth century Mediterranean. Aeschylus came to the city sometime in the 470s to develop a version of his play *The Persians* and even dedicated an original piece called *Women of Etna* to Hieron.[10] Aristotle cites Syracuse as one of the birthplaces of comedy, thanks in particular to the work of Epicharmus, who, he tells us, was the first author ever to work in the genre. Only fragments of his output remain, though we can deduce from the titles alone – 'Odysseus', 'Cyclops' and 'Trojan Men' – that these were mythological satires. Other works, like 'The Sausage', and 'Country-Folk', seem to have been bawdy farces, exploring more domestic, everyday issues. Today we tend to think of comedy as a form of light entertainment. In the context of the Mediterranean in the fifth century BC, though, where literature was largely confined to epic poetry, the emergence of this genre was a radical development which enabled audiences to express discontent with the established order of things. It's important not to overstate this. Hieron was an authoritarian ruler who made little effort to institute suffrage or sortition of the kind seen in Athens. His celebration of free expression, however, and enthusiasm towards building civic spaces, marked a significant step away from the closed-off oligarchies of previous centuries, and towards a rudimentary form of democracy.

In the fifth century BC the vast majority of Syracusans were involved in the agricultural economy and worked as subsistence farmers, day labourers on large estates or as slaves. Still, for the *gamori* and anyone lucky enough to dwell in their inner circles, the urban lifestyle was relatively comfortable. We know from vases, coins and remains of jewellery, that the city's elite were well-coiffed, elegant people, who paid great attention to their appearance. They also seem to have eaten well. Syracuse was home to one of the world's first cooking schools, and its chefs were in high demand across the Mediterranean. Towards the end of the fifth century BC, one of them, a man named Mithaecus, wrote an important volume on the art of cuisine which was later transcribed by scholars on the Greek mainland. Only one recipe remains, for a scabbardfish which the author instructs should be gutted, beheaded, rinsed, filleted and served with oil and cheese.[11] Based on later evidence from the poet Archestratos, we know that his book contained meat recipes, and that Syracuse's wealthier residents were also dining on tuna, swordfish, shellfish, eel, copious wine and sesame desserts.[12] Roman writers would look back approvingly at this life of relative luxury in centuries to come. At the time, however, many mainland Greeks saw the behaviour of the Syracusans as unduly, immorally, sybaritic. When Plato first visited the city in 388 BC, for example, he felt compelled to write a letter expressing his outrage at the decadence he witnessed:

> My first impressions on arrival were those of strong disapproval –
> disapproval of the kind of life which was there called the life of

happiness, stuffed full as it was with the banquets of the Italian Greeks and Syracusans, who ate to repletion twice every day, and were never without a partner for the night ... No city could remain in a state of tranquillity under any laws whatsoever, when men think it right to squander all their property in extravagant excesses, and consider it a duty to be idle in everything else except eating and drinking and the laborious prosecution of debauchery.[13]

There are a few reasons to be sceptical of this account. In 414, the philosopher's home city of Athens had attempted to confront Syracuse in a naval battle, and suffered what many observers in the ancient world had considered to be a spectacular and humiliating defeat. If Plato ostensibly came to Sicily to meet a friend, then he almost certainly wanted to learn more about this mysterious power that had so successfully resisted his city's fleet. Plato's idea of Syracuse was further coloured by the coincidence of his journey with the reign of Dionysius I, one of the city's most notorious tyrants, who held onto power for the first few decades of the fourth century BC. Famously paranoid and despotic – a narcissist and an apparently awful poet – Dionysius was immortalised in Dante's *Inferno*, where he can be found trapped in a river of boiling blood.[14] Gelon had, with a few exceptions, adopted a defensive stance when faced with minor Carthaginian threats. Dionysius, by contrast, went on the offensive and ordered a series of gratuitous attacks on Punic settlements in the west of the island. In 396 BC his armies laid waste to two of Sicily's most important Phoenician cities, Motya and Solus, killing hundreds of civilians in the process. These assaults were certainly excessive, though it's worth noting they were not motivated by anything resembling modern xenophobia. The tyrant ordered similar assaults in 390 BC against the Greek cities of Southern

Italy, including Thurii and Crotone in modern-day Calabria. Similarly, when the Greco-Sicilian cities of Catania and Naxos attempted to protest against his despotic mode of governance, he simply besieged them, and forced the majority of their inhabitants into slavery. Dionysius may not have been involved in ethnic cleansing. He was, however, a megalomaniac. In Syracuse he relied upon a large force of Spartan mercenaries to enforce order in the streets. He commissioned an imposing castle, the Euryalus Fortress, to be built to the north of the city to house this private army, and, according to later folkloric accounts, transformed the surrounding caves into his own personal torture chambers.[15] If the *gamori* were free to enjoy the hedonistic pleasures of Mediterranean life, the majority of the city's population were most likely living in fear throughout his reign.

Unfortunately, no reliable chronicle remains of Plato's encounter with Dionysius. In a later account, written in the first century, Plutarch claims the philosopher directly accused the tyrant of being an unvirtuous coward, upon which the conversation is said to have degraded into mutual calumny.[16] The extent of Plato's disgust with Sicilian rule, though, is most evident in the *Gorgias*, a dialogue the philosopher wrote shortly after his return to Athens. The title refers to a nomadic Sicilian sophist who had been active in the fifth century BC and whom some scholars consider the first nihilist philosopher.[17] On the surface, the text is a debate on rhetoric, and specifically whether it should be considered a legitimate object for philosophical inquiry. One suspects, though, that Gorgias was just a scapegoat here. Really this was Plato's chance to lay into Dionysius's approach to government. Gorgias makes two claims in the dialogue. He first argues that language and Truth are inherently divorced from one another, and that words, by implication, can make no claim on objective reality. As a result, he goes on to suggest that rhetoric – by which he here means political speechmaking – should be considered an 'art' precisely because it stands in for this 'absence', and creates the illusion of meaning.[18] Unsurprisingly, Socrates vehemently rejects the sophist's view. Rhetoric, he claims, is nothing more than a trick that those lacking in genuine knowledge use in order to manipulate the masses to their own ends. Gorgias, he insists, has confused philosophy with mere persuasion. The dialogue concludes in predictable fashion with Socrates proposing dialectical reasoning as the legitimate means of reconnecting language with Truth and morality: 'All flattery, to ourselves or to others, few or many, we must shun,' he says. 'This is how we should use rhetoric, always in the direction of justice.'[19]

This is not one of Plato's most coherent works. The Athenian's logic breaks down on several occasions, his examples are disjoined, and, based on surviving evidence, his straw-man arguments have little to do with the points that Gorgias, and other sophists, actually put forth. Nevertheless, there are few better examples of how alien and indeed superficial Sicilian politics seemed to the Athenian elite. In fact, Plato returned to this 'problem' throughout his life. In 367 BC, after Dionysius's death, which legend maintains followed a particularly indulgent drinking session, the philosopher returned to the island, on the invitation of his good friend Dion, to tutor the tyrant's son. While more studious than his father, Dionysius II enjoyed a similarly lavish lifestyle, and, despite believing himself a true philosopher, proved unable to keep up with his teacher's demanding syllabus. A more serious obstacle, though, came from the *gamori*, who, fearful of what Plato's teaching might imply for their own positions, fed the tyrant rumours that the 'Athenian spy' was plotting a revolution. Plato was promptly imprisoned, and forced to return home.

Yet even this was not enough to dissuade the philosopher. In 360 BC Plato returned to the island to make one last attempt to understand its political culture. If anything, though, this trip proved even more disastrous than the last. By this point in his reign, Dionysius was losing his grip on power. Shortly after the Athenian arrived, Southern Sicily was taken over by rioting. Once again, the tyrant had Plato imprisoned, believing him to have had a role in organising the uprising. This time Plato only managed to escape thanks to the help of some friends on the southern Italian mainland who presumably paid a hefty bail for his release. These events filled the Athenian with uncharacteristic pessimism. For most of his life the philosopher had endeavoured to make sense of Syracusan politics and had even mooted the city as a possible destination to build his utopian Republic. In old age, however, he came to look back on this fantasy as one of his worst errors of judgement. Sicily, he concluded, was a place of immeasurable woe. It was too chaotic, too intrinsically corrupt, to serve as a blueprint for any future society.

The tyrannies of the fourth century BC marked a low point in the otherwise rather grand history of ancient Syracuse. In the years following Plato's death in 347 BC, the city returned to prominence, and re-established its reputation as one of the Mediterranean's most prosperous and civilised ports. This fate was linked closely to the rise of Alexandria, and particularly its Great Library which was built in the third century BC and which was reachable from Sicily's southern coast in a couple of days' sail. The library, also known as the *musaeum* (literally, a 'temple of the muses'), was a cosmopolitan environment whose patrons, the Ptolemaic dynasty, were concerned with surpassing tribal, military divisions to develop universal human knowledge.

Its members included philosophers, poets, mathematicians and engineers from across the known world, from Egypt in the west to India in the east, who would gather to debate texts, and translate literature across cultural and linguistic divides. Many Syracusans established a reputation among the library's community, including Theocritus, the founder of bucolic poetry, Timaeus, the historian and geographer, and, most famous of all, Archimedes, who refined his famous theories on density between Sicily and Egypt. The stories of each of these individuals are fascinating. For our purposes, though, it is the cultural geography itself that is significant. In the third century BC, Syracuse was not only, or not even primarily, a 'Sicilian city'. It was, in many respects, 'closer' to Alexandria, Antioch, Ephesus and Gaza than the smaller, relatively insular, settlements to the north of the island.

Syracuse's new-found prosperity was accompanied by a long period of stable government. In 270 BC Hieron II came to power and ruled for over fifty years, until 215 BC. Much like his earlier namesake, Hieron II was a passionate patron of the arts. During his reign he oversaw the renovation of the city's historic fifth-century monuments – which had fallen into decline under the tyranny of Dionysius – at great expense. He also commissioned a new entertainment district, expanded the theatre and constructed several new agorae. Traders from North Africa and the Middle East flocked to the city's harbours, bringing new artworks and commodities with them. As a result, a 'Hellenistic culture' began to thrive in Sicily; a nostalgic reinvention of older Greek aesthetics which developed in dialogue with artists from the Middle East. Examples of this can be seen in crafts, in the work of ceramicists who developed new terracotta works inspired by grotesque pottery from across the Levant; or the silversmiths who began emulating plates, necklaces and jewellery in a style that imitated Persian specimens which were most likely brought to the city from Persepolis. The greatest innovations, though, took place in sculpture. Before the third century BC most Sicilian artists had limited themselves to depicting idealised, typified images of the gods. During Hieron's rule, however, the islanders started to create more dynamic, individualised and emotionally expressive figures. Many of these pieces were created and exchanged across the Mediterranean as part of an increasingly global art market. Some, like the bronze Dancing Satyr of Mazara del Vallo (c. 250 BC), which depicts a spinning figure engaged in a Dionysian ritual, exhibit such a complex blurring of Greek, Punic, European and African influences that scholars continue to debate where they were made, and how they found their way to Sicily.

The third century BC was a kind of 'golden age' for Syracuse. Looking at the island as a whole, though, this was a turbulent period characterised by unprecedented conflict. In 264 BC, the first signs of serious unrest came when a small party of Roman soldiers made their way into Sicily. They caught the island's rulers entirely off-guard. Before the third century BC, Rome's history had been largely separate to that of the island. Since it was founded in 753 BC, the rulers of the Italian city had focused on growing their population and holding off assaults from local tribes. By the time of Hieron II's rule, however, Rome was a large, wealthy republic, and its ruling class was beginning to consider military campaigns against the Greek cities in Southern Italy. Initially the Romans intervened in Sicily to confront the threat of a group of 'Mamertine' bandits who had occupied the port of Messina, the closest point to the peninsula. What actually motivated Rome into action, though, was the fact that these bandits were supported by Carthaginian forces. The Roman move south, then, was no innocuous scouting party. It was a strategic expedition that aimed to gauge and potentially halt the African power from expanding northward towards Italy. This became increasingly clear in the weeks to follow. The well-trained Roman legions made short work of the disorganised Mamertines. Rather than returning to the mainland, however, they spread their forces along Sicily's north coast, and, over the next three years, gradually began to raid Greek and Carthaginian settlements in the area around modern-day Palermo. Hieron wisely paid a tribute to the invading force in order to shield his city from these attacks. Just a few miles from Syracuse's walls, however, Sicily was in flames. In 261 BC the Romans fought, and won, a significant victory against the Carthaginian army outside the southern city of Agrigento. From this moment, having secured as much as half of the island already, the Roman elite decided to consolidate their efforts, and set out to expel Carthaginian civilisation from Sicily altogether.

The First Punic War, which historians usually date from 264 to 241 BC, was the largest and most important conflict in Sicily's ancient history. While the island's city-states had always fought among one another, this was the first time that political leaders on both sides of the Mediterranean framed the island explicitly as a geopolitical frontier. To a certain extent one could, with some justification, point to this moment as the origin of the great and increasing division between Europe and Africa. The reality, though, is rather more nuanced. For many residents in the affected areas – in south-west Sicily, Tunisia and Libya – life continued much as normal. Even in the heart of the war years, people not only continued to trade, but began to send increasing numbers of gifts and gestures of friendship, pledging to maintain bonds beyond the emerging cultural divisions. Likewise, it's important to remember that, in the third century BC, Carthage was in fact as much a part of the Hellenistic world as anywhere else in the Mediterranean: the city's elite communicated in Greek and were inspired by the same mythology and political traditions that were commonly held in Syracuse or Alexandria. Nevertheless, as far as Sicily is concerned, the Romans did succeed in their aim of ousting the Punic influence from the island. Most of the battles took place at sea, sparing the inland cities further destruction. During the conflict, however, Rome gradually succeeded in pushing its influence as far as modern-day Trapani on Sicily's western coast, claiming a series of Phoenician settlements in the process. By the time the Carthaginians surrendered in 241 BC, following defeat in a naval battle near Favignana, an island just off Sicily, the invading force had spread out to take control of their first trading posts in the south-west. In 227 BC Rome officially declared Sicily its first 'province'. From this moment on, the island's inhabitants were required to adhere to, and participate in, the legal and state structures of the Republic.

There was one exception to this. For a decade following the war, the Romans, out of respect for Hieron II, permitted Syracuse, still Sicily's most powerful city, to retain its independence. In 215 BC, however, following the tyrant's death, the diplomatic truce came to an end. Hieronymus, Hieron's successor, was just fifteen years old when he took power. His advisors, fearing for their status in the Roman-dominated world, encouraged the young ruler to confront the occupying forces directly, arguing that it was only a matter of time before the Italian army made an attack against the city. Hieronymus was easily convinced. In 216 BC, as the Carthaginians regrouped and attempted a new offensive towards the European mainland, he pledged Syracusan troops to support them. This proved a fatal mistake. Pro-Roman

Sicilians promptly assassinated the ruler and, despite attempts from the city elite to broker a deal, the peace was broken. In 214 BC a large army of Roman legions surrounded Syracuse in a siege that has gone down in legend as one of the most dramatic of the ancient world. Apocryphal accounts attest that Archimedes helped hold off the assault by appeal to a series of fantastical weapons, including a grappling hook that could apparently lift ships out of the water, and, even more spuriously, a 'death ray' made of bright metals that reflected intense beams of sunlight and set fire to sails. These stories are clearly absurd. Nevertheless, they convey how momentous this showdown was, and, to some extent, the genuine resilience of the Sicilian city's defence. The Romans sieged Syracuse for two long years. When they finally broke through in 212 BC, the troops were so inflamed that they burnt down temples, executed the nobility and killed hundreds of citizens, including Archimedes. The city would never fully recover.

The transition from 'Greek' to 'Roman' rule might sound definitive to modern ears, but for most of the island's residents, life in second-century BC Sicily continued much as it had previously. While Latin became the new administrative language, Sicilians continued to speak Greek, alongside various local dialects, well into the Middle Ages. The islanders were free to practise their religious rites and faced no discrimination for doing so. On the contrary, rather than replace what they found, the Romans adopted a process of syncretism by which they simply absorbed and adapted stories and rituals from their conquered lands to suit their own needs. Over time, the islanders came to know Artemis as Diana, Persephone as Proserpina, Aphrodite as Venus and so on. This process took place over a long period and there are

no clear date parameters. It's worth noting, though, the fundamental role that Sicily played in this process. The island was not
just any colony. It was Rome's first foreign acquisition, and, as
such, it provided the Italian city with its first sense of proto-
imperial identity. Defenders of Rome often present syncretism
as if it were an enlightened and actively benevolent process; as
if the Republic's leading figures had consciously, and sensitively,
begun to reflect on the relative merits of Greek and Punic ideals.
In fact, this process was made possible, by and large, as a result
of the actions of various corrupt colonial governors who looted
the island's religious sites and traded its exotic Hellenistic statues
among one another as status symbols.[20] While it's true that Rome
did develop its own hybrid, pluralistic identity in the centuries to
come, this was a result of, not a counterbalance to, their subjugation of the local population.

One class of Sicilians suffered in particular as a result of
Roman rule: the slaves. Before the invasion, most of these individuals had worked in and around small-holds and independent
farmsteads which produced mixed crops to support the Greek
and Carthaginian settlements. After conquering Syracuse,
however, the Romans constructed a new system of *latifondi*, far
larger estates which were geared towards the intensive mono-
crop production of cereals, grapes and olives. Rich families from
the mainland began to purchase farms as business opportunities, and managed them from afar. The landowners were keen
to profit from the new opportunity to export to the capital, and,
as a result, it seems they forced the slave population to work
longer hours in worse conditions.[21] Many of these individuals refused to be treated in such a manner. In 136 BC Eunus, a
Syrian-born slave from Enna, in central Sicily, killed his master
following a dispute over what he saw as excessive disciplinary

measures in the fields. In response, hundreds of other slaves, armed with farming equipment, clubs and occasionally swords, rose up to support Eunus and began attacking landowners across the island and burning the crop supplies. This unrest lasted for two years and Rome was forced to send a dedicated military mission to Sicily to restore order. The discontent, though, was so great that in 104 BC, three decades later, a new generation of slaves repeated the feat. This time they were more organised. The rebels built their own armies, complete with cavalry units, and attacked the legions in the open field. Between 103 and 102 BC, while most of the Republic's army was distracted fighting Germanic tribes in northern Europe, Sicily's slaves effectively took control of the *latifondi* themselves, and worked the land as free individuals. Rome eventually mobilised troops down to the island, and they slaughtered the last rebels in 101 BC. Nevertheless, the story of this short-lived independence movement quickly passed into legend, and some Sicilians continue to point to these events as the origins of the island's tense relationship with mainland Italy.

The slave revolts are an important punctuation mark in Sicily's early history. First and foremost, they offer a rare glimpse into the lived experience of the island's lower classes, and give some sense of the changes they experienced. More generally, they demonstrate how relatively unimportant Sicily was in the eyes of decision makers in the capital. The fact that the slaves were able to block the supply of grain for such a long period, and to repeat that feat, shows the island was far from a priority. At the same time, while Sicily was the definition of 'provincial', it was not a mere backwater. The island continued to exert a cultural fascination that far exceeded its political status. In 75 BC Cicero served as a public official on Sicily, and he seems to have been overwhelmed by the unique landscape and old temples. In a letter addressed to friends in the capital he boasted that he had, apparently, discovered Archimedes's tomb in Syracuse, and he would speak regularly in admiration of the ancient Greek past for the rest of his life.[22] The fact that this esteemed politician was so keen to celebrate this exotic history is revealing. While Sicily was Rome's rather rebellious breadbasket, it was clearly far more than this. It was also a key part of the Republic's identity, a symbolically important geography onto which the ruling elite proudly projected a fantasy of their own Hellenistic origins.

In 27 BC, following the assassination of Julius Caesar and the subsequent period of civil war, the Roman Republic evolved to become an empire. The following centuries, until roughly 180 AD, have become known as the *pax romana* on account of their relative peace and prosperity. While there were some exceptions to this, the epithet holds largely true in Sicily's case.[23] Throughout this period the Romans made considerable investments on the island, building roads, bridges and aqueducts. For the first time in Sicilian history, wealth was distributed in a meaningful way beyond Syracuse. Trapani, on the west coast, came to prominence as a primary producer of *garum*, a fermented fish sauce that was a staple on the Roman table. Messina and Taormina, in the east, expanded to become key trading posts, facilitating the exchange of goods between North Africa and mainland Italy. The most noteworthy transformation took place at the foot of Mount Etna, in Catania, which became a tourist destination for wealthy Roman citizens. Despite centuries of raids, earthquakes and volcanic eruptions, the city's amphitheatre, odeon and bathhouse survive today as testimony of its historic role as a centre for leisure and entertainment.

The most important development of the early imperial era, though, was the spread of Christianity. No one knows exactly when the first converts arrived in Sicily, or how widely the islanders took up the faith. The Acts of the Apostles (28:12) suggests that St Paul introduced the religion to Sicily during his journey to Rome in 59 AD. Later scholars have linked it to the Jewish–Roman wars, a series of conflicts in the Middle East which erupted over the drive to create a new Jewish homeland.[24] The earliest archaeological evidence we have is a group of Christian burial chambers in the south-east of the island, which date to 250 AD. Whatever the precise chronology, the development of Christianity presented problems for the Roman elite that far exceeded those of the slave revolts. In its early incarnation, Christianity was an uncompromising, apocalyptic, revolutionary faith, whose followers believed in an imminent resurrection of the dead and overturning of the established order. One of the most seductive aspects of this new cult was its promise of a heaven-like space, a paradise for followers of the one true God and his only son Jesus Christ. For a suffering populace, faced with the constant threat of plague, war and famine, the prospect of justice on earth and eternal peace for the spirit proved intoxicating.

During this period, Christianity was a pluralistic movement which spread quickly, both across and beyond the Mediterranean, taking on localised versions as it travelled. Sicilians, like many others, were particularly fixated on the idea of martyrdom. Across the empire, peaking at the beginning of the fourth century AD, Roman soldiers arrested, killed and tortured Christians as part of a long and controversial policy of persecutions. Many of those who were rounded up accepted their fate and repeated the doctrine that was so central to the early movement: that to die in sacrifice for God was a surefire way to heaven. In Sicily this defiance was manifest in the rebellion of two saints from the south-east of the island: St Agatha of Catania and St Lucy of Syracuse. Their stories are remarkably similar. Both of the women are said to have been devout believers who were forced into arranged marriages with non-Christians and refused to be wed on account of their faith. Both were tortured as a result. Agatha suffered the fate of having her breasts burnt off by iron pokers, and has since become venerated as the saint for survivors of rape. Lucy, whose eyes were gouged out, is the protector of the blind.[25] Today worshippers around the world recognise these figures as models of virtue. For Sicilians, though, these women are not just religious martyrs. They are just as significant as local heroines, as civic figures who stood up to the oppressive powers of the state. In later centuries Sicilian Christianity would develop to take on a more explicitly Catholic-authoritarian character. In these early years, however, the cults are better understood as a democratic expression of local, popular resistance to Roman rule.

The covert aspect of Christianity came to an end at the start of the fourth century when Emperor Constantine decriminalised the faith across the Roman Empire. Soon after this, at the Council of Nicaea in 325, influential members of the early church agreed upon a uniform creed and formalised some of the religion's most important festivals, including Easter. The coincidence of these two events was an epochal political event, and marked the beginning of Christianity's evolution from a grassroots protest movement into one of the world's most important institutional powers. The consequences for Sicily were profound. For the next five centuries, with the exception of occasional invasions by Goths and Vandals, rulers in Constantinople governed the island as a Byzantine Christian territory. During this period the church began to position itself as an important landowner. In the past, many Sicilian Christians had been forced to conduct their worship in makeshift cave churches and underground grottos. Byzantium, by contrast, provided funds for the construction of small chapels and monasteries in rural areas. In the larger, older cities, the clergy transformed Roman basilicas, the rectangular buildings which had been used for civil processes during the imperial era, into larger churches for Christian worship.[26] This was a slow but profound process which enabled the clergy to spread the faith to increasing swathes of the population, while gradually obtaining economic and political control over the island as a whole.

There were a few exceptions to this. While the church authorities grew in influence in the first centuries of the new millennium, parts of the Sicilian nobility, mainly rural landowners, seemingly refused to convert. The power of these individuals was minimal compared with the Christian elite. Nevertheless, these figures continued to play an important role in Sicilian society, both as agricultural managers but also, in some instances, as unwitting protectors of Hellenistic culture. One unusually clear example of this can be seen at the Villa del Casale, a rural estate in the centre of Sicily. The enormous building, which was built in the fourth century AD, is thought to have been home to a second-tier member of the ruling class, on account of the relative absence of expensive marble. While fairly modest, it nevertheless boasts one of the largest and best-preserved collections of Roman floor mosaics anywhere in the world. The main subjects are Greek mythological figures which include Hercules, Polyphemus and other well-known characters. Yet there are secular images too, including a group of female gymnasts who are depicted running with weights and playing with a ball, clad in what look like modern bikinis. The most interesting examples of all show animals:

there are hunting scenes populated with rabbits, boar and deer but also extravagant processions of lions, elephants, tigers and a rhino on their way to Rome. These are unique works and, as a result, it would be unwise to extrapolate from them to make generalisations about the island's culture as a whole. Clearly, though, despite the political victory of the church, the classical past continued to exert at least some influence over some of the islanders' imaginative lives.

In 660 Syracuse briefly returned to some degree of prosperity when Emperor Constans II decided to move to the city, and, for a while, considered it a potential capital for the empire. During this period the ecclesiastical elite funded the construction of a large cathedral on the site of the Temple of Athena, ensuring that this majestic site, built under Gelon's rule in the fifth century BC, would live on in another form. The unusually large amount of gold coinage that was in circulation at this time also suggests that the city was relatively wealthy. Some historians argue that Constans most likely raised taxes around this time and that this was one of the motivations that led his chamberlain to assassinate him in 668. With the exception of this violent act, though, Syracuse was a relatively peaceful place. The Jewish community, in particular, grew significantly, and these individuals were free to congregate without significant discrimination. The city is still home to one of the oldest functioning *mikveh* (ritual baths) in the world, and several crypts dating to this period include tombs in which Jews and Christians are buried side by side. Compared with the aggressively sectarian climate of Constantinople, scholars looked to Sicily as a safe place to study. Syracuse was home to a renowned ecclesiastical library and played an important role in debates around canonical law. Most of the subject matter was theological, concerned with the intricacies of the Justinian legal code, though the collection did hold its secrets. Amid the religious tomes were important works of classical philosophy that had been salvaged or copied from the Library of Alexandria before its destruction in the third century. Many of these, including works by Ptolemy, the Greek-Egyptian mathematician, and several treatises by Aristotle, would remain there for centuries when intellectuals from across Europe would seek them out as reference points in the development of the Italian Renaissance.

At the end of the eighth century Sicily was a prosperous if fairly typical Byzantine outpost, similar in status to many other territories along the Balkan and South Italian coasts. Beyond the spectacle of colloquies and episcopal conferences, however, the island's unique history continued to exert some background influence over everyday affairs. While the Sicilians did not challenge the orthodoxy of the rulers, and offered little resistance to the strictures of the church, neither did they entirely forget the extraordinary mix of cultures that had shaped the island's ancient past. On the contrary, as we shall see throughout this book, this heritage continued to shape politics and society in quite unexpected ways in the centuries to come.

2

The Polyglot Kingdom (826–1182)

Life in the Emirate, Norman Conquest,
Hybrid Architecture

There is no peaceful life save in sweet Sicily's shade, under a dynasty which surpasses the Caesars. See these royal palaces, where joy has made its abode, a marvellous home to which Allah granted perfect beauty.

Abd ar-Rahman al-Itrabanishi, Sicilian poet, c. 1150

[Palermo] is an ancient and elegant city, magnificent, gracious, and seductive to look upon. It is a wonderful place, built in the Cordoba style ... [King William II] roams through the gardens and courts for amusement and pleasure ... The Christian women follow the fashion of Muslims, are fluent of speech, wrap their cloaks about them, and are veiled.

Ibn Jubayr, geographer, 1185

By the eighth and ninth centuries, following a long period of civil war, the Abbasids, a Sunni dynasty from modern-day Iraq, emerged as leaders of Islam. Like Christianity, the faith was born as a revolutionary movement, premised on restoring the 'original' order of god, Allah, to the world. Between 610 and 632 the prophet Muhammad, who claimed to have a direct relationship with the divine, led a campaign against the 'pagan' polytheistic cult members in Mecca and the 'false' monotheisms of Christianity and Judaism. His religious motivation was to spread the direct word of god. It's important to recognise, though, that he was also inspired by a political task: to unify the disparate groups across the Arabic-speaking world into a single body. The faith's early militarism was not, therefore, a question of opposing all competing religions, or not only. First and foremost it was a symptom of a more complex, ultimately secular, dispute among competing tribes.

The Abbasids came to power at a decisive moment, when the vast majority of the Arab world had converted to Islam. They were reformists who were concerned above all with redefining Muslim society in terms that would prioritise the quest for knowledge over combative martyrdom, faith over ethnicity and cooperation over tribalism. Their capital in Baghdad was well positioned to absorb the wealth of the silk route and became a meeting point for the many Muslims that shared their vision. At the city's House of Wisdom – a precursor to the early modern university – Sunni and Shia scholars worked together to translate ancient Greek and Roman texts, bringing the city in line with the Hellenistic cultures of the ancient world. Literature flourished thanks to the work of poets like Abū Nuwās and Abū Tammām, while the philosopher Ibn Sīnā, or Avicenna as he is known in the West, achieved global renown for his theories of individual consciousness. The city's scientists pursued innumerable innovations in medicine, astrology and engineering, most notably in the field of hydraulics. Al-Khwārizmī, a Persian mathematician, revolutionised trigonometry, and it is to the Latinisation of his name, Algorithmi, that we owe a word that is so central to our own times: the algorithm.

Today we often think of the history of Christianity and Islam as one of innate opposition. In reality, the ninth century was a moment of reorientation for all parties, characterised by complex patterns of conflict and cooperation. Byzantine scholars were welcome in Baghdad, and Muslims in Byzantium; and despite political misalignments, trade between the cities was active. Islamic culture even had an influence on the evolution of Christianity, as manifest in the practice of iconoclasm, in which Byzantine Christians destroyed representations of religious figures (while the protagonists never saw this directly as an attempt to implement Islamic aniconism – i.e., a ban on representing God in figurative terms – the two were clearly related).

The notion of ideological opposition is further complicated by the fact that Constantinople was as threatened by developments in western Europe as it was with events in the east. Abbasid expansion in Asia Minor was one thing, but the city's elite were equally concerned by the rise of Charlemagne, the king of the Franks and Lombards, who was appointed Emperor of the Romans in 800 and seemed to possess expansionist ambitions of his own. As far as Sicilians were concerned, the biggest threat to their safety was an increase in raids from 'Saracen' pirates – a loose term that medieval Christians used to refer to a diverse group of fighters from Arab territories who were particularly active in the Aegean. In 700, a group of these Saracens actually colonised Pantelleria, a small island to the south-west of Sicily, and used it as a trading hub for looted goods. This was not, though, an ideological or geopolitical move. It was, at best, an opportunistic landgrab which if anything served to demonstrate how comparatively weak Byzantine naval power was in the region.

At the start of the 820s Arab rulers began to consider the more ambitious move of taking Sicily itself. The instigators were the Sunni Aghlabid dynasty, who were tasked with managing territory in the old Carthaginian heartlands in Ifrīqya on behalf of the Abbasids. Their capital city, Kairouan – which still stands in modern Tunisia – was an important site for Islam, home to one of the oldest places of Muslim worship, and a diverse population including Berbers, Mudar and a range of Syrian factions, all of whom had different customs, interpretations of the religion and often long-standing rivalries. As had been the case in Muhammad's time, the city's elite saw a jihad, a holy war, as a useful pretext for uniting the potentially disparate groups. Despite this, many in the Aghlabid ranks were reluctant to initiate an all-out conflict with Byzantium. In 826, however, after years of discussion, the leaders eventually came to a resolution when a Greek general called Euphemius declared himself a rival emperor and attempted a revolutionary coup in Syracuse. Euphemius failed in his effort. In the aftermath, however, he appealed to the Aghlabids for assistance, and offered an annual tribute in exchange for military support against Constantinople. The Muslim rulers in Kairouan accepted. It was, they agreed, the perfect smokescreen behind which to commence a full-scale invasion.

The Islamic conquest of Sicily began in 826 in Mazara del Vallo, an ex-Phoenician colony on the island's south-west coast. When the Aghlabids landed this was little more than a fishing port with limited military infrastructure. In the coming decades, however, the Arabs would transform it into an international centre for Islamic law, with close links to Ifrīqya. From this point on, however, the 'secret' campaign progressed slowly. While the army made short work of Euphemius's forces, following a battle around the hilltop town of Enna, it took them over fifty years to

obtain control of the island as a whole. This was as much a consequence of the nature of the mission as it was the spirit of Sicilian
resistance. The invaders were not enacting a kind of extended
Saracen raid. They aimed to build a long-term presence on the
island, to bring it under the influence of the faith as a whole, the
dar al-Islam.

Much of the Sicilian population seems to have conceded without
opposition. Many of those in coastal settlements simply converted
on the spot, seeing an alliance with Islam as an opportunity for
respite from attacks by pirates. Parallel to this, as the Aghlabid
army moved from west to east, the generals decommissioned soldiers to set up new villages and repopulate abandoned ones. Their
influence is still visible in the names of towns across the west of
the island: Marsala comes from the Arabic *Marsa Alī*, God's harbour; Misilmeri means 'resting place of the emir'; and Corleone
most probably takes its name from a prominent Arab military
commander, Kurliyun. All of the 'castel' prefixes that survive to
this day across Sicily, as in Caltanissetta and Caltagirone, signpost
where the army constructed fortified castles to consolidate their
power and establish a new system of territorial management.[1]

In the instances where local populations did fight back, the
Arab troops deployed excessive force. Muslim historians like Ibn
al-Athīr and Al-Tijani wrote tracts celebrating stonings in conquered cities and described how the invading army strung heads
along the various cities' walls to humiliate the dead.[2] While the
Christian representation of Islam as a kind of 'pagan revival'
conducted on the service of Satan himself was certainly framed
in rather paranoid terms, it was not, therefore, entirely without
justification.[3] The most significant massacre took place in Syracuse, which remained the centre of Byzantine power throughout
the period of Muslim conquest. While the city had continued

to decline since the time of the Republic, its natural advantages and strong walls still posed a problem for the invading forces. Like the Romans before them, it took the Arabs over a year to breach the fortifications, and when they finally did, in 877, this was largely thanks to naval support from Ifrīqya. Theodosius, a monk who was imprisoned during the city's capture, has left us a first-hand description of the ferocity with which the invading troops razed the city. According to his chronicle, the Arab forces killed all the Byzantine military personnel, looted and burnt churches and residences and enslaved all citizens who agreed to surrender.[4] This was the final blow for that once great city. Since antiquity, Syracuse and its surrounding province had been the centre of the island's cultural and political life. From the Arab conquest onwards, it was the north-west of the island, and Palermo in particular, that would shape Sicily's history.

When the Aghlabids took control of Palermo in 831 the city was in a sorry state. Its civilian population was dwindling, its architecture decrepit and its harbour insignificant. The Aghlabid generals, though, immediately recognised the potential to develop this site, which was surrounded with rich, fertile land, and well positioned for trade with North Africa. In fact, they were so attuned to the city's geographical advantages that they decided to make it their capital, renaming it Bal'harm (the origin of Palermo) from the previous Panormus. One of the first things the new rulers did to mark the city's importance was to construct mosques. According to the travelling historian Ibn Hawqal, who visited Palermo in the early tenth century, the urban area was home to as many as three hundred such spaces.[5] These were not only religious buildings. They also had an important civic function, as courts with municipal offices.

Arguably their most important role was as Koranic schools, which aside from religious law taught basic literacy skills, mathematics, and art and crafts to Muslim migrants as well as new converts from the Greek-speaking population. Under Byzantine rule, Palermo had been governed by a small ecclesiastical elite, flanked by a modest community of merchants and soldiers and a mass of illiterate peasants. From the very beginning of Arab rule, the Aghlabids worked to educate large parts of the population. Within decades of the Islamic conquest, Palermo was Sicily's most literate city and was home to a whole new class of bureaucrats and scribes.

Post-conquest, life in the capital was relatively tolerant. While Muslims enjoyed priority in state services, and it was illegal to read from the Bible or Torah in public, Christians and Jews were free to live and trade and practise their religions in private. Even Theodosius, who wrote his aforementioned account of the destruction of Syracuse from a prison cell, marvelled at the diversity of residents and travellers in the west of the island. He described Palermo as being 'lively' and 'well-populated', a place where 'citizens and foreigners gathered together' and would sing in the streets.[6] While there was, in reality, considerable segregation between religious groups, particularly in wealthier neighbourhoods, the popular districts were melting pots. The area around the port, now Vucciria, was once filled with hostels that provided temporary accommodation for mercenaries, maritime workers, and smugglers from across the Mediterranean. Two souks, now known as Capo and Borgo Vecchio, obtained renown for the quality of their meat, and the skill of their predominantly Jewish butchers.[7] The city's most important market, Ballarò, also came to prominence around this time and provided a centre for the sale of imported goods like spices, medicines, fabrics and other luxury items, which Arab merchants imported from Baghdad.

During the period as an emirate, Palermo's topography evolved according to models developed in the Islamic world. North Italian cities – particularly those like Florence or Siena which flourished in the medieval period – are usually structured around Greco-Roman models, with the piazza as the basic urban unit. Palermo, by contrast, bears a closer resemblance to Maghrebian cities, like Kairouan and, to some extent, Cairo. The 'centre' of Palermo, for example, is not a square but a long road called the *cassaro* (now Via Vittorio Emanuele) which runs east to west, connecting the port with what was at the time the central mosque, now the site of the city's cathedral.[8] This area was surrounded by a labyrinthine network of subsidiary streets and blind alleys called *aziqqa* which correspond to the two central residential districts of Capo and Albergeria. These are now suffering visibly from neglect. In the tenth century, though, they were home to prosperous businessmen who conducted their trade on the nearby *simāt*, a commercial street. Separate to this, a few hundred metres to the east of the port, was Al-Khalesa, now known as La Kalsa, which served as a kind of 'city within a city', and provided a home for the emir, the state administrators and delegates from other Muslim territories. The entire city was well supplied with amenities thanks to a system of *qanats*, underground tunnels that the Arabs built to bring clean water from the nearby hills for drinking and bathing.

During the reign of the Fatimids – an Egyptian Shiite dynasty who took control of all of the Ifrīqyan territories, including Sicily, in 909 – citizens across the Islamic world came to admire the island as one of the faith's most important possessions. One significant factor in this was the spread of new agricultural techniques in the surrounding countryside, like terracing and irrigation, which dramatically improved the island's crop yield.[9] Throughout the tenth century, farmers in the west of Sicily began to produce large quantities of rice, bulgur, lemons, oranges, melons, prickly pears, cucumber, aubergine, spinach, dates and cane sugar, along with various herbs and spices like sumac, tarragon, jasmine, saffron and of course the now-ubiquitous almond and pistachio nuts. Of course, the majority of the population did not have access to such bounteous goods. The historian Yaqut al-Hamawi describes how the diet of the peasants in the inland villages was limited to 'stinking food' like onions, and we know from other sources that rural residents would mainly have sustained themselves on dried fava beans, peas, chard and snails.[10] Nevertheless, the urban elite, which was relatively sizeable, were able to enjoy new delicacies like almond and lemon *granita* which local chefs made using snow from Mount Etna, and which they stored in deep ditches known as *neviere*, as well as some form of *cannolo*, the famous tubes of fried dough filled with ricotta cream and candied fruit. While the Qur'an forbids Muslims from consuming alcohol, many Sicilian Arabs seem to have taken a liberal approach to this rule. It was in the tenth century that the islanders came to develop what we'd now call 'dessert wines', including some version of Zibibbo, an aromatic drink produced using dried grapes, which they drank in large quantities.

Today, many Sicilians are proud of the Arab influence on their cuisine. The fact is, though, that very few original recipes remain from this period. This heritage is more a case of 'invented tradition' than it is of traceable legacy.[11] Most of the evidence for this historic connection can be seen in later 'fusion' foods: many of the sweets that people now enjoy on Christian saint days, for example, including marzipan fruits, *nucàtoli* (date biscuits), *torrone* (nougat) and the caramel-and-sesame bites called *giurgiulena*, were in fact created by Muslim chefs. Other more general tendencies, such as the islanders' preference for sweet and sour flavours, may well go back to the time of the emirate.

Perhaps the best example of the long-term legacy of this moment, though, is *pasta con le sarde*. According to folkloric tradition, this dish, which calls for sardines to be cooked in a sauce of wild fennel tops, was originally a Byzantine naval staple that was invented as a form of medicine, to cover the tangy taste, and nauseous side effects, of eating old fish. Under the Arabs, migrants from North Africa seemingly began to add nuts, raisins and sometimes saffron to the dish, to balance the bitter taste of the greens. This sauce was most likely served with couscous, which is still popular on the island, and which was, incidentally, the first form of dried pasta to be consumed anywhere in Italy.[12] Nowadays, though, most of the islanders, particularly in Palermo, eat the sauce with *bucatini*, long hollow noodles that are common in the country's southern regions. There are clearly some significant gaps in this story. Nevertheless, the sheer popularity of this dish is a fitting illustration of how, despite centuries of subsequent colonisations, the islanders continue to celebrate certain aspects of their Arab heritage.

While Sicily's Muslim leaders presided over a series of impressive cultural and technological achievements, their emirate was never particularly stable. Throughout the tenth century, Palermo was witness to almost constant revolts, most of which were the result of disagreements between the original Sunni colonisers and later Shiite Fatimid administrators. In addition to this there was the question of the Berber peoples, who were isolated from positions of influence and who were treated as second-class citizens by the ruling elite. Their tribes regularly assaulted the island's fortresses and, in many parts of the island, these peoples were effectively operating as bandits within the Islamic territory. In 1019 a particularly large group of Berber horsemen, supported by black African slaves, launched a ferocious riot in the capital, during which they demanded the right to their own protected lands, and representation within the political establishment. By 1040, these combined tensions gave way to a full-scale civil war in which multiple factions claimed to represent the authority of the caliphate.

As Muslim rule faltered, bishops in Rome and Constantinople plotted to take the island back in the name of Christendom. Sicily was no longer a 'peripheral' question, but a decisive battleground for the future of the faith. Relations between the Eastern and Western church had degenerated significantly during the two hundred years of the Sicilian emirate. Age-old theological disputes – surrounding the Creed, the nature of eucharistic sacrament and celibacy among other things – had been replaced by more pressing concerns regarding the exertion of political power and, more concretely, territorial disputes in Southern Italy. Popes and patriarchs jostled to assert dominance over one another, clashing continually over the question of how far the sovereignty of the Western church should extend.

Finally, the two powers reached a historic impasse. In 1054 Pope Leo IX and Michael Cerularius, Patriarch of Constantinople, issued mutual excommunications to one another, thereby inaugurating what has become known as 'the Great Schism'. From this point on, the two institutions – the Eastern Orthodox and Catholic church – were considered entirely separate powers. This schism is rightly recognised as one of the most important events in Christian history, and it had quite specific implications

for Sicily. Taking the island back was no longer just a question
of 'liberating' a territory from Muslim rule; it became a competition between the two churches, one that would determine which
would have dominance in the region.

It was the Papacy that proved the most opportunistic. In 1059
another pope, Nicholas II, held a conference in Melfi in Southern Italy, during which he reached out to an unexpected ally, the
Normans, for aid. This was far from an obvious decision. In the
tenth century this then recently Christianised mix of Vikings,
Celts, Franks and Romans had made significant inroads into
Southern Italy, and had taken land from the Papacy, Byzantium,
and the Lombards in modern-day Puglia and Calabria. In 1053, in
the run-up to the schism, they had even kidnapped and ransomed
Leo IX during a successful attempt to gain land in Benevento,
a key military outpost near Naples. Despite the fact that many
cardinals opposed this dubious conduct, Nicholas reasoned that
these renegade soldiers were at least nominally tied to the Catholic church and, as such, could, under the right circumstances, be a
useful weapon against both the Arabs and the orthodox authorities. At Melfi, on 29 August, he therefore made an offer to Robert
Guiscard, head of the Hauteville family, and one of the most
powerful Norman leaders. The Papal States would refrain from
attacking his strongholds in Southern Italy, and actively support
them in a campaign to conquer Sicily. In exchange, Robert would
be required to hand over control of all the churches within his
territories – many of which were Byzantine – and pay a regular
tax to Rome. Understanding the value of papal protection and
keen to expand his own peoples' influence, Robert agreed. Sicily
became the testing ground for this new alliance.

In May 1061 Robert and his brother Roger led an army from
Calabria across the straits of Messina to the island's east coast.

They set out under the banner of Archangel Michael, the warrior saint whom many Christians adopted as their protector en route to the crusades in Jerusalem. Despite the iconography, however, this was not an especially xenophobic campaign. The commanders were open to strategic alliances with Muslim forces. During the first months of the invasion an emir, Ibn al Timnah, assisted the Christian forces to gain peaceful control of various cities in the south-east. After pausing to construct castles and other bases, the Normans then made a significant breakthrough in 1063 at the Battle of Cerami which enabled them to expand their influence across the centre of the island. Yet the campaign faltered after this first major victory. While William of Normandy would conquer England in a matter of months, it took Robert and Roger nine years to fight their way to the Sicilian capital. Even as they pushed across the island, the Hauteville brothers were repeatedly forced to divert their attentions to attacks against their territories on the southern mainland. At several points their troop numbers dwindled to the mere hundreds.

Finally, in 1072, taking advantage of factional tensions between Arab groups, the Normans organised a prompt siege of Palermo and successfully took control of the city. Robert appointed himself as the island's first duke and returned to Puglia, his obligations to the Papacy completed. Roger remained in his place, under the title of count, to govern over the new Norman territory.

Any residual image of this Christian reconquest as a jingoistic affair must be counterbalanced by consideration of Roger's subsequent administration.[13] Rather than radical rupture with the Arab rule, the new count extended and revitalised the island along similar guidelines that had motivated the Aghlabids and their successors. In a land that was still overwhelmingly populated with Muslims – the rest being more or less Greek-speaking Christians – Roger recognised that he would have to demonstrate moderation and tolerance if he was to succeed in establishing a new governmental system. He forbade the Norman soldiers from unnecessary pillaging, and took personal responsibility to limit the massacre of Muslims post-conquest. He ordered mosques that had been built on church foundations to be reconverted, but allowed original structures to be left intact. Many Muslims were impressed by these policies. Others continued to resist his rule: small-scale independent emirates continued to fight on for another twenty years, and guerrilla warfare was widespread for longer still. By the 1090s, as Norman forces began to consolidate their power, many Muslims decided to emigrate. Among them was the poet Ibn Hamdis, whose verses about his lost homeland, which he wrote during a period of extended exile, serve as a fitting eulogy to the years of Fatimid governance:

> I remember Sicily as agony,
> reflection tortures my soul.
> The land of my youthful pleasures,
> once inhabited by the greatest of people,
> is but a desert now.
> I have been banished from paradise,
> and I long to tell you why.[14]

Powerful as they are, Hamdis's words are hardly representative of Sicily's Muslim population as a whole. Just as the Christians under Arab rule had adjusted to new political circumstances, so too, over the twelfth century in particular, the relationship between Norman administration and Arab communities would be one of ever-increasing collaboration. Roger himself seems to have been fluent in Arabic, which remained a state language on equal standing with Greek, Hebrew, Latin and now Norman French; and he selected Muslims to be some of his closest advisors. Similarly, Roger elected to keep the financial system largely in the hands of Arabs, and to populate his bureaucratic class with those that had been so well trained in the Koranic schools. Just as importantly, he also gave money to Sicilian Greeks to rebuild the orthodox churches and monasteries that had declined under the emirate. As long as these communities cut administrative ties to Constantinople and pledged themselves politically as subjects of the Papacy, he promised, they would be free to worship according to their own rituals and in their own language.

None of this is what Pope Nicholas II had imagined when he made his deal with Robert in Melfi in 1059. While Catholicism was, in theory, the new state religion, the politics of the new country explicitly rebuffed the cultural oppositions and theological disagreements that had fuelled the Great Schism. The Papacy had expected Roger to manage a transition to a Catholic monoculture. Instead, the count encouraged a new Norman version of syncretism, in which the orthodox and Muslim traditions were incorporated wherever possible into the new state. In 1097, these tensions came to a head when a new pope, Urban II, ordered all European Christians to embark on the First Crusade and Roger refused to provide his support to the venture. In response, in a show of force designed to intimidate the Norman ruler, the Papacy appointed a new Bishop of Troina and Messina as an apostolic legate on the island, without the count's consent. Shortly after his landing, Roger had him arrested. This kind of direct provocation could have constituted a declaration of war coming from most other rulers. By this point, however, the Normans had become so influential in European affairs that

Urban, who was concerned primarily with ensuring his success in Jerusalem, could not afford to make enemies of them. Roger himself was well aware of this fact. When he met the pope in person the following year, he refused to back down. In fact he won some remarkable concessions. During their discussion, the Papacy agreed to all of Roger's terms: not only would the Normans have control over appointment of all of Sicily's bishops, they would also have the right to vet subsequent papal legates in advance of their arrival from Rome. This was an extraordinary diplomatic victory. It also marked the beginning of a long power struggle with the Vatican, which would prove an increasingly important part of Sicily's political history in the decades to come.

When Roger I died in 1101 he was widely revered for his achievements both as a soldier and as a statesman. Under Roger II, who ruled Sicily from 1105, Norman Catholicism continued to fuse with the island's other pre-existing cultures within the context of a more mature, constitutionally defined, social order. We don't know much about the early period of the younger Roger's rule. One of his first notable actions as count, in 1114, was to aggressively assert his father's newly won right to control the religious authorities by deposing the archbishop of Cosenza in Calabria. In 1129, he took the even riskier and more dramatic step of supporting the claim of an antipope, Anacletus II, in his challenge against the incumbent pontiff. If that campaign had failed, the rebellious young Hauteville may well have faced the threat of an invasion from the mainland. Fortunately for Roger, Anacletus did indeed ascend the papal throne the next year and, as a reward for his loyalty, offered him a crown.

On Christmas Day 1130 Roger II was pronounced Sicily's first king. He celebrated in lavish fashion with a vast procession of horses followed by an extraordinary banquet with gold and silver cutlery and servants clad in expensive silk. One observer, who made the journey down from Southern Italy, noted that 'the glory and wealth of the royal abode were so spectacular that ... it instilled not a little fear in all those who had come from so far away. For many saw there more things than they had even heard rumour of previously.'[15] This witness's shock is understandable. If nothing else, the presence of Muslims in the court must have seemed strange indeed to a traveller from the mainland. Yet Roger's coronation was also a significant 'rags to riches' story. Just a century before, most of Europe's elite had thought of the Hautevilles as nomadic mercenaries and troublemakers. Now they were claiming the conventions of royalty as their own, and doing so in the most ostentatious manner.

In 1131 Roger commissioned a new cathedral at Cefalù, a coastal town to the east of Palermo, to mark a new era of 'royal power'. In many respects this building serves as a visual manifesto for his subsequent rule. Roger I had accepted that a monotheistic divinity could be worshipped in diverse ways according to different cultural traditions. At Cefalù, though, Roger II strove to give this philosophy a concrete form. The frame of the cathedral – the pillars, apses and fonts, as well as the external façade, with its dual bell towers – is essentially Romanesque in style and recalls the Hautevilles' French origins and the churches of Normandy. The ornamental details, however, demonstrate the family's subsequent fusion with the cultures of the south. A subtle Arabic influence permeates the building, in the floral and geometric patterns, and some of the fantastic beasts that decorate the ceiling. Artists from Constantinople produced a series of golden mosaics of saints in the choir. These, together with the Madonna and angels on the apses, are purely Byzantine. At the centre of the building is a Christ Pantocrator, which stares down majestically from the cathedral's dome with a Bible in his hands. The text, tellingly, is in Greek with a Latin inscription. Looking at this building today it's hard to remember that this was, and remains, a functioning Catholic cathedral. The aesthetics of the space, which combines all of the artistic skills that had been developed across the Mediterranean in previous centuries, would have stunned contemporary worshippers. This was not just a religious building. It was a creative piece of political propaganda, articulating a new and esoteric vision of what the Sicilian state might look like.

Roger was obsessed with the task of building unity among the different cultures in his kingdom. In order to achieve this, he worked to develop a new form of centralised government. In 1140, a full century before King John approved the Magna Carta in England, he and his aides drew up the Assizes of Ariano. These early constitutional documents provided the political consolidation of the ideals that had been expressed visually at Cefalù. The main purpose of these forty-four laws, many of which were imported from other Norman territories in France, was to provide a new feudal structure for the island. Indeed, the Assizes mark the formal birth of a system of knights and landowners who, while they could only be appointed by royal authority, could pass power down according to a strict notion of hereditary lineage. In exchange for various privileges, these knights were required to police their land against all kinds of criminals and vagabonds, to provide hospitality for friends of the king, to protect the church, and treat peasants with compassion. The Assizes forbade the fighting between factions that had been so endemic under Arab rule, making this a crime punishable by execution. More generally, Roger's document highlighted the need to tackle corruption, particularly within religious institutions. It clearly states that the sale and bartering of relics of saints and martyrs should be made illegal, and that nobody should be able to buy their way into the priesthood. A sizeable section of the document is concerned with regulating female sexuality. Woman adulterers were no longer condemned to death, as they had been under Muslim rule, but nonetheless faced the grim prospects of a 'slitting of [the] nose' or 'public flogging'. Prostitution, in a more humane move, was decriminalised and pimping defined as the 'worst kind of crime'. Perhaps the most intriguing clause in the document is its call for all the island's subjects to tolerate one another's religious and cultural differences, with the proviso that they did not come into tension with, or contradict, the absolute rule of the crown.

It's impossible to know exactly what the Sicilian population made of Roger's vision of society. Based on the limited archaeological finds, we can deduce that these constitutional documents had at least some bearing on the actual administration. The implementation of the cosmopolitan state was physically present in everyday commercial life. A piece of early coinage, called the *tarì*, was emblazoned with a *T* shape on one side, symbolising resurrection in the Greek Orthodox tradition, while the other contained Arabic lettering and the message 'Allah is the only God'.[16]Another object, a tombstone belonging to the mother of one of the king's priests, which is inscribed in four languages (dating to 1148 in Latin, 6658 in Greek, 543 in Arabic and 4904 in Hebrew), demonstrates that parts of the ecclesiastical establishment felt relatively at ease in this environment. Similarly, it's clear that Norman Sicily provided fertile conditions for scholarship. Throughout Roger's reign, scientists, artists, philosophers and musicians from North Africa, Andalucía and the Middle

East began to arrive on the island in ever-increasing numbers. Translators, such as the South Italian physician Filagato Ceramide, worked to produce Latin and French versions of ancient Greek and Arabic texts, while George of Antioch, an admiral and Christian emir of Syria, and Nilus Doxopatres, a Byzantine theologian, produced original works of poetry and short fiction. According to Henry Aristippus, a Catholic intellectual who lived on the island in the twelfth century, the libraries in both Palermo and Syracuse were filled with 'new' works by Euclid, Aristotle, Themistios and Plutarch among other writers, and there was a rich culture of debate.[17]

Roger himself was deeply invested in the intellectual life of his court. Between 1136 and 1154 the king developed a particularly close relationship with a Moroccan-born geographer named Muhammad al-Idrisi, whose contributions to cartography rank among the most significant of the medieval world. Al-Idrisi was well travelled, and after studying in Córdoba spent his life on the move between Portugal and Damascus. He lived in Palermo for several years, during which time he worked with the Norman monarch on a hugely ambitious project which aimed to collate unprecedented information about the natural and human geography of the known world. As part of this initiative Roger and Al-Idrisi worked together in examining ancient texts. Meanwhile they tasked the island's scribes with conducting a census of Sicily's biggest port cities. By interviewing travellers, and embarking on small-scale surveying missions, the state administration collectively developed an atlas of the world's rivers, coasts, forests and mountains, as well as roads, fortresses and other human infrastructure. The results, published as the *Kitab Rudjdjar* (the *Book of Roger*) were sufficiently accurate that in the fifteenth century Christopher Columbus was still using these findings as a key reference during his voyage to the Americas.[18] Alongside its scientific value the book also served as a detailed cultural encyclopaedia, and is filled with wry and, in retrospect, rather amusing observations. It describes, for example, how the Norman territories in modern-day France were 'a land of abundance, comfort, and insensibility' but home to a population 'characterised by their ignorance and coarse disposition'.[19] Britain, meanwhile, is deemed to resemble 'the head of an ostrich', with a population of 'patient, determined and resolute' people, yet it's cursed by 'an endless winter'.[20] Sicily, unsurprisingly, is 'the pearl of the age' on account of its 'uniqueness' and powerful leaders.[21] In recognition of this, the accompanying map faces south rather than north, with Palermo positioned along the central axis.

For Roger himself the *Kitab Rudjdjar* seems to have been, primarily, an intellectual endeavour. While he embarked on a small-scale imperial project in North Africa – claiming the island of Djerba and several settlements on the Tunisian mainland – he was motivated more by a need to protect Sicily's commercial interests, than to impose political rule over the local populations. In 1147 Roger, like his father before him, refused to set out on Pope Eugene III's Second Crusade. Instead he used the opportunity to reinforce his defences against Byzantium in and around Southern Italy. In the very few cases where the king did authorise offensive military missions, as in Tripoli in 1143, he was mainly interested in expanding the Norman trade routes. Despite these occasional acts of aggression, Roger maintained good relations, and even friendships, with rulers across the southern Mediterranean such as Al-Hafiz, the Egyptian Fatimid caliph. In the context of a Christian world that, elsewhere, was beginning to describe religious war in fundamentalist terms, as an eternal conflict between 'civitas christiana' and 'civitas diabolica', the monarch's vision was, without doubt, exceptional. While his state was hierarchical, it did aim to provide a social structure that avoided discriminating based on ethnicity or religion and, in this sense, at least, was more enlightened than many other European kingdoms.

During the late period of Norman rule, which ran from Roger's death in 1154 to around 1194, Sicily's absolute monarchy gradually weakened. While the nature of the state itself remained formally unchanged under the following Hauteville rulers, the island's knights and barons became increasingly confident in challenging the centralisation that Roger had established. These centrifugal energies ultimately served to undermine the social fabric. In 1160 a charismatic knight named Matteo Bonello succeeded in raising support among his fellow barons, who were frustrated at what they saw as the over-representation of Islam in the state administration. In November that year Bonello's rebels orchestrated the assassination of one of Sicily's most important Muslim officials, Maione da Bari, in the streets of Palermo, which snowballed, quite suddenly, into attacks against the island's Arab communities. Protesters, who were paid by the barons, burnt down the city's mosques and bathhouses, broke into the royal palace, and emptied the treasuries. While the plot collapsed soon after – Bonello was imprisoned and died in 1161 – these events seem to have unleashed a latent xenophobia in the south and east of the island. Ibn Qalāqis, an Egyptian scholar who travelled across Sicily around this time, details how the barons, particularly around Syracuse, began to impose higher taxes on Muslim subjects.[22] And while the geographer Ibn Jubayr was impressed by the state of coexistence he saw in Palermo, he was horrified by the subjugation of his fellow believers in the port of Messina.[23]

A few isolated aspects of Roger's vision endured for a while longer. William II, who governed from 1166 to 1189, continued to commission Muslim artists to design and decorate his state buildings. This is particularly visible in the Genoard, the one-time royal park and hunting ground, which owes its name to Arab rule when it was known as Gennat al-Ard (Paradise on Earth). Today the area corresponds to the city's south-western suburbs and looks, at first, like a typical modern urban enclave. In the twelfth century, though, it was a green oasis, a sanctuary of palm, fir and orange trees which expanded outwards into a wild area of lakes, rivers and woodland.[24] Most of the Genoard's palaces have been destroyed, though a few, like the enigmatic Cuba, a tall Islamic-style building which even crops up in Boccaccio's *Decameron*, are in surprisingly good condition. The most luxurious and best preserved of all is the Zisa, which served as a royal retreat. The three-storey rectangular building, home to several *muqarnas* (typically Islamic honeycomb-like structures) on the vaulted ceilings, bears a close resemblance to the architecture that was developing at the time in Tunisia and Egypt. The main structure is built around a cavernous *iwan*, the walls of which are adorned with a series of mosaics that represent Islamic symbols of immortality: the peacock, whose spread tail feathers are synonymous with the universe, and the palm tree which Muslims revere for its capacity to survive harsh conditions. The centrepiece, an interior fountain marked by an eagle, a symbol of imperial power common to both ancient Rome and Egypt, flows out from the palace into the garden: a poetic tribute to the links between Europe and Africa, and earthly and man-made paradise. This was an intellectual game, a private 'theme park', where William could retreat to escape the demands of politics. While it tells us little about life in the city as a whole, it is, nevertheless, a powerful indicator of the esteem that the later Norman kings seem to have held for the emirate that their ancestors had conquered.

William's greatest legacy, however, was a Christian building – the Abbey of Monreale, which at the time was just a small village at the edge of Palermo in the foothills of Monte Caputo. Completed in 1174, this was not just another church. Instead it represented a full maturation of the aesthetic project that Roger II had begun forty years earlier in the cathedral at Cefalù. Local legend holds that William came up with the idea of building a religious monument at this site after encountering a vision of the Virgin Mary during a hunt at the limits of the Genoard. It's clear, though, that he was motivated by personal and political concerns. In 1168 Walter Ophamil, the king's former tutor and one of the island's most important religious authorities, received approval from Rome to oversee a new development at Palermo's cathedral. We might therefore see William's decision to commission Monreale as an effort to impress his master, to demonstrate his skills as a religious patron, and to maintain direct control over what would, for a while, be the island's most important religious building. The proposed location – on the foundations of an orthodox chapel that had been neglected under Arab rule – ensured the Papacy gave swift approval to the project. The speed of construction was similarly impressive. William invested enormous sums into the site, and, as a result, a combined workforce of Christians, Jews and Muslims succeeded in completing the cathedral's exterior in just two years and the interior within a decade. Given the beauty of both, this was a remarkable feat.

Like Cefalù, the rather simple façade at Monreale recalls the Romanesque features of Norman French architecture. In this instance, though, the Islamic influence is more explicit – visible, for example, in the interlocking arches and elaborate geometric patterns of the rear apse. The interior is cavernous, its transept over a hundred metres long and forty-three metres high and dominated by large granite columns, as well as one anomalous pillar made from green cipollino marble. William ordered two sets of bronze doors, from Tuscany and Puglia, to be shipped to the island presumably in order to demonstrate that, unlike Ophamil, he was able to afford that age's finest artisanship. Most striking of all are the wall mosaics which far surpass those of Roger II's own cathedral. There are 7,000 square metres of gold tesserae at Monreale, which are divided into 130 scenes. Those in the nave depict the story of Genesis, from the Creation to Jacob's wrestling with the angel. The aisle, meanwhile, is dedicated to the New Testament, and, while decorated with scenes of saints and martyrs, it is taken up largely with the story of the Passion. The papal authorities were impressed. In 1182, Pope Lucius formally recognised the new archbishopric and declared Monreale the greatest architectural accomplishment since ancient times.[25]

Understandably, most visitors to the abbey spend the majority of their time admiring the nave. There's a case to be made, though, that it's the cloister that really ties the building together, and, arguably, the Norman period itself. The design is a perfect square, boasting 228 elaborate columns decorated with orange limestone, black lava and coloured rocks. The marble capitals, which here push the boundaries of Romanesque convention, mirror the biblical scenes of the interior. The influences, though, go further back still. Alongside Noah, Samson and John the Baptist, visitors can admire Hellenic-looking figures and more anomalous, grotesque bodies hidden behind the sculpted foliage. An Islamic-style fountain designed in the shape of an enormous towering palm tree unites the immortal symbolism of the Muslim world, as seen in the Zisa, with the religious ritual of Christian baptism. Yet even these are just surface details. The interaction of elements in Monreale's cloister is so complex and esoteric that art historians continue to disagree as to which specific styles might be attributed to which cultural traditions. The fact that such a dizzying array of influences are synthesised into such a harmonious design here is one of the great hallmarks of Sicily's history. While the everyday realities of the island's society remain frustratingly mysterious, buildings like Monreale give at least some insight into the imaginative world of the Norman kingdom and the cosmopolitan ideals that its rulers sought to uphold.

3

The Anti-Christ of Palermo (1182–1347)

An Emperor-King, the 'Peaceful Crusade', Sicily's War of Independence

[Frederick] is joined in odious friendship with the Saracens; several times he has sent envoys and gifts to them, and receives the like from them in return with expressions of honour and welcome; he embraces their rites; he openly keeps them with him ... he cause[s] the envoys of the sultan to be honourably received and lavishly entertained throughout the kingdom of Sicily.

Papal bull deposing Emperor Frederick II, 1245

In 2015 the world heritage organisation UNESCO formally recognised Palermo's Arab-Norman architecture as protected sites, citing them as 'the material testimony of a particular political and cultural condition characterized by a fruitful cohabitation of people of different origins'. This reverence is understandable and valid to some extent, though it shouldn't be exaggerated. The apparent 'golden age' of coexistence was short-lived, and was confined, by and large, to four or five rulers over a period of just eighty years. Even here we can note several paradoxes.

While Roger II and William II were enamoured with Greek and Arabic aesthetics, by the end of their dynasty Sicily's population was almost entirely Catholic. If the Norman kings valorised Byzantine and Islamic art, the very act of placing these influences within a Christian framework served, inevitably, to dilute the complexity of the systems of thought they so admired. Some historians have even gone as far as to argue that the Normans reduced entire societies to a crude form of political propaganda or, in the case of the Genoard, a form of entertainment for the elite.[1]

Perhaps the most significant problem with Norman-Sicilian culture, however, is how reliant it was on the individual personalities of a few rather impressive leaders and the ideology of absolute monarchy. While the relative lack of unrest during this period might well indicate that Sicily's inhabitants lived happily side by side, with fewer cultural and ethnic divisions than under the emirate or subsequent administrations, this can't be taken for granted. If a Byzantine or Arab invasion had been successful anytime throughout the twelfth century, it is equally possible that this tolerant pluralistic society would have collapsed.

It's often said that when powerful monarchs die, social crises follow in their wake. In the case of Sicily this maxim was proved correct in 1189 when Tancred I, an illegitimate grandchild of Roger II, took the Sicilian throne. Tancred was a capable soldier, but a poor administrator. He therefore depended on his knights to enforce domestic order to a degree that far exceeded his forbears. Delegating power, though, was a dangerous move. Only thirty years had passed since Bonello and his rebel nobles had tried to overthrow the Hautevilles, and many of those who were now advising the king had almost certainly supported that coup. Recognising Tancred's weakness, they once again worked to assert their dominance over the island's affairs. And again they focused their ire at the island's Muslims. In 1191 the barons in Southern Sicily increased their discriminatory anti-Islamic taxes and began to confiscate lands and goods from these communities by force. In response to this, a general named Muhammad Ibn Abbād, based in the still predominantly Arab port of Mazara del Vallo, led a furious reactionary jihad in which he organised his fellow Muslims to attack the Christian landowners. In a matter of months, the ancient, apparently obsolete geographic divisions between Sicily's south and west resurfaced for the first time in centuries. Tancred tried to contain the violence, but his efforts were in vain. By the time of his death in 1194, civil war had, in all but name, returned to the island.

Some historians mark this moment as the beginning of Sicily's infamous and dramatic decline, from a centre of world civilisation to one of Europe's most oppressive kingdoms. There was, however, one further moment of cultural flourishing in the island's medieval history. Sicilians still remember Frederick II, who ruled from 1198 to 1250, as one of their most important and influential leaders. His reputation is nothing short of legendary. To this day his name is emblazoned on street signs, piazzas, hotels and restaurants across the island. Internationally too, Frederick has a reputation as being one of the most exceptional individuals of his age. And while some revisionist scholars have sought to challenge this notion, presenting the king more soberly as a 'man of his time', it's fair to say that, by now, the story has taken on a life of its own.[2] He was, according to the famous scholar of Italian art and culture Jacob Burckhardt, 'the first ruler of the modern type anywhere in the world'.[3] Nietzsche saw him as 'the first European[4] ... an atheist and hater of the church [and] one of the people most closely related to me'.[5] In the twentieth century, the philosopher Giovanni Gentile described Frederick's rule as representing 'an awakening of consciousness' which set the groundwork for what he saw as the glories of Mussolini's fascism.[6]

Frederick was born in 1194 in Iesi, central Italy, the child of Roger II's daughter Constance and the Holy Roman Emperor, Henry VI of Swabia. This was a watershed alliance which marked the end of the direct Norman Hauteville line and the ascendency of the Germanic Hohenstaufen dynasty to power in Sicily. The conditions surrounding the monarch's birth give some insight into what was at stake during his reign. Frederick was not just a royal baby: he was the physical incarnation of a synthesis between the esoteric Norman kingdom of the south and the great sprawl of the Germanic territories. His very name, Federico Ruggero, Frederick Roger, combined the names of his two grandfathers, and by extension those two, previously separate, political realities. When Constance and Henry died within a year of one another in 1197 and 1198, they left behind not only a human being, a four-year-old king, but a political chess piece. There are various accounts of Frederick's upbringing, some more romanticised than others. His biographer, the historian Ernst Kantorowicz, presented the young king as a kind of orphan prodigy, a wild and curious boy who absorbed the wisdom of the Palermitan souks via a kind of cultural osmosis:

> At eight and nine years old the young King wandered about without let or hindrance, and strolled unchecked through the narrow streets and markets and gardens of the semi African capital at the foot of the Pellegrino. An amazing variety of peoples, religions and customs jostled each other before his eyes: mosques with their minarets,

synagogues with their cupolas stood cheek by jowl with Norman
churches and cathedrals, which again had been adorned by Byzantine
masters with gold mosaics, their rafters supported by Greek columns
on which Saracen craftsmen had carved in Kufic script the name
of Allah.[7]

We know for certain that Frederick was, like his Norman forbears, capable of communicating in both Arabic and Hebrew as
well as Latin, French, Greek and German. The fact, though, that
his instructors included the rather more sober figure of Cencio
Savelli, later known as Pope Honorius III, suggests that his real
education was closer to that of a standard medieval 'scholastic'
education than Kantorowicz's portrayal might suggest. From a
young age, Frederick was concerned with securing his birthright
as emperor-elect. In 1212, he left Sicily for Germany with a small
army and successfully defeated a series of Saxon factions that had
made a rival claim to the title. In order for him to be able to take
on the role of emperor, in theory at least, Frederick should have
had to relinquish the Sicilian crown. The Papacy, after all, was
concerned with limiting the power of its rivals, and the idea that
one individual might enjoy political control over an area stretching from Sicily to the Prussian borderlands far exceeded what
most Catholic bishops deemed acceptable. Frederick, though,
made a persuasive counter-argument: by wielding both imperial
and royal titles, he claimed, he would be in a better position to
mobilise forces from across Christendom to participate in future
crusades. Honorius III, having known Frederick since he was a
boy, conceded, though not without hesitation. This was a serious
delegation of authority and one that far surpassed that which
the Norman kings had secured. Nevertheless, in 1220, Honorius
declared the Swabian monarch both the king of Sicily and the

Holy Roman Emperor. At just twenty-five years old Frederick was arguably Europe's most powerful political leader, second only to the pope himself.

Frederick travelled incessantly during his reign, though he remained personally attached to Sicily, which he considered a home of sorts. One of his priorities, as far as the island was concerned, was to contain the jihad in the west, which, by the start of the 1220s, was gaining in intensity. During the king's campaigns in Germany, a group of Ibn Abbād's rebels established a small, independent emirate at Corleone, just 50 km from Palermo. In 1216 they used this base to launch a ferocious attack against the cathedral at Monreale during which they kidnapped the local bishop and confined the Christian population to slavery.

In response to these provocations the emperor took a dramatic step. In the winter of 1220, just weeks after securing his imperial title, he ordered the forced deportation of 20,000 Sicilian Muslims to live in exile in the small settlement of Lucera, in modern-day Puglia. This was an undeniably violent act. It's important to recognise, though, that the emperor's decision to take such drastic action was not motivated by the same intolerance that was rife in the Papacy. Frederick did not see these individuals as demons or animals. On the contrary, he actively invested funds to ensure that, once established in Puglia, Muslims had sufficient resources to build mosques, and they were, from this moment on, free to practise their faith without discrimination. In fact, in the following decades, Lucera flourished, and developed a sizeable agricultural economy as well as its own small-scale textile and ceramics industry. This was Frederick's hope all along. The emperor well understood that the Muslims were among his most dangerous and militarily powerful subjects. By deporting these individuals to a city that was just miles from the Vatican's own territories, his main goal was to send a message to all those who had questioned Honorius's wisdom in granting him control of both the crown and empire. The community in Lucera provided a solution to the unrest in Sicily, but it was also a thinly veiled warning to the Papacy, not to interfere by further limiting his ambitions.

As emperor first and king of Sicily second, Frederick was forced to engage in this kind of high-level strategic thinking throughout his reign. In northern Europe, order was maintained by different means than in the south. In Germany, for example, where conflict was particularly intense between the pro-papal Guelphs and the Ghibellines, who supported an expansion of imperial power, Frederick actively armed nobles that supported his claims. In Sicily, on the other hand, where these divisions were less pronounced, and where the barons had proved themselves less trustworthy, he maintained his authority by a series of strict laws. He seized properties from historically rebellious families, limited the influence and territories of individual vassals and forbade marriages among the ruling class without his own express consent. To enforce this, he employed a diverse range of military factions, which included both Teutonic knights and Arab soldiers from Lucera, to whom he allocated castles across the island's interior. This approach, while certainly despotic, also provided a pragmatic means of ensuring that there was a basic degree of unity among the different ethnic, religious and cultural groups that lived in his territories.

In 1224 Frederick took a more concerted step towards realising his centralised pan-European vision by establishing the University of Naples. This was an exceptional act. At the time, the vast majority of Europe's educational facilities were managed directly by the church. This university, by contrast, was a secular institution that was chartered by royal decree. It was, technically speaking, the first non-sectarian, state-funded university anywhere in the world. The curriculum was particularly weighted towards legal studies, and served the purpose of training a new class of state bureaucrats. While many important religious thinkers passed through its corridors – most notably Thomas Aquinas, who studied there around 1239 – this degree of secularisation was unprecedented. The university was a remarkably open institution and the imperial administration provided food and lodging to generations of students from across the continent, and from all backgrounds, in exchange for their future services to the crown and empire. By offering education to such a diverse group of individuals, Frederick clearly hoped to build a bridge between the different sides of his domain. Of course, he could not openly present the institution in these terms. If he had made any attempt to unify his territories in an administrative sense, the Papacy would, without doubt, have declared war. After graduation, Frederick therefore stipulated that the majority of graduates remain in Southern Italy and Sicily, to manage what were, after all, his favourite cities. Palermo, in particular, benefitted from this arrangement. In the late 1220s, after decades of administrative chaos, the capital was gradually repopulated with a class of highly educated anti-papal, pro-Ghibelline youths whose primary loyalty was not to the church but to the new secularised state.

Though Frederick had been cautious not to overplay his hand, conflict with Rome proved inevitable. In 1227 a new pope, Gregory IX, excommunicated the emperor, ostensibly for delaying his obligation to embark on a crusade and thereby breaking the fundamental condition on which he had been permitted to maintain his dual titles. In response to this, indeed directly contradicting this measure, Frederick set out the following year on his own mission to the Holy Land, independently of papal authorisation. Unlike the 'formal' crusades, which the popes had conducted as military operations, Frederick kept his armies at bay. Instead the emperor approached the rulers of Palestine and Egypt as a legitimate heir to the throne; a diplomat, interlocutor and potential ally.[8] Specifically, he reached out to Al-Kamil, an Egyptian sultan who had successfully defeated the Christians' Fifth Crusade in 1221, to try to strike a deal. Al-Kamil was a moderate figure and was, at the time, facing serious domestic unrest. Eager to avoid further conflict, he permitted Frederick to proceed uninhibited to the Holy City on the condition that, among other things, Muslim communities were able to maintain control of two of the most sacred sites: the Dome of the Rock and the Mosque of Omar. Frederick accepted. On 18 March 1229, the Hohenstaufen emperor peacefully marched his troops into Jerusalem, flanked on either side by Christians and Muslims, and crowned himself king with no priest present and none of the bloodshed that had plagued the city in previous decades.[9]

The ramifications of this move sent shockwaves across medieval Europe. Pope Gregory deposed the emperor a second time, and even sent his own 'crusade' against Sicily in 1230. His forces, though, were unable to make progress against the island's formidable navy. In the months that followed, a papal bull circulated across Germany containing apocalyptic prophecies which described Frederick as a chimeric apparition of the Anti-Christ itself:

A beast full of blasphemous names shaped like a panther and with the claws of a bear and the mouth of a lion has risen from the sea raging and spewing forth blasphemies against the name of God. Hungry to destroy everything with its claws and to trample everything under its hooves it has been secretly scheming against the faith ... it openly builds war machines, erects schools capable of leading astray the souls of the faithful and rises against the redeemer of humankind, Christ himself. Do not be amazed to see it unsheathe its sword against us for its lofty aim is to wipe out the name of our lord from the earth. In order to oppose its lies with the clarity of truth and refute its deceptions with the purity of argument look carefully upon the head, the body and the tail of the beast Frederick going by the name of Emperor.[10]

In 1245, another pope, Innocent IV, would eventually strip Frederick of his imperial title altogether. By this stage, however, the Hohenstaufen king had already consolidated his authority in both the political and, as he saw it, spiritual realms. After his success in Jerusalem, Frederick increasingly came to present himself as the natural inheritor of what he saw as a classical Roman-imperial genius. In 1231, he issued a new golden coin called the *augustale*, which was embossed with an eagle in reference to the great emperor Octavian, and which depicted him clad in a toga and wearing a laurel crown. He announced that he wished to be buried in a red porphyry sarcophagus, of Hellenistic imitation, which had originally been designed for Roger II, and which was widely considered the finest Greek-style artwork of the medieval world.[11] Previous Sicilian monarchs, including Roger himself, had appropriated such aesthetics in order to convey a sense of mystique and transcendental allure that would appeal to the island's many cultures. Frederick was not seeking any such communion with a divine force. His attitude towards this distant past was not reverential. He was instead aiming to demonstrate his own dominance over these previous ages and to instil a sense of majesty and fear into his subjects.

None of this is to suggest that the emperor was lacking in the subtler tools of governance. Indeed, if anything, Frederick's later policy decisions were more nuanced than those of his youth. This is particularly evident in his Constitutions of Melfi, legal documents that he published in 1231. The purpose of this text was to further limit powers of the secular and religious elite: among other things he banned magistrates from judging cases where their family held estates, and, for the first time in the island's history, dictated that the king himself become the ultimate authority in defining and punishing heretics, and that priests be tried under his own secular law.[12] The constitutions introduced several measures that seem progressive to this day: they limited barons from cutting forests and woodland down without royal consent, and placed a blanket ban on burning toxic substances near rivers as part of an effort to limit pollution. Extraordinarily they even legalised a form of divorce, allowing nobility to separate in cases where, among other things, they could prove adultery had taken place. While some forms of annulment were possible in other parts of the world, and the conditions strongly favoured the male party, these were remarkably liberal policies by the standards of thirteenth-century Europe. In fact, following the emperor's death, Sicilians would not regain this particular right until 1974.

Beyond his relatively 'modern' conception of state power, Frederick made important contributions to Sicily's intellectual and artistic culture. Under the Hauteville kings, the royal court had been firmly based in Palermo. During Frederick's reign, however, it evolved to become an itinerant community of scholars, artists and performers who followed the emperor on his many journeys. Much like Roger II before him, Frederick hand-picked his courtiers from around the world. He was particularly interested in harnessing the talents of intellectuals from the Maghreb and Arab Andalucía; though, more than his predecessors, he also invited figures from northern Europe – from Germany and Britain – to join the court. His inner circle included Theodore, an Arab Christian from Antioch with whom he discussed Aristotle; Judah ben Solomon ha-Kohen, a Jewish mathematician from Toledo; Ibn Sabain, a Sufi philosopher who advised him in questions related to lucid dreaming; and Michael Scot, a polymath, philosopher and alchemist who travelled from the Scottish borderlands to Sicily to serve as the royal astronomer. Just as Roger II had worked alongside Muhammad al-Idrisi to develop a geographical treatise, so Frederick collaborated with his advisors to develop a scholarly work of his own. The result, in this instance, was a scientific study, *On the Art of Hunting with Birds* (1240), which combined philosophical assertions, empirical experiments and illustrations, to offer a comprehensive manual to the art of falconry. It was one of the most important works of natural philosophy of the age.

Frederick's court is best known, however, for its contributions to the field of literature. Between 1230 and 1266 a group of writers, including Pietro della Vigna, Cielo d'Alcamo and Giacomo da Lentini, worked together to develop a new poetic form that would express the glories of their patron. Their experiments gave birth to what is arguably the most influential poetic structure of all time: the sonnet. Today many people think of this form as a 'pure' Western-Christian invention, which originated in central Italy during the Renaissance. It might therefore be surprising to learn that it was actually created 200 years earlier, within the cosmopolitan environment of Frederick's court. Most of the poets that contributed to inventing the sonnet held key roles in the emperor's state administration. Della Vigna, for example, was Frederick's chancellor, while Cielo d'Alcamo was a notary of some kind. The first proper example is thought to be da Lentini's poem 'My heart is set on serving God' (c. 1230). Its content, a ballad to courtly love, was typical of European poetry at the time, but the form – the rhyme scheme and metre – was entirely new. Da Lentini's work artfully combined tropes that were popular in Palermo and Southern Italy, from ancient classical and Arab erotic verses to the songs of southern French troubadours, to create an entirely novel means of artistic expression. Unfortunately, all of the original twelfth-century poems have been lost. The works we read today are in fact Tuscan transcriptions of later performances. The fact that scholars in Florence and Rome were so admiring of these pieces, however, demonstrates how profoundly Frederick's scholars influenced the development of Italian culture as a whole. In the *Divine Comedy*, Dante Alighieri explicitly celebrates the work of da Lentini and the other Sicilian poets, and credits them as having invented the 'sweet new style' that had so inspired his own, more-celebrated, work (*Purgatorio*, canto 24).

The poets of the Sicilian school performed their pieces in a 'high tongue' which bore little resemblance to everyday speech. On a daily basis, the members of the court probably communicated in Latin as well as various *koine* (a mix of Greek dialects which were spread in different forms from Southern Italy all the way to Persia). Beyond the elite, however, a new kind of popular language also began to develop throughout the thirteenth century. Norman Sicily had been a polyglot society, dominated by a mix of Latin, Greek and Arabic dialects. By the time of Frederick's rule, however, Sicilians of all social classes were beginning to speak to one another using a distinctive romance language with common Latin-rooted grammar and syntax. Scholars continue to debate at what point this might be called 'Sicilian'. It's nevertheless worth noting how the previous centuries of cultural mixing impacted on the language. Many Sicilian words, particularly those related to food, were taken from ancient Greek: *pistiari*, to snack, is rooted in *esthìo*; *cirasa*, cherry, comes from *kerasos*; *babbaluciu*, snail, from *boubalàkion*. Other ancient words survived to describe craft and household objects such as *cartedda*, basket, from *kártallos*; and *bucali*, pitcher, from *baukalion*. We saw in the previous chapter how Arabic vocabulary left an enormous legacy in place names, sweets and spices. In the later medieval period, though, northern European influences began to creep in, providing several verbs and nouns to do with commerce and trade. The Norman French *acater*, for example, gave birth to the Sicilian *accattari*, to buy. Its later Angevin inflections provided denominations for several professions like *vucceri*, butcher, which comes from *bouchier*; and *custureri*, tailor, from *cousturier*. Under Frederick, new Sicilian-Germanic words entered the vocabulary such as *sparagnari*, from *sparen*, to save money; and *guastari*, from *wastjan*, to waste it. Given their subject matter, fiscal responsibility, one suspects these entered into common usage thanks to Swabian state administrators that had graduated from Naples.

Over the centuries scholars have produced vast numbers of codices, dictionaries and linguistic studies which together demonstrate how, over generations, the Sicilian language has come to absorb foreign influences into its own unique grammar. What's less often considered, though, is how these exchanges impacted on the cultural life of the islanders themselves. Academic studies are useful in that they provide an intellectual basis by which we can define Sicily's linguistic cosmopolitanism. In order to understand how the wider, largely illiterate population experienced the changes, though, we have to turn to other texts, to folk tales, and transcribed accounts of the oral tradition in particular. Luckily, thanks to the work of anthropologists like Giuseppe Pitrè, we know, for example, that Sicilians were sharing tales of King Arthur as early as the eleventh century.[13] One version, transcribed by an English lawyer named Gervase of Tilbury, suggests it was imported to the island along with the Normans sometime after 1066. There were a few transformations along the way. In the Sicilian version, Avalon is not located around Glastonbury Tor in Somerset, but at the island's own Mount Etna. Neither does Arthur die at the close of the stories. Instead he is said to be sleeping under the volcano, his life sustained by the Holy Grail. Other northern European influences seem to have crept into Sicily's popular culture during Frederick's reign. In later centuries Sicilians continued to tell stories that evoke creatures which are typically associated with German fairy stories, (such as dwarves, goblins and gnomes), and over time they would go on to develop their own versions of Cinderella, Rapunzel and Puss in Boots among others.

We can trace other aspects of Sicily's folk culture quite directly to cities in the southern Mediterranean. It's clear that many islanders, most likely merchants and fishermen, kept in close contact with Arabic speakers from Africa and the Middle East. A good example is the character of Giufà, a figure that crops up under different names across the region, including Giuha (Tunisia), Jeha (Morocco), Goha (Egypt) and Nasreddin Hodja (Turkey). Giufà's characteristics differ from place to place. In Sicily, though, he is a capricious figure, an 'innocent rogue' who, however dim-witted he might seem on the surface, always ends up on the upper hand of an argument. Giufà sometimes appears alongside another character called Firrazzanu, a sly Palermitan trickster and urban Robin Hood who steals from the local nobility, not to redistribute money to the hungry populace, but to better his own fare. Firrazzanu possesses *furbezza*, a devious intelligence. Giufà, meanwhile, succeeds in his own endeavours thanks to a blind, and possibly feigned, ignorance. Most of the stories are domestic comedies that involve this character 'inadvertently' winning extra food or money at the expense of his relatives. In more profound tales Giufà profits from the untruths, anxieties and deceptions of a far broader range of authority figures including sultans, kings, father figures and tax collectors. In one of the more explicit stories the Sicilian boy even urinates 'accidentally' on a police officer.

On the whole these are light-hearted allegories that serve variously as stories for children or even as bar-room jokes. Nevertheless, several cultural historians have pointed to Giufà as one of Sicily's most important folk personalities. The Palermitan journalist Salvatore Marrone, for example, has argued that the young man embodies the extreme paradoxes and contradictions that characterise life on the island; he is a kind of philosophical 'metacharacter' who permits his audience to connect to a different reality, beyond the ideological conditioning of institutional powers.[14] For all his 'tricks' and apparent amorality, Giufà is never consciously malicious. Instead this candid young man outwits his superiors because of their own greed, incompetence or abuse of office. Giufà does not urinate on the police officer in the aforementioned tale as an act of protest; the unfortunate man simply finds himself in the wrong place at the wrong time during a countryside patrol that should, in theory, be beyond his remit. Giufà's 'stupid' responses mirror other, more foundational, injustices. He is the spokesperson of a 'pure' humanity that rejects the tendency of politicians, priests and other influential figures to impose identities on their followers. Giufà, Giuha, Jeha and Goha are all free to cross the Mediterranean, without any concern for borders.

A final word should be left for a medieval story in which Frederick II plays a starring role. The legend of Colapesce concerns a young orphan boy named Cola who has a reputation for being a particularly brilliant swimmer. Hearing of Cola's talent, the emperor challenges him to retrieve a series of treasures from the bottom of the Strait of Messina. First, he throws in a goblet, which the boy easily retrieves. Next, he throws in a chest full of coins, which, again, he promptly returns to the surface. Finally, when tasked with rescuing a tiny ring from the deepest and most dangerous waters, Cola vanishes, never to return. Parents sometimes tell this story to their children to warn them not to swim off alone at the beach or take part in dangerous games. There is, however, a fantastical alternative ending, which gives a broader insight into the development of Sicilian culture more generally. According to the citizens of Catania and other communities in the east of the island, Cola does not perish under the waves. Instead, having dived down to the very bottom of the sea, he makes two startling discoveries. The first is that he is not in fact a human, but a demigod, a child of Neptune. Below a certain depth he transforms into a kind of man-fish with a fine pair of flippers, and gills. His second discovery is rather more troubling: Sicily, he learns, is not simply floating on the water, it is propped up by three stone pillars, each of which is sinking with alarming speed into the seabed. Cola is forced to make a split-second decision: he could swim away and turn his back on his homeland, or else sacrifice himself, using his superhuman strength to hold the pillars afloat in order to save those on the surface. It goes without saying that, in this version, he chooses the latter option. Legend maintains that he remains there to this day, at the bottom of the sea, literally holding the island on his shoulders, without any hope of reward or recognition. He is, for this reason, the island's first recognisable proletarian hero.

For all the marvels of his court, Frederick spent his final years politically isolated. Increasingly, he confined himself to Puglia, wrought by spiritual worries and locked in esoteric philosophical debate with his advisors. He died there of dysentery in 1250. Despite the emperor's altercations with the Papacy, many contemporary chronicles judged his legacy in favourable terms. In the year of his death European scholars awarded him the popular epithet *stupor mundi*, wonder of the world, on account of his political and cultural achievements.[15] He was succeeded by three children, none of whom would make a lasting imprint. Manfred I was a fine leader, who enjoyed considerable support among Sicily's knights. Unsurprisingly, though, he was incapable of managing the diplomatic crises that his father had left in his wake. By the mid-thirteenth century the conflict between the Guelphs and Ghibellines was intensifying across Europe. The Papacy, keen to contain the implicitly Ghibelline energies that were rife in Sicily, openly schemed to overthrow the Hohenstaufens. In 1266 a French-born pope, Urban IV, declared that his fellow countryman, Charles of Anjou, a pious crusader and count over a large territory in northern Europe, was in fact the rightful king of Sicily. Incensed, Manfred ventured out personally, as head of a cavalry unit, to defend his kingdom and his title. He died in battle the following year, outside the southern Italian city of Benevento. With his death the island passed automatically into the possession of the French Angevins.

Over the next twenty years, Sicily, and Palermo in particular, was reduced to provincial status. Despite his title, Charles preferred to govern from Naples, a city that over these two decades would develop magnificently at the expense of the Sicilian capital. Nonetheless, the Angevin king did take his task of re-establishing papal authority on the island seriously. On coming to power, one of his first acts was to strip all Hohenstaufen lords of their titles and confiscate their lands. While a few families guilefully changed their names to claim Greek, Byzantine and Arab heritage, Charles handed out the majority of Sicily's largest estates to families from France. The Angevins ignored the Constitutions of Melfi, and, as a result, Frederick's bureaucratic state, with its finely tuned fiscal regulations, anti-corruption measures, and newly defined social and environmental protections, collapsed on itself.

Some groups of exiled pro-Hohenstaufen forces attempted to resist Charles. In 1268 a small army of Swabian sympathisers tried and failed to overthrow a French garrison in the south of the island. An even bigger uprising took place that same year in Lucera, where the Muslim community took up arms under Frederick's banner to defend the legacy of the man who, despite having evicted them from their homeland, had proved himself a tolerant and generous leader. Charles responded to these threats with brutal force. Starting in the 1270s the king deployed a permanent unit of soldiers to police public spaces in Palermo, and arrested and executed dozens of citizens whom he suspected of posing a threat to his kingdom. The terrain was set for the largest and most oft-recounted conflict in Sicilian history.

On Easter Monday 1282 the French military presence in Palermo was particularly heavy. That day a large shipment of Sicilian grain and horses was due to depart for Naples and the ports were filled with boats. Rumours were circulating across the island that groups of pro-Ghibelline forces were planning to sabotage the operation in protest against the king. What took place instead was akin to a full-scale revolution. Remarkably, one of the instigators, John of Procida, a physician who had served at Frederick's court and who had lost his lands during the Angevin expropriation, left a first-hand account of what took place. In his chronicle, Procida himself takes credit for raising the funds and being the strategic mastermind behind the revolt, which he claims was made possible thanks to a secret donation from Constantinople and organised through a vast network of conspirators across Europe. The immediate trigger, he writes, came when a French soldier raped a local Palermitan woman at the Church of Santo Spirito, just outside the city's ancient walls. In a propagandistic flourish, Procida adds that this woman was groped 'zealously' and that 'this kind of molestation had occurred in the past'.[16] On witnessing this abuse, he goes on to explain, a good man, a heroic Palermitan burgher, stepped in and laid waste to the woman's attacker, thereby protecting the honour of both the assaulted woman and the Sicilian people themselves.

At this point, in Procida's account, the bells rang out for Vespers. As the streets began to fill with churchgoers, groups of enraged citizens, encouraged by the pro-Hohenstaufen nobility, turned their swords and daggers against the Angevin troops, many of whom, he states, were drunk in the taverns. A large crowd of rebels began to push their way across the city, from the Porta Mazzara, in the west, towards Ballarò, the Arab souk, burning buildings and killing as they went. According to some anti-Ghibelline accounts the rioters did not limit themselves to targeting soldiers but slaughtered children, the elderly and, apparently, pregnant women too. Whatever the truth of such tales, the scale of the violence was considerable. As the Angevins attempted to regroup near the cathedral, the rebels set the local government buildings alight and the island's predominantly French bureaucrats were forced to flee to the small blind alleys of the old Aghlabid *aziqqa*, where, having cornered themselves, they were butchered. Procida claims that the rebels killed over 3,000 people that night alone, and while most historians consider this an exaggeration, there's little doubt that the events were among the largest-scale examples of urban rioting anywhere in medieval Europe.

By morning Procida and his fellow rebels had taken control of Palermo. They raised the Hohenstaufen flag in the streets and retreated to Monreale to consider their next steps. From the safety of the hills the nobility worked to shape their mass revolt into a sustainable coup. Procida, together with a close circle of his most loyal knights, formed a temporary government to delegate administrative tasks. They sent a message to Spain, to Peter of Aragon – representative of one of the most powerful anti-French dynasties in Europe and the husband of Manfred's daughter Constance – inviting him to take the crown. While the knights authored communications to monarchs across Europe, informing them of the events, the insurrection spread from Palermo to Corleone, then west towards Trapani and east to Catania, where French soldiers fled without resistance. Only in Messina, where Charles's navy was based, was the response more muted. Even here, though, the local population set fire to the city's principal castle. Finally, in September, Peter arrived from Catalonia and was, informally, crowned king. For Procida, this was a moment of triumph, the definitive end of the revolt and cause for a didactic reflection. The events, he wrote, were a warning to 'all those lords of kingdoms, cities, lands and castles, and those in every other position of authority', to 'avoid the use of humiliation and injury against their vassals and their serfs'.[17]

In reality the uprising of the Sicilian Vespers was the prelude to a larger war that raged for two decades and spread far beyond the island's shores. Between 1282 and 1301 battles took place across the Mediterranean and the European mainland, as the French and Spanish forces sought to settle their dispute. Initially both sides hoped the crisis could be contained. Peter and Charles even arranged a duel near Bordeaux in 1283 in which they and one hundred of their best soldiers agreed to fight eye to eye to resolve the matter. On the arranged day, however, each side turned up at different times, and both declared themselves victorious. The conflict snowballed. In the months following the farcical stand-off, Byzantium entered more definitely into the war on the side of the Sicilians, and for a brief moment, as had been the case during the Norman conquest, the island became the centre stage of a proxy conflict between the Eastern and Western church. Few battles took place in Sicily itself. Nevertheless, the Aragonese rulers, who remained firmly placed in Barcelona and Valencia throughout this tense period, implored the island's nobility, including Procida, to pay vast taxes to fuel military campaigns across the continent. Finally, in 1302, with all the major players in financial disarray, the church facilitated a compromise. Pope Boniface VIII formally permitted Frederick of Aragon to reign in Sicily as 'King of Trinacria' (one of the ancient names for the island) while Charles II of Anjou would maintain control of Naples and Southern Italy (though oddly he was allowed to maintain the title 'King of Sicily'). Things could hardly have been more convoluted.

The War of the Vespers had no clear winner. Despite its muted ending, however, many Sicilians remember the events in rather idealised terms as a tale of democratic liberation. The reality, though, was far less rosy. Procida and other leaders within the Sicilian nobility did succeed in securing some minor democratic reforms, and convinced Frederick to grant an annual parliament in which the leading families would be called upon to advise the king. There is no evidence, however, that the decision-making process had any impact on royal policy. Instead, just as had happened during the transition to Angevin rule, a new generation of Spanish nobles migrated to the island to take over rural estates and fiefdoms, and the management of government affairs. To cover the costs of the war these officials diverted money away from key infrastructure, and dramatically downsized the state in Palermo. Rural roads fell into disrepair and the barons were ordered by royal command to cut down the forests to provide timber for Spanish ships. With the island now politically separated from Naples and its university, literacy rates dropped dramatically.

For almost 400 years, Sicily had been governed by an urban elite in Palermo. Following the Vespers, though, power moved progressively away from these individuals, and into the hands of rural landowners and church authorities. This would have catastrophic consequences for the majority of the islanders. If the Sicilian people had indeed stood up against the combined power of both the Papacy and one of Europe's most powerful kings, their victory was a bitter one. In the ashes of that conflict a new form of provincial despotism began to develop on the island which would undermine the concepts of law, order and justice for centuries to come.

4

A Silent Scream (1347–1693)

Black Death, the Spanish Inquisition, Spells and Incantations

The Sicilians generally are more astute than they are prudent, sharper than they are sincere, they love novelty, they're argumentative, flatterers and jealous by nature; subtle critics of their rulers' actions, they maintain how easy it would be to realise all they said they would do, if they were in their place. Their nature is made of two extremes: they are supremely timid and supremely reckless … they are very self-interested and like many protean types will submit to anyone who will facilitate to help them in those ends.

Scipio di Castro, 'Warnings to Marco Antonio Colonna
on undertaking the role of Viceroy in Sicily', 1577

In October 1347 a Genoese trading expedition returning from the Black Sea was forced to make an emergency stop in Sicily's eastern port of Messina when the crew was struck by a particularly lethal strain of plague. Medieval populations were accustomed to outbreaks of pestilence, but even those used to such sights expressed shock at the scenes on the island. One witness, a traveller called Michael Platiensis, left a chronicle in which he describes how the affected people developed boils on their thighs and upper arms and 'felt a pain throughout their whole bodies' before 'vomiting blood without intermission' for three days. He concludes his initial evaluation with the observation that 'anyone who only spoke to [the infected] was seized by a mortal illness and in no manner could avoid death'.[1] These are some of the first European descriptions of what would later become known as the Black Death. The pandemic caught Sicily entirely off-guard. The soldiers in Messina immediately closed off the docks, but they were given little guidance from the Palermitan elite and failed to quarantine the local population. As a result, the plague spread quickly across the island. As Platiensis continues:

> The Messinians resolved to emigrate. One portion of them settled in the vineyards and the fields, but a larger portion sought refuge in the town of Catania, trusting that the holy virgin Agatha of Catania would deliver them from their evil. [Yet] the population of Catania was so godless and timid that no one among them ... offered [the refugees] shelter. If some relations in Catania had not secretly harboured a number of people from Messina, they would have been deprived of all assistance. Thus the people of Messina dispersed over the whole island of Sicily ... and with them the disease.[2]

Modern estimates suggest that the plague killed up to half of Europe's population, rising to as much as 70 percent in the case of Sicily.[3] It is highly likely that Catania and Trapani, two of the largest cities, lost their entire populations. The most immediate implication of the pandemic, though, was to accelerate the exodus from Palermo. As we saw in the previous chapter, the island's capital had already entered a period of profound decline in the wake of the War of the Vespers. This was exacerbated in the context of the Black Death as almost all of the noble families, old and new, retreated to their rural estates in the south of the island. This was, of course, an ineffective means of escaping the disease. While the urban poor were disproportionately hit by the plague, many noble families, confined in close-knit communities, were also infected. One of Sicily's best-known frescos, *The Triumph of Death* (c. 1446), depicts a skeletal horseman shooting arrows at well-dressed figures in an allegorical satire of the ruling class's hopeless attempts to escape the unfolding apocalypse.

The peasantry, for their part, won some small gains in the midst of this crisis. During the Norman and Swabian period, serfs had laboured on the land without pay, in exchange for lodging and the right to farm for subsistence purposes. During the Black Death, however, as both manpower and food supplies were hit, rural workers were able to demand better conditions and even succeeded, on occasion, in gaining remuneration for their work. The luckiest were able to escape their feudal bonds altogether.

This was a hugely traumatic experience for those who lived through it. While written sources are unfortunately scarce, artworks give at least some insight into how the islanders responded. From the fourteenth century onwards, the bright gold Byzantine mosaics of Sicily's churches and chapels began to be replaced by darker, stranger pieces. Monks continued to depict saints and Madonnas, but these were increasingly accompanied by grotesque figures, like dog people, humans with multiple heads, unicorns and other more ambiguous monsters.[4] The figure of Jesus himself was totally transformed. Instead of the majestic Christ Pantocrator, like that which adorns the Norman cathedral in Cefalù, many plague-era renderings show an emaciated man, himself resembling one of the diseased, his face contorted in pain and suffering. Two hundred years previously, the Hauteville artists had portrayed Christ surrounded by palm trees and peacocks. Now Sicily's painters began to depict him immersed in medicinal herbs and winter plants like hemlock, cyclamen and rosemary. For centuries, the islanders had come to see the Messiah as a divine leader and a source of inspiration; a reflection, ultimately, of the values of absolute monarchy. During Aragonese rule he became a more intimate figure, a fellow man, struggling to survive in a cruel world.

The Black Death reached its peak in Sicily around 1350, but its effects would extend far further. The plague continued to spread across the island for years after and by the end of the fourteenth century it had wiped out many of the families that had ruled the island for much of the medieval era. Those who did survive briefly attempted to seize control of the government. In 1392 a Norman family, the Chiaramonte, contested the legitimacy of King Martin I, arguing that the island should be ruled from Palermo and not, as it was at the time, from Barcelona. Together with a number of like-minded noblemen, Andrea, the head of the family, developed a proposal for an independent Sicily which he suggested would be presided over by a Spaniard, perhaps from the House of Aragon, yet potentially allied with the French Angevins in Naples. Martin I easily laid waste to these plans. That June he travelled to Sicily with an army, bribed the southern barons for their loyalty, and beheaded Andrea for treason. To ensure no further conspiracies were able to take place the king then awarded titles to some of his young soldiers, most of whom came from the countryside around Valencia, and allocated them land in Sicily. This was the first time these men had tasted power. In many cases they felt compelled to prove their legitimacy by engaging in direct armed conflict with the last dregs of the incumbent nobility. Starting around 1400, in the small town of Sciacca, a port in the west of the island, a veritable civil war broke out between the Luna nobility from Catalonia and the historic Norman rulers, the Perollo. This bloody conflict lasted for two centuries and killed hundreds. Similar smaller-scale feuds broke out across the length of the island. As the Spanish gradually came to dominate, the nobility itself came to take on a new character. While always prone to factionalism and in-fighting, under the Normans and Swabians this class had been constrained to present itself as offering at least some semblance of stability and order. In the years after the Black Death, however, these families, being so far from royal oversight, were free to pursue their own agendas. They effectively became an anti-state force, governing their lands according to what some historians have come to refer to as a kind of 'feudal anarchy'.

In 1469 Ferdinand of Aragon married Isabella of Castile, thereby unifying mainland Spain. As a result, Sicily became a Spanish 'possession', a colony in all but name. From this moment on the island would be governed by a long line of foreign rulers. Over the next 200 years, few kings even visited Palermo. Instead a group of viceroys took over the everyday administration. In theory these individuals were responsible for enforcing the laws that were written in Madrid and ensuring that, if nothing else, the nobility paid their taxes. In many cases, however, the viceroys were closely linked to the new ruling families, and were perfectly comfortable in distributing favours to their associates in exchange for bribes. During the fifteenth century these state administrators were at the centre of a sophisticated corruption ring in which they distributed new noble titles and honours to the highest bidders. The ruling families could effectively rise through the social

ranks and gain influence over one another based on how well
they managed to negotiate this parallel economy. If Frederick
II's state had been highly centralised and well disciplined, the
political system in the new Spanish Sicily was one that openly
rewarded avarice and competition.

Parallel to this, the church authorities obtained a political
power that had been previously unimaginable on the island. For
most of the medieval era Sicilian Catholicism had been represented by a relatively benign, and rather heterogeneous, sect:
the Benedictines. Following the union of crowns, however, they
were eclipsed by the evangelical and authoritarian Dominicans,
whose founding tenet holds that Christ himself came to earth
with a sword in hand to enact a holy war.

This might sound like a purely semantic shift, but in fact it
had several devastating consequences. The most serious was a
dramatic increase in anti-Semitism. At the start of Ferdinand
and Isabella's reign, Sicily's Jewish population numbered around
30,000. On account of their private religious schools, these individuals were among the best educated on the island and were
well known for their skills in banking and metalwork. Certain
Christian groups had long resented this fact. As in much of
Europe, a conspiracy theory circulated widely in Sicily during
the Black Death insisting that the disease was not natural but the
result of a Jewish plot to poison the water supply, to kill their
religious opponents. In 1369, partly in reaction to this paranoia,
the crown had ordered that all the island's Jews would, in fact, be
required to wear a light-coloured badge and to trim their beards
in a distinctive fashion, so as to distinguish themselves from
other citizens. Starting in 1453, however, when the Ottomans
took control of Constantinople, thereby plunging the Christian
world into political crisis, Dominican priests successfully lobbied

the Sicilian viceroys to more strictly enforce anti-Semitic laws. Spain banned sexual intercourse between Jews and Christians and introduced legislation which stated not only that Jews were forbidden from constructing new synagogues but that it was illegal to repair old ones.

These racist policies soon devolved into bloodshed. On the morning of 15 August 1474 the Christian population of Modica, a town in the south-east of Sicily, went to the Chiesa di Santa Maria di Betlem to bless the summer harvest and mark the festival of the Assumption. The celebrations that year, though, were marked by tension. Around lunch-time a Dominican priest named Fra Giovanni da Pistoia gave a particularly inflammatory sermon. In it he condemned the Jews as enemies of Christianity and explicitly incited his followers to attack those in the local community that followed the Israelites. This was an unusual development. In previous centuries the 'shire' of Modica – a noble fiefdom which had been managed by the Chiaramonte and included the small towns of Alcamo, Caccamo and Calatafimi – had been renowned for its tolerance. At the time it was home to the largest community of Jews on the island. These events, though, were a turning point in these previously peaceful relations. Following the service, hundreds of members of the congregation marched through the city streets chanting, 'Long live Maria, death to the Jews!' On arriving at the neighbourhood of Cartellone, where most of this population lived, a group of men, armed with swords, spears and apparently crossbows, began attacking the residents indiscriminately. It's estimated that the mob killed 350 people that day, including children and the elderly. At the peak of the violence, as the blood began to dry, the crowd burnt the synagogue to the ground. Many Sicilians were shocked by these events. The viceroy, Lopez Ximenes Durrea, travelled from Palermo to Modica to put those responsible on trial. The hearing, though, was inconclusive and Fra Giovanni remained free. In the following days a series of copycat attacks took place in towns and villages across Sicily. On 18 September in Noto, not far from Modica, another Dominican priest galvanised a similar pogrom which claimed the lives of at least eighteen people. No one was arrested.

In 1492 Ferdinand and Isabella signed the Alhambra Decree which officially proclaimed Judaism illegal in all Spanish territories. This rule was to be enforced by the secular state but reinforced by a new religious tribunal: the Inquisition. This institution had first been established in Spain in 1478 as a means of ousting Muslim communities from Andalucía. Sicily, though, had its own branch which, initially at least, was largely occupied with formalising the repression of Jewish people. From the moment the Alhambra Decree was passed, all individuals openly practising the religion were legally required to hand over their most valuable belongings or face deportation. Sicilian authorities ordered raids on Jewish homes and synagogues, and confiscated money and other valuable items from believers. A new viceroy, Don Ferdinando Acuña, introduced taxes designed to ensure that worshippers could not re-establish themselves if they tried to flee the persecution. In 1493 at least 10,000 Sicilian Jews left the island. They headed first to Calabria and Naples, and later to Rome, Venice and the wider diaspora across the Mediterranean. Sicily's border police were ruthless: they only permitted these individuals to take a single pair of clothes with them on their journey, along with a mattress, some bed sheets, basic foodstuffs and a small sum of money. The guards searched the emigrants' body cavities to ensure they were not trying to smuggle out hidden gemstones. A small number of practising Jews converted to Christianity in the hope that they might avoid such a fate.

Sadly their efforts proved futile. In 1500 the state passed a further law which explicitly forbid new converts from leaving Sicily without a special permit, which, inevitably, required a hefty down-payment. Those without such funds were permanently separated from family members who had already fled. Judaism in Sicily died along with these individuals.

In theory the Inquisition's legal remit was confined to defining and identifying 'heresy'. In reality, their power extended much further. They were also a political force, designed to reinforce royal authority and hold the colonial apparatus to account. In Spanish Sicily, the state and church effectively shared governance, and the lines between the two powers were frequently blurred. For example, while the Inquisition ordered executions, they were not legally permitted to enact them. Instead it was the viceroys who had the responsibility for taking the final decision (though, of course, opposing such advice would most likely have been considered a heresy). The result was a strange paradox. On the one hand the Inquisition was a top-down authoritarian force which manifested its power through spectacular events such as public burnings, the so-called *auto-da-fé*. While Protestant historians have often exaggerated the frequency of these proceedings there were indeed several such occasions. In 1513 – to take one particularly brutal year – thirty-nine burnings were recorded in Sicily, claiming nearly one hundred victims.[5] On the other hand, it's important to remember that the inquisitors, like the nobility, also worked to undermine the state and used constitutional loopholes to justify their actions. The tribunal was not a totalitarian institution. Its power came less from its drastic enforcement of religious orthodoxy than the fact that nobody was exactly sure how it worked. In the past, Roger II's Assizes of Ariano and Frederick II's Constitutions of Melfi had provided explicit guidelines regarding the punishment of heretics. The tribunal, by contrast, was dominated by corrupt individuals, and secured its authority by a combination of nepotism, obscurantism and improvisation.

At different moments in its history, the Inquisition acted both as part of Sicily's clientelist economy, and as the main institution that policed it. From the very beginning of its activities, in 1489, an agent named Marin obtained a reputation for accepting bribes from rich families to denounce their rivals, and for selling exemptions to ensure they escaped punishment. This was far from an isolated case. Indeed such stories were sufficiently widespread that in 1514 Sicily's parliament voted to vastly limit the power of the Inquisition in an effort to tackle their excesses head-on. Unsurprisingly, given the limited powers this institution had, there were no immediate consequences. Nevertheless, Sicily's politicians refused to back down. Two years later, in 1516, the indignant nobility organised a revolt against a particularly corrupt viceroy named Hugo de Moncada, who had been siphoning off grain profits, and the inquisitor, Miguel Cervera, who had been assisting him. In March that year, a group of mercenary soldiers, funded by members of parliament, broke into the poorly guarded Spanish military barracks in Palermo, stole weapons and distributed them among the working population. The local people seem to have taken to the streets enthusiastically. In fact their numbers were so great that Moncada was forced to flee the city disguised as a servant. The protesters then chased Cervera out of the capital amid chants that he was 'not a catcher of heretics, only of money' and pelted him with rocks.

As a result of these events, the Inquisition ceased its activities in Sicily for several years. But this pause was short-lived and by 1554 the institution redoubled its influence on the island. If at first its agents had been focused on catching Jewish individuals, in this second phase of their activity they extended their gaze to persecute a wider variety of people including witches, prostitutes, necromancers, blasphemers, homosexuals and, where they could find them, Protestants.[6] The sheer diversity of those that they targeted can be seen today in the Palazzo Chiaramonte-Steri, which from 1600 served as the Inquisition's official headquarters and prison. Visitors to this enormous fortified building can enter the old cells where, remarkably, graffiti that the prisoners themselves made is still visible on the walls. These are not just a few etchings but chamber after chamber of poems, prayers, jokes and images which the inmates scribbled using ground-up terracotta floor tiles, and even food. There are names, testimonies of innocence, simple words like 'courage' and various descriptions of anger, fear and physical illness. What's particularly striking, though, is the range of languages on display. The prisoners did not only write their messages in Sicilian, but in Arabic, Greek, Hebrew and Latin among other tongues too. There are entire sonnets on the walls, Sicilianised verses of Dante and even an English translation of the Apostles' Creed. One piece shows a vast naval battle that scholars have now identified as Lepanto; another a remarkably well-proportioned map of Sicily. The most iconic image depicts the Inquisition itself which the artist has transfigured into a terrifying monster spreading its vast jaws over sixteen predominantly Old Testament figures. It is a powerful, irrefutable symbol of how Sicily's religious police did indeed serve to devour the very faith they professed to protect.[7]

Historians continue to debate the function of these works. On the whole, though there are plenty of occult symbols among these illustrations, the majority depict Christian scenes, of saints and martyrs. One theory holds that the prisoners created these pieces in an attempt to gain a pardon from the guards. There's no evidence, however, to suggest that such attempts were successful. The Inquisition's methods were based on a rather crude process by which the agents used torture to elicit a confession, and then offered absolution and punishment. While in most cases this meant having property taken away, or being forced to march the streets in a penitential garment called a *sanbenito*, some who ended up in the Inquisition's prison would have remained there for life, or been burnt outside Palermo's cathedral.

A final sketch, tucked away in the latrines, where presumably even the guards would not have dared to venture, captures the desperation of the incarcerated people. It shows a pompous-looking inquisitor sitting on his horse, which, appropriately to the context, is taking a rather large dump. It's a simple picture. Of all the images, though, it's one of the most intensely human expressions of the fear, loathing and resignation that was confined inside the prison walls. The Palazzo Chiaramonte-Steri was a place where people of all classes came to their end, where Sicily's proto-modern justice system was replaced by mob rule, and its historic cosmopolitanism was finally eclipsed by a Catholic monoculture.

Sicily's relationship with Spain was never a straightforward one of foreign oppression, as Italian nationalists would later frame it. By the dawn of the seventeenth century the majority of the islanders had, on the surface at least, adapted to fulfil the cultural expectations of their new rulers. This was not, at the end of the day, a difficult transition. After all, it was the Norman-Hohenstaufen nobility that had invited the Aragonese to intervene in the island's affairs in the first place, and alternative political alliances, a union with France, or occupation by the rapidly expanding Ottoman Empire, offered few obvious advantages. The fact that Spain was a global superpower, and was feared across the European continent, aided the Sicilians' sense of belonging to something larger than themselves. While the islanders frequently lamented the absence of kings, they quickly found other 'celebrity' figures, military heroes and strong leaders to champion. Residents along the south coast particularly idolised Pedro Téllez-Girón, the dashing Duke of Osuna, who despite spending most of his time in Andalucía used Syracuse as his base for a series of successful offensives against Muslim forces, culminating in a decisive victory against the Ottomans at the Battle of Cape Corvo in 1613. This was the first time since the days of the Hohenstaufens that Sicilians had felt able to bask in their reputation as a major naval power.

It's perhaps surprising to note that, for all its political problems, early modern Sicily was not an especially poor place. After 1492, when Europeans began to colonise the Americas, the Mediterranean began its decline as a centre of world trade. The consequences of this were particularly severe for maritime republics like Venice and Genoa, as is well known. To some extent, though, Sicily's relationship with Spain protected it from these changes. The nobility and merchant class both benefitted from imported conquistador plunder, which made it to the island from Mexico and the Caribbean via Valencia. The colonial administration also systematically introduced new crops onto the island, like tomatoes, potatoes, bell peppers and the now endemic prickly pears. Starting in about 1620 the islanders even began to produce luxury goods of their own. The dry land around Agrigento, in the island's south, proved ideal terrain for growing cane sugar, which was a valuable commodity in its own right but which also fuelled the expansion of a small rum industry. In nearby Modica, local chefs combined this harvest with imported cocoa to produce a bitter, grainy chocolate that was based on the Aztec recipe *xocoatl*. At the dawn of the seventeenth century, under Philip III, Sicily was home to over forty guilds, and thanks to advances in naval technology, local manufacturers were able to export cloth, silk and salt in ever larger quantities. Sicily was not exactly wealthy. Still, there was a certain dynamism to the economy that defies the stereotype that the island was, by this point, a mere backwater in the midst of a provincial lake.[8]

This is not to suggest that resources were evenly distributed. On the contrary, while some peasants enjoyed the benefits of a small-scale market economy, these developments largely ben-efitted the small class of independent landowners. Most Sicilians were still reliant on navigating fluctuating harvests, grain prices and harsh taxes in order to survive. Urban workers did, occasion-ally, organise limited uprisings in an attempt to claim their basic rights. In 1647, for example, a year of severe drought, the resi-dents of Palermo took to the streets and burnt down tax offices and the treasury in protest against shortages of bread. Their main demand was for a cut in tariffs on what were known as the 'five gabelles': wine, wheat, meat, oil and cheese. Observing the size of the crowds the viceroy, the Marquis of los Vélez, immediately conceded this. While echoes of the revolt spread to other parts of the island, and Messina in particular, no organisations or leaders emerged that were able to sustain the momentum.

Most of Sicily's population was forced into subservience by their commitment to their religion. Throughout the seven-teenth century, the Spanish developed Catholic celebrations into extraordinary spectacles, with more elaborate processions, rituals, dances and associated foodstuffs to ensure that the island-ers became more culturally invested in the Christian worldview.

These were not just 'foreign imports'. Many of the events were deeply rooted in Sicily's past, and the long history of its first martyrs and saints. The ancient celebrations of St Agatha of Catania and St Lucy of Syracuse, for example, evolved from being liturgical services, confined to religious sites, into mass events that encompassed the whole urban area. Local artisans produced ornamental floats for the occasions which, then as now, were processed through the cities accompanied by music, street theatre and poetry. Several of the island's most beloved traditions were born in this period. It was during a resurgence of bubonic plague in 1624–30, for example, that the population of Palermo came to venerate St Rosalia, now their patron protector, when she apparently intervened to save the capital from annihilation.

These new forms of mass congregation might suggest that the islanders had begun to develop some degree of unity around a homogeneous Christian identity. In reality, while Spanish-Sicilian culture was indeed almost exclusively Catholic there was also an extraordinary diversity within the apparently uniform idea of the church. During the sixteenth and seventeenth centuries, for example, several new orders began to compete with the Dominicans for political dominance within and beyond the structures of the Inquisition. The most powerful were the Jesuits, who prioritised education, and a more individualised, intimate form of devotion, over the established order's millenarian crusading. Starting in 1549 they set up colleges across eastern Sicily, most notably in Messina, Catania and Syracuse. While these institutions played some role in counteracting Sicily's illiteracy, they were primarily a means by which the sect sought to influence the viceroys and crown. Other orders, like the Augustinians and Carmelites, opposed the wealth of the incumbent clergy, and quietly promoted charity work, visits to the sick, and asceticism.

The most radical of all were the Capuchins, who arrived in Sicily from the Italian mainland in 1534. In contrast to their clean-shaven and extravagantly dressed colleagues, members of this order distinguished themselves by growing beards and wearing simple hooded robes. They preached an apocalyptic, eternal struggle between good and evil which was directed not only against external enemies like the Ottomans, but, just as significantly, against traitors within the faith itself.[9] Unsurprisingly, both the Papacy and the Inquisition would identify a number of heretics within their ranks in the years to come.

In fact the more one looks beyond the Sicilians' most theatrical displays of devotion, the less straightforwardly obedient the population seems to have been. Catholicism may have become the dominant symbolic vocabulary on the island, but its local permutations were far less orthodox than the political rulers might have wished. When venerating their patron saint, San Vito, for example, the residents of Mazara del Vallo continued to use bay leaves to ward off 'evil spirits' in accordance with ancient 'pagan' exorcist practices. When the inquisitors questioned this custom, the local clergy simply attached red ribbons to the performers to render the activity 'Catholic'. This was fairly a typical strategy across and beyond the region. In Sicily, however, many residents took things a step further. Some openly worshipped polytheistic deities. Each spring, for example, villagers in the north-eastern villages of the Nebrodi mountains would flock to the 'Megaliths of Argimusco', a series of rocks known as 'the Sicilian Stonehenge', to conduct fertility rituals, calling on fairies and spirits to protect prospective pregnancies. Peasants in Naro, an isolated town in the south of the island, worshipped the Greek goddess Persephone well into the early modern period. To mark the festival of St John the Baptist, on the summer solstice, hundreds of islanders would pay homage to the saint by dancing, drinking and engaging in orgiastic practices in what was, presumably, a continuation of the festivals to Bacchus and Dionysus.

In private, away from the eyes of religious authorities, many Sicilians practised magical rituals. Given the intimate nature of this activity it's hard to ascertain precisely how widespread various phenomena have been over time. Later anthropological surveys conducted in Southern Italy, though, suggest that at least some of the local population would have consumed menstrual blood or urine in order to obtain what they believed would be superhuman powers. Another common praxis was to distort prayers, or hijack biblical verses to add chants or incantations that could help the subject to seduce a lover or curse a rival.[10] We know that peasants across the Sicilian countryside shared tales about the *donne di fora*, ghostly figures, inspired by the Moroccan figure of the *jnuun*, which apparently 'haunted' small villages, punishing 'disorderly' families; and that, in the cities, 'high magic' like divination was widespread. In seventeenth century Palermo, a woman named Antonina Lombardo offered to read her clients' futures by creating patterns of fava beans, cereals and other foodstuffs. A gentleman, Santo Gasparo, claimed he could interpret the sounds of animals, particularly the whine of pigs, to diagnose the health of his customers' souls. Anyone wishing to purchase a magical object could have headed to Ballarò market, which obtained a particular reputation for its stockpiles of amulets and jewellery that were commonly used in the practice of necromancy.[11]

There are hundreds of similar examples. These few cases alone, though, demonstrate that throughout Spanish rule the Sicilians experienced a complex process of adaptation and integration which combined public devotion and apparent obedience with private subversion. Some historians have suggested that, faced with the Inquisition's oppression, the islanders developed a form of 'occult resistance', by which they adopted feigned ignorance and opportunistic subversion as alternatives to outright revolt. The displays of obedience, then, may well have been accompanied by an individualistic form of rebellion that was hard for the authorities to identify. Further evidence for this interpretation can be seen in the widespread popularity of a folkloric tale called the Beati Paoli, a secret society that apparently flourished during Spanish rule.[12] According to legend this vigilante sect kidnapped corrupt members of the ruling class, including clergymen and state officials, and organised secret 'show trials' during midnight tribunals in which they confiscated wealth and distributed it to the poor. As the journalist Vincenzo Linares wrote of them in the nineteenth century:

> [The Beati Paoli] would meet in secret at the touch of midnight. Echoes of the trials would be heard in the piazzas, the streets, inside houses ... they came from all the social classes, and they could appear anywhere. Their meetings were brief, and close-cut cases were put to public opinion in a free vote, with immediate and ferocious penalties. The voice of the people, the voice of God, so they said ... and like God they did not distinguish in their judgement. The corrupt magistrate, the leading nobleman, a colluding worker, all were put under severe exam. It was not unusual that one would see a powerful nobleman, on the same day as his trial, killed on the boundaries of his land; or a judge appearing dead after declaring an unfair sentence.[13]

There is little evidence to suggest that the Beati Paoli ever existed. The fact that this legend is so popular, though, reveals much about how Sicilians remember Spanish rule. While some, including Linares, have tended to condemn the actions of this 'illegal cult', the majority of later cultural representations, such as Luigi Natoli's popular novel *I Beati Paoli* (1912) or Pino Mercanti's film *The Hooded Sect* (1948), have served to implicitly vindicate their actions. One might be forgiven for thinking that many of the islanders do indeed seem to wish that the organisation had been real. In the twentieth century, Leonardo Sciascia, one of Sicily's most respected novelists, went as far as to suggest that there was a direct link between the legend of the Beati Paoli and that of the modern mafia. The Beati Paoli is not just a story, he argued, it is an expression of Sicily's 'unchangeable constitution'; an essential, almost metaphysical, resistance to governance.[14] Umberto Eco's reinterpretation of this rather idealistic statement perhaps comes closer to the truth. Rather than drawing concrete parallels with the present day, he focuses on the fictional nature of the Beati Paoli as constituting 'an illusory project of resistance and liberation', one which was 'born to oppose Power' but in fact served as little more than 'a state within a state … another form of domination'.[15] Just as Cosa Nostra mirrors the failings of modern Italian institutions, Eco suggests, so the Beati Paoli once reflected the intolerance and fear of the Spanish colonial project. In the absence of collective resistance, they offered a much needed illusion of justice.

One commonly held misconception about Spanish Sicily is the idea that the island was entirely unaffected by the developments of the Italian Renaissance. It's certainly true that the feuding nobility, unscrupulous viceroys and harsh religious authorities combined to block the kind of flourishing in art and science that took place on some parts of the mainland. Between the fifteenth and seventeenth centuries Sicily did not develop a tradition of political republicanism or artistic patronage of the kind that thrived in city-states like Florence during the same period. While a small handful of humanists were educated on the island, most notably the influential Neoplatonist translator and philosopher Luca Marineo, most of Sicily's intellectuals were forced to emigrate to the peninsula, or just as often to Spain, to Valencia in particular, to continue their work. No major Sicilian institutions attempted to orchestrate a classical revival, and while individual artisans produced beautiful silverwork and elaborate Catalan-Gothic ornaments, the island has no equivalent to Michelangelo or Botticelli.

There are, however, some important exceptions. Antonello da Messina, who was born in Sicily in 1430, was one of the most important and most often overlooked protagonists in the development of early Renaissance painting. Antonello trained in Naples, where, under the tutelage of Niccolò Antonio, he developed an innovative technique that was inspired by the hyper-realistic 'Flanders style' of northern Europe, and particularly the work of Jan van Eyck. In his *Lives of the Artists* (1550), Giorgio Vasari even goes as far as to credit da Messina with having brought oil painting to Italy.[16] While subsequent investigations have contested that claim, he was certainly one of the earliest Mediterranean artists to master the technique. Among da Messina's works, the *Portrait of a Young Man* (1478) and *Ecce Homo* series (1470–75) stand out in particular for their anatomical accuracy and unusually confident grasp of perspective. The artist's most important piece by some distance, though, is the *Virgin Annunciate* (1476) which depicts Mary at the moment of the Annunciation. The painting, which is dominated by a vast shawl of blue drapery, is notable for its use of colour. Yet it's the composition that is most striking. The majority of Italian artworks at the time were 'flat' allegorical pieces. Da Messina, though, structures his work such that the viewer takes on the role of Gabriel presenting the news to Mary. This was one of very few paintings from this period that attempted to draw the viewer into the piece, not only as a witness but as an active participant in a three-dimensional scene. For this reason alone, both the painting, and the artist, are surely worthy of renewed interest.

In a similar vein, the Gagini family, who dedicated much of their professional energy to beautifying the churches of Palermo and other towns in the west of the island, produced hundreds of statues of a standard that is comparable to those that one might expect to find in a museum like the Uffizi Gallery. Antonello, the family's main representative, who was active between 1478 and 1536, was once considered among the geniuses of his age, though art historians have largely forgotten his legacy. In fact, this is less a reflection of Sicily's 'innate' marginality than a consequence of the loss of several of his most important works due to earthquakes, fire and negligence. His masterpiece, a twenty-five-metre-high Tribuna depicting Christ exiting the tomb upon resurrection, was one of the most ambitious works of the sixteenth century. Unfortunately, though, it was completely destroyed in 1780 during a particularly aggressive renovation of Palermo cathedral. Thanks to a group of Sicilian architects led by Salvatore Rizzuti, international audiences can now view a 3D model of the work, which gives some idea of its original form. Based on his team's reconstruction it's clear that the façade, which was decorated with forty statues, was a masterpiece of craftsmanship. More interesting still, it confirms that the proportions and scale of the piece were fully conversant with the 'golden ratio', the Euclidean formula on which the architectural norms in Northern Italy were based. Of all the island's lost artworks – and there are unfortunately a great many – this is arguably the most significant.

While there are a few other exceptions to the general idea of Sicily's cultural stagnation under Spain, there's no escaping the fact that the island's most important surviving Renaissance treasure was a hand-me-down from Florence. In 1554 Francesco Camilliani built the so-called Praetorian Fountain (Fontana Pretoria) for a private patron, Luigi de Toledo, in the Tuscan capital. Contemporary observers were astounded by this piece. Vasari described it as 'stupendous' in its composition, and 'one of the most beautiful in all of Italy'.[17] By the time the work was finished, though, Toledo was heavily in debt and had no choice but to sell it. The Palermitan elite, eager to demonstrate their high cultural tastes, were the first to take up the offer. In 1574 a team of stonemasons carefully dismantled the fountain into over 600 pieces and sent them to the Sicilian city where they reconstructed it at great expense in a square directly in front of the town hall. Given that the majority of the forty-eight statues depict nude pre-Christian figures, including nymphs, satyrs and muses, this was a controversial acquisition to say the least. Locals nicknamed the piece the 'Fontana della vergogna', the fountain of shame, perhaps on account of what they perceived to be its lewd and blasphemous subject matter. Other equally convincing theories, however, maintain that this was an objection to the sum the administration spent to ship the artwork south, or, more simply still, that it was just a popular slur against the viceroys and parliamentarians themselves.

The strangest thing about the Praetorian Fountain, though, is how uncannily it captures the ideals of Sicily's ancient Hellenistic history. Camilliani first conceived of the design as an academic exercise. It was, to his mind, a tribute to a far-off and exotic classical world. That reality, though, was not at all so alien for Sicilians, who, unlike the Tuscans, had played a central role in the original flourishing of Punic-Greek culture in the third century BC. The result is a unique historical peculiarity. While the Palermitan administration purchased this fountain in the sixteenth century as a retort to those who thought of the city as relatively backward, it was, in a strange sense, a 'return' to artistic and aesthetic norms that had characterised the island's pre-Christian past. Whether one sees this piece as a vindication of Sicily's classical cosmopolitanism or a superficial foreign distortion of that era is irrelevant. Either way the fountain is a particularly stark indicator of how limited the Inquisition's grip over Sicily actually was. While the island may not have undergone a conventional renaissance, memories of the pre-Christian world clearly continued to hold significance in some of the islanders' imaginations. Perhaps, then, the Sicilians did not conform so strictly to the dogmas of Spanish Catholicism as one might be tempted to believe.

PART II: The Hypocrisies of Nationalism

5

Decadence and Parlour Games (1693–1860)

Baroque Towns, Legendary Bandits, Folk Politics

The Sicilians, so far from their king, who they do not know except through viceroys, are used to thinking of rulers as old pensioners who they can take advantage of, they make a show of offering free gifts ... they're always ready to accept a new sovereign, that will offer them better conditions, but in the case of a tyrant they turn to the known systems of revolt.

Dominique Vivant, French diplomat, 1788

At the start of January 1693 two major earthquakes, each with a force of about 7.5 on the moment magnitude scale, struck Sicily's south-eastern corner somewhere along the Ionian coast. They were, and remain, the largest seismic events in Italy's history. The initial shocks reduced more than fifty towns and cities to rubble, destroying houses and monuments, temples and churches. To make matters worse a series of smaller quakes also took place at sea, resulting in a ten-metre tsunami which devastated fishing villages across the coast from Messina in the north to Pachino in the south. Sicilians still point to the events of that winter as being among the worst disasters the island has ever faced. At least 60,000 people died, around 5 percent of the island's population, and tens of thousands were left homeless.

The long-term political consequences of these events proved even more significant than the tragedy itself. For the first time since the War of the Vespers, the administration in Palermo was forced to pay serious attention to the realities of life on the island's southern coast. On account of its distance from the capital, this area had long been among the last places to receive news of legislation. With the notable exception of Frederick II, most monarchs had left the towns and villages here in the control of a few noble families that had managed agricultural production far from royal oversight. The barons were, as a result, particularly renowned for their vendettas, and the peasantry their unruliness.

The year 1693 was one of the few moments in which Sicily's foreign rulers sought to confront these problems head-on. In the weeks following the earthquake, the Habsburg king Charles II, who was based in Madrid, responded by ordering the construction of a series of new towns to house displaced people. The central conurbation, he proposed, should be located in the Hyblaean Mountains to the south-west of Syracuse, and ideally in the vicinity of Noto, an old medieval town with a modest community of scholars, which had previously served as a small cultural centre for the area. At the time of the earthquake, archaeologists were only just beginning to unearth Southern Sicily's extensive classical heritage. Nevertheless, Charles and his advisors, like most of Europe's educated elite, were familiar with tales about the glories of ancient Syracuse and its esteemed citizens such as Archimedes, and they strongly associated this corner of the island with idealised notions of progress and political stability. By investing so heavily in this region, they certainly wished to assist those royal subjects that had been affected by the earthquakes. At the same time, though, they sought to take advantage of the situation, to offer a forward-looking vision of the Habsburg monarchy that would present Spanish Catholicism as something that had surpassed the achievements of the classical world.

Most of Sicily's settlements are a chaotic mix of Greco-Roman, Norman, medieval and modern builds, with little evidence of organised design. Noto, by contrast, is the apotheosis of Spanish city planning. Much of this is the result of work conducted by a Dutch military engineer called Carlos de Grunenberg, who Charles commissioned to design the street map. De Grunenberg constructed his scheme around a rigid grid system, which he and his collaborators conceived as a physical representation of the hierarchical values their patron so revered. The entire city is based around two parallel roads which were planned to run from west to east, in order to catch the sun at all times. At the mid-point, one finds the administrative buildings, the cathedral and the town hall. These are surrounded by the most important noble residences which were designed in a distinctive mix of Romanesque and, later, neoclassical styles by architects from across the peninsula. Art historians often describe the overall effect, the convergence of curves and ovals, and dramatic experiments with shadow and light, as constituting a 'Sicilian baroque'. Geometry is an important part of the style, particularly in religious buildings, though it does have other distinguishing features. Its secular form, in particular, is characterised by an abundance of gargoyles and other grotesque ornaments. The most overt example in Noto is the Palazzo Villadorata, which once housed the noble Nicolaci family, and which is home to balconies that depict a whole menagerie of griffins and mermaids among other fantastic beasts.

Today tourists happily photograph these statues as if they were purely decorative ornaments. In their original context, however, these were not mere adornments to the villa. They were guardians, whose purpose was to intimidate superstitious passers-by and to protect the property, the private space, from those looking in from outside.

It's easy to be seduced by the golden glow of Noto's unique 'peach' limestone, which shines so brightly in the midday sun. Yet there's something sinister about this town. Outside of its central grid Noto contains almost nothing of historic or artistic value. Just metres from the cathedral, the extravagance of the Palazzo Villadorata quickly gives way to poor-quality low-rise housing with few amenities or public spaces. This is, of course, an immediate consequence of twentieth-century planning. To some extent, though, it also reflects the essence of de Grunenberg's original design. The Spanish elite never did intend Noto to be a community space. The city was to be a display of power and dominance, and nothing else.

Local residents were well aware of this fact from the beginning. In fact, in 1694, in the early stages of the construction, inhabitants of the old town organised a plebiscite in which they explicitly rejected de Grunenberg's plan. The most militant opponents of the works actually attempted to sabotage them by organising raids on the construction sites, during which they vandalised the new buildings and dismantled scaffolding. In response to these acts of defiance the Habsburg soldiers executed dozens of working-age men and forced the rest of the population, largely women and children, to live in shanty towns at the edge of the new conurbation well into the eighteenth century. Today Noto's population is just over 20,000, but the contrast between luxury and squalor remains atypical for such a small place. So while this beautiful town well deserves its reputation as 'capital of Sicilian baroque' it must also be seen, in context, as one of the bloodiest emblems of Spanish despotism.

Elsewhere on the island, in Catania in particular, the rebuild took a different and arguably more democratic form. Once again de Grunenberg sketched plans for long, wide promenades which were designed to cut through the ruins along a symmetrical axis. In this case, though, it proved impossible to impose such a 'pure' model on a city that had an urban area which was much larger than Noto, and where many of the old foundations, including those of Roman buildings, remained intact. The process itself was more anarchic. Architects from across Spain and Italy flocked to the city to build palaces along the new promenades, but also, rather haphazardly, across the old destroyed urban area. The most important protagonist in this process was Giovanni Battista Vaccarini, a Palermitan architect who had studied in Rome in the 1720s. On his return to his homeland, he was awarded commissions to develop some of Catania's most important buildings, including the town hall and cathedral, which he designed according to models first developed by Gian Lorenzo Bernini in the grand, central-Italian city. There was, however, a major difference between his and Bernini's work. Part of the allure of Rome's Piazza Navona, with its iconic baroque fountains, is the quality of the building material: bright travertine marble. The architects that reconstructed Catania, by contrast, were forced to do so using black igneous rock from the foothills of Etna. As a result, while the city's monuments appear elegant and stately, they are, in fact, built from the same relatively cheap material that was used to construct many more-humble abodes, among the residences that spread out to the suburbs. Noto's architecture is hermetic, confined to a few streets. Catania, by contrast, is sprawling, dark and dusty, and the lines between the wealthier and poorer parts of the city are more blurred than is usual in Sicily.

One project in particular captures the new urban spirit that took root in Catania following the earthquake: the renovation of the university. This institution is, in fact, the oldest on the island, and was opened by the Spanish king Alfonso I in the fifteenth century. Due to the Black Death, however, and the strong influence of Jesuit colleges in the nearby area, the student body rarely surpassed a few dozen individuals. After 1693 the institution took on a new life. Vaccarini and his team constructed a new library and administrative buildings which provided a more spacious environment in which to study. More importantly still, a host of new scholars took control of the curriculum. When the university was founded, the institution was, like most medieval academies, focused overwhelmingly on law and theology. Following the rebuild, however, several departments opened which were focused on secular subjects, including mineralogy and geology, economics and commerce, philology and literary criticism. By 1750, over 1,000 individuals from as far away as Malta, Rhodes and Palestine were present in the city, dedicating themselves to these studies. Parallel to this, several reformist bishops obtained influential positions on the governing board. One of them, a man named Salvatore Ventimiglia, who was appointed by his colleagues as rector in 1758, went as far as to encourage his students to read works by Descartes and Spinoza, despite the fact that studying such texts was expressly forbidden by the Inquisition. When the Jesuits objected to this and proposed that their order take direct control of the university, the students responded by occupying the new buildings, and even organised a series of demonstrations calling for the sect to be removed from the city altogether. Thanks to their efforts the offending texts remain in the library to this day.

Stories like these are a recurring part of Catania's history. Starting in the seventeenth century the city developed its own independent identity, often challenging and contradicting decisions made in Palermo. Its most iconic monument, the Fontana dell'Elefante, is a celebration of this anomalous, outsider status. The fountain, which sits at the very centre of the city in the main piazza, just a few metres from the cathedral, is not a single, unified piece, but a hodgepodge of elements. The most obvious feature is a basalt sculpture of an elephant, *u Liotru*, which locals maintain is a reference to the name of a wizard who once lived in the city and kept such an animal as his steed. The statue itself, which was heavily damaged in the earthquake, actually dates back to the Roman era. When Vaccarini heard the tale of the wizard in the 1730s, however, he was so thrilled that he ordered the sculpture be repaired and placed on a rather extravagant baroque plinth. During the restoration work Vaccarini also made the rather strange decision to graft another object on its back: a seventh-century Egyptian obelisk which probably arrived in Catania as plunder from one of the crusades. The combination of these elements – an ancient pagan statue, North African loot and an extravagant Italian-inspired base – in a single object is disorienting to say the least. The result, though, is a fitting testimony to how esoteric Catania's civic identity was in the aftermath of the 1693 earthquake. In most instances Sicilian baroque was the symptom of a Spanish-led effort to bulldoze Sicily's long and complex cultural history, and replace it with the fantasy of a homogeneous, ordered society. In Catania, more than anywhere else, the citizens defied this logic and instead came to celebrate the island's hybridity as the guiding principle for a new and increasingly metropolitan society.

~

Looking at Catania in isolation it might seem as though Sicily was developing along similar lines to other parts of mainland western Europe. By the mid-eighteenth century the city's population reached 45,000, it had a nascent middle class, was pushing for some degree of political secularisation, and even began to develop small-scale industries, in glass and paper in particular. While noble families still controlled most of the city's businesses, a growing number of influential merchants succeeded in establishing a foothold in the city's property market, forming a small but powerful bourgeoisie. Usually these combined phenomena could be considered as representing an early form of 'modernisation'. In reality, though, Catania was the exception, not the rule. To some extent, despite its awful human cost, the earthquake had been a gift to the city. The disaster had destabilised the ruling class, opened a space for new political players to enter civic life, and enabled artists and intellectuals to rethink what might be possible in society as a whole.

Elsewhere on the island, and particularly in the west, which had been unaffected by the events of 1693, things looked rather different. Palermo was, at the time, experiencing an economic slump. By 1700 the city's population had grown to over 110,000 people. Yet despite this, the capital was not home to any of the innovations or new forms of industrial production that were seen in Catania. Intellectual life was still dominated by the church, and there was no form of secularisation analogous to that in the island's second city (astonishingly the capital was not home to its own university until 1808). To make matters worse, unemployment was rife and inequality was growing to the point that most of the population, those who were untrained in crafts, were forced to beg, steal or do odd jobs in order to survive. Nevertheless, at the same time as the underclass swelled, the wealthy nobility began to return to the city in ever-larger numbers to take advantage of the relatively easy access to high-value luxury products that were being imported from Spain, such as tea, coffee, tobacco and sherry. Noble families commissioned extravagant residences like the Palazzo Sant'Elia and Palazzo Valguarnera-Gangi, which was immortalised in the ballroom scene of Luchino Visconti's film adaption of *The Leopard* (1963), where they held parties and literary salons. These buildings, which were decorated with gilded furniture and *trompe-l'œil* ceilings, exhibited a degree of opulence and wealth that far exceeded anything on display in Catania. While Sicily's second city was itself unequal, as a commercial hub it at least offered some chance of gainful employment for its poorer residents. In the capital, the class structure was essentially unchanged from medieval times, with a small handful of noble families ruling over the masses as if they were bound by feudal bonds. Crucially, the bourgeoisie was nowhere to be seen.

The negative consequences of this became particularly apparent following the Bourbon accession to the throne of Sicily in 1735.[1] Today this dynasty holds the reputation of being one of the most oppressive in the island's history. In reality, particularly in the early stages of their rule, they were relatively benevolent in their approach. The family's first, and finest, representative, Charles V (later Charles III of Spain), was what we might now call an 'enlightened despot'; an absolute monarch, yes, but still one of few early modern rulers who even thought to try to solve the problem of urban poverty in his kingdom. Unlike the Habsburgs, who had largely governed Sicily from Madrid, the Bourbon kings were firmly based in Naples. While Charles, like many of his contemporaries, spent vast sums of money constructing lavish palaces, he was also keen to demonstrate that his rule would have material benefits for the working classes. One of his first actions on taking power was to dramatically raise taxes on the nobility in order to fund poorhouses that would provide welfare to those in need. While Sicily's wealthier families resisted this proposal, arguing that it was the church's job to provide this service, the island's poor were hugely supportive of the measure, and many came to celebrate Charles as a liberating figure. In 1740 the Spanish king came into similar tensions with Sicily's religious authorities when he signed an edict allowing Jewish traders to return to live and work across Southern Italy. The ecclesiastical authorities organised furious protests in response, and after six years, the king was forced to revoke this policy.

Later in his reign Charles refused to succumb to the seemingly total intransigence of the Sicilian elite. In 1767 he took the drastic step of expelling all Jesuits from the Bourbon territories. The same year, he cut all funding to the Sicilian Inquisition, and as a result it effectively ceased to function altogether. The impact of these combined measures was immediate. Across the island, Sicilians began to take advantage of their increased freedom of expression. In the south-east, a community of dialect poets began composing bawdy verses that openly mocked the church and local elites. A whole community of actors, mimes, clowns and other performers ridiculed priests, barons and viceroys. Street theatre became more risqué. Palermo, in particular, was scene to an explosion of eroticism. Large quantities of pornographic materials began to be imported to the capital from France and the phenomenon of *cicisbeismo*, in which noblewomen would pay working-class men for sexual services, was widespread. A number of libertine figures came to prominence in this licentious climate. The most famous of all was Giuseppe Balsamo, otherwise known as Count Alessandro di Cagliostro. Born in 1743 in

Albergheria, a poor working-class neighbourhood in Palermo, Balsamo amassed a considerable fortune by selling false antiquities and bogus potions, and offering questionable services such as fortune-telling to the elite across Europe. He is best known internationally as a con artist. In Sicily, though, many people still think of Balsamo as a local hero who, through his admirable intelligence, was able to infiltrate and extort the highest ranks of the continental nobility.[2]

For the peasantry the early years of Bourbon rule proved rather more fraught. State tax records from 1748 show that the number of independent landowners and other smallholders increased dramatically in this period. While this may seem like a positive development, it's worth pointing out that the vast majority of rural workers were still bound by contracts that bore a close resemblance to those of the medieval manorial system. Most peasants rented their land from the nobility and, in exchange, were permitted to farm, or work in trade, with certain strict conditions (typically handing over a certain amount of the crop yield). In some extreme cases, in particularly poor parts of the island, individuals were still forced to work the land simply for the right to live and eat. Nevertheless, as the noble landowners began to move back to Palermo they needed to employ people to keep control of the estates in their absence. To do this they selected small groups of ambitious independent farmers who, in exchange for a share of the agricultural profits, agreed to police the land, and ensure the poorer peasants paid their rents. Members of this new class, who from the nineteenth century became known as *gabellotti*, were infamous for abusing their power. These 'middlemen' did not take over the estates for free. They too had to pay rent to the landlords. For this reason, they did everything they could to shift the burden of these costs onto the shoulders of the rural workforce. Later accounts, from the time of Italian unification, describe how these figures charged extortionate fees for lending out seeds and farming equipment, invented new charges and fake taxes, and, on occasion, simply stole goods from those under their authority. This was not yet the mafia, but it was not far off.

This violent system of territorial management began in earnest in 1759 when Charles's son Ferdinand took control of the Bourbons' southern Italian territories. It was an awkward transition. Ferdinand lacked his father's liberal qualities; he was poorly educated and prone to long bouts of illness. He also faced considerable practical challenges. In the 1760s, a series of famines spread across central Sicily and the *gabellotti* were particularly brutal in repressing the peasantry's attempts at rebellion. As a result, instead of an uprising, the island seems to have been struck by a peculiarly large wave of banditry. Highwaymen were a common presence in most of early modern Europe. Following the famine of 1760, however, a series of more organised groups, sometimes known as brigands, began to establish themselves in Sicily in large numbers. Antonino Di Blasi, otherwise known as Testalonga, was one of the most famous early leaders. Between 1761 and 1767 he and two deputies led a force of three separate bands, comprised of ten to fifteen men each, which were stationed at different points across the island's semi-deserted interior. This was no rag-tag bunch. Testalonga's cells were heavily armed, and his men were equipped not only with swords, but with muskets and horses. Brigand groups focused on the routes between Palermo, Messina and Catania where they orchestrated ambushes on the poorly maintained roads. Over the course of that decade, stories began to abound of robberies and kidnappings and animals being stolen. Legend holds that anyone who passed directly across the centre of the island during the early years of Ferdinand's rule would have been forced to pay up to these bands. In 1767 the Bourbon police caught Testalonga and executed him along with several of his captains. The very fact that these men had succeeded in building such a sizeable and dangerous armed force in such a short space of time, however, and that other smaller groups were also active, is a good indicator of how fragile the rule of law on the island had become under Spanish domination.

Much of Sicily's rural working class seems to have supported the brigands. While the reality is that many of these figures worked alongside the *gabellotti* to persecute peasants, folklorists spoke of bandits in favourable terms as defenders of the common people. Perhaps the most famous story of all is that of Pasquale Bruno, who is said to have lived in the area around Messina between 1780 and 1803. According to most accounts, Bruno was radicalised into action against the ruling class as a young man after his mother was raped and killed by the count of a small town called Bauso. Disgusted, Bruno ran away to seek refuge in the nearby agricultural area of Barcellona Pozzo di Gotto where he lived and worked alongside the peasants. After a few years of labouring in the fields, Bruno returned to Bauso, and, on doing so, fell in love with a servant at the count's castle, named Teresa. Bruno was sufficiently enamoured that, for a brief while, he was willing to put aside his vendetta. The count, however, was less accommodating, and forbade the two from marrying. Furious, Bruno returned to Barcellona Pozzo di Gotto and rallied his friends among the peasantry. For several years throughout the 1790s, he and his band conducted a campaign of armed resistance across the island during which they attacked the nobility and *gabellotti* alike and apparently redistributed their wealth to the local poor. The state was unable to catch the bandit leader. It wasn't until the count threatened to burn down Bauso unless the outlaw ceased his activities that Bruno, who considered himself a 'man of honour', turned himself in. He was taken to the town's square and was executed in front of a large crowd which, out of respect for the condemned man, apparently remained silent throughout the proceedings.

It's tempting to think of tales like these as stories about heroic individuals. What makes them truly remarkable, though, is their collective dimension. Before the eighteenth century, the church had been the only significant community force in Sicily. During the early years of Bourbon rule, though, a whole manner of alternative social groupings began to emerge, which, while manifest in different forms, from urban street performers to vigilante cells, were stretched across the length and breadth of the island. As the Sicilian people discussed and debated these phenomena, they came, in the process, to develop an embryonic form of class consciousness, or at the very least a sense of shared identity that was rooted in more than just a vague feeling of injustice. Perhaps the most important, and esoteric, illustration of what this process looked like can be seen in the growing popularity of the puppet theatre (*opera dei pupi*). Today, we tend to associate puppets with children's entertainment. In Sicily, though, the *pupi* have a quite specific history within working-class education. Church authorities first introduced them in the Norman era as a way of teaching the island's illiterate populace about the stories of the saints. By the time of the Bourbons, however, thanks in part to Charles's liberal reforms, these shows began to incorporate secular content, including stories of figures like Testalonga and Bruno. The most popular tale from the beginning was the Carolingian cycle, a Renaissance poem which narrates the adventures of Orlando Furioso and describes his heroic actions during Charlemagne's conflicts with the Saracens. This might, at first, seem like a straightforward swashbuckling tale. For Sicily's working-class population, however, it also provided a rare chance to reflect on the island's pan-Mediterranean history, and, in particular, aspects of their shared identity that predated the Spanish occupation.

What really makes the puppet theatre important, though, is the sense of ownership that the audience seems to have felt over the art form. From the start of the nineteenth century, audiences grew to such numbers that, in the capital at least, the puppeteers were able to put on nightly shows. The performers used the opportunity to make jokes about the noble families, and to spread and critique local gossip. The puppets themselves began to take on different forms in the east and west of the island, and each city came to develop its own locally specific characters.[3] The crowd screamed and shouted and laughed at the stage during these events, and many people chose to stay behind after the shows to discuss the moral dilemmas they raised. Unlike the top-down education that the clergy offered in their sermons, the puppet theatre was a true civic space, where history and politics were treated not as dogmas but as ideas to be debated. This was more than just entertainment. It was the island's first form of mass media and it played an important role in enabling Sicily's poor to recognise themselves as protagonists in a new, common story.

In 1789 the events of the French Revolution sent shockwaves around Europe. Across the continent the bourgeoisie, propped up by working-class support, moved to abolish absolute monarchies and replace them with new constitutional, national, democracies. Southern Italy was no exception to this. In 1798 armed Jacobin groups laid siege to the Bourbon palace at Capodimonte in Naples where they set up their own government, the so-called

Parthenopean Republic, and forced Ferdinand into exile in Palermo. Keen to avoid similar scenes in Sicily, the king sent private militias across the island on his arrival to weed out any potential rebels. In reality the Sicilians were not planning anything as ambitious as their cousins on the mainland. The return to an 'inquisitorial' atmosphere and the sudden intrusion on their newly won liberty, however, did galvanise resentment among some of the islanders. In 1799, groups of Jacobin sympathisers in Catania worked to organise a fairly sizeable revolt against the king's police forces. While there was nothing revolutionary about their intention – at least not yet – neither was this mere banditry. It was the first mass uprising that brought peasants and intellectuals together, and, as such, was one of the most serious acts of collective opposition that the residents in this part of the island had forwarded since the War of the Vespers in the thirteenth century. As the Catanian poet Domenico Tempio put it:

> Since time immemorial
> there's no record
> of our people ever
> rising up in insurrection.
>
> Ever pliant and docile,
> submissive and obedient
> they bear their loads
> like patient donkeys.
>
> Even when beaten
> with incredible violence
> they've never lost their patience
> over these lashings.

If they had something
to eat, straw and fetid
leftovers, they stayed quiet,
afraid even to bray.

They never showed their rage
in words, or deeds,
just like a donkey
with its drooping ears.

But virtue has its limits.
The donkey is an animal,
and like all other beasts
it has its brutal instincts.[4]

The uprising in south-east Sicily represented an important shift from fragmented individual protests, which were intended to resolve specific disputes, to a more general attack against the social order. Even in Palermo, where the working class was most loyal to the Bourbons, parts of the nobility, together with traders that were well informed about the developments in Naples, began to call for systemic changes. Liberated from the Inquisition, the most educated islanders were free to discuss Enlightenment ideas that went far beyond the benevolent monarchy that Charles had represented. Prominent lawyers began suggesting that the Bourbons might do well to recognise a 'social contract' as an alternative to divine order, emphasising the importance of consensus between governors and the governed. Theologians began to talk of 'rational Christianity' as an alternative to absolute faith. Scientists proposed new methods for understanding the laws of physics. In 1788, the mathematician Lorenzo Federici invented a new kind of sundial in the shape of a dodecahedron which was positioned in such a way that the viewer could read multiple time zones at once. He later placed it, rather provocatively, on top of a statue of Atlas, the Greek Titan, in Palermo's first public park, the Villa Giulia. Inspired by this, in 1801, the priest Giuseppe Piazzi developed his own 'meridian', now visible on the floor of Palermo cathedral, which encouraged the local population to read time according to French convention with noon as the 'centre' point (rather than sunset, which had previously been conventional on the island). Sicily was, in a very literal sense, becoming synchronised with events on the European continent.

Ferdinand was shaken by these developments. These sceptical, scientific and materialist worldviews were dangerously Napoleonic in character, and he viewed them as potentially subversive. In 1806 his worst fears were confirmed when an army of Napoleonic soldiers did indeed push southwards and took control of Naples. For the second time in a decade, the Bourbon monarch was forced to flee his capital and take refuge in Palermo. Sensing the changing mood among the ruling elite, Ferdinand locked himself in a villa on the outskirts of the capital. Once there he isolated himself from the outside world: he ordered entire estates to be moved out of the way to make space for his personal hunting grounds, and had the interior of the house decorated at great expense with orientalist frescos of cherry blossoms and other far-eastern flora, in order to please his wife, Maria Carolina of Austria.

Throughout his stay Ferdinand relied on the British, who had established a strong foothold in nearby Malta, to protect his personal and political interests. In 1808 Ferdinand gave permission for the Royal Navy to dock permanently in Palermo's port. Both parties benefitted from this arrangement. Ferdinand was able to ward off the imminent threat of a French invasion. The British, meanwhile, were able to take advantage of exclusive trade contracts. Ferdinand offered favourable tax rates on a range of valuable exports including olive oil and citrus fruit. Two merchants, John Woodhouse and Benjamin Ingham, created an entirely new market for Marsala wine, the sickly-sweet mix of Grillo and Catarratto grapes from the west of the island which the local residents had been drinking without ceremony for generations. (It is thanks to them that the drink became one of the staple goods to be found in the home of any self-respecting bourgeoisie, alongside port and sherry.) Sicily's most important export by some distance, however, was sulphur, which was a central component of gunpowder, textile production and oil refining. At its peak the island was shipping 44,653 tonnes of this 'yellow gold' per year to Britain.[5] The human cost of this was enormous. The working conditions in the mines were notoriously poor. Sicily's landowners employed children as young as ten years old to delve into the depths of the pits to retrieve the raw ore, and the older teenagers often suffered from blindness and severe physical deformities. This horrific practice played an important and often under-acknowledged role in fuelling Britain's much-celebrated Industrial Revolution.

The ties between Sicily and the United Kingdom went far beyond trade. With Ferdinand incapable of governing, the island was, from 1806 to 1815, an unofficial protectorate of the empire, and a key part of Britain's wider strategy to limit Napoleon's influence over the Mediterranean. Imperial officials even came to have a direct role in matters of state. One of them, a soldier and liberal politician named William Bentinck, played a particularly important role in modernising the island's political system. When he first arrived in Sicily, Bentinck had been shocked by the state of the local administration; by the scale of the banditry, the vast inequalities of wealth and the violence of landowners against their employees. In 1812, keen to prevent what he saw as an imminent revolution, he drafted a new constitution for Sicily which, had it been fully realised, would have abolished the final remnants of the feudal system. As well as calling for an end to the right of the nobility to control land beyond their own private estates, Bentinck's document outlined a dramatic expansion of the commons and new laws to protect freedom of expression and the independence of the judiciary. Its most radical proposal was for a new two-chamber parliament, in the Westminster style, which Bentinck suggested might be implemented in Palermo and which would play a major role in drafting and authorising legislation. Had these proposals been successfully implemented, there's little doubt that Sicily's small bourgeoisie would have rallied to support the incumbent monarchy. This was not to be the case. Initially Ferdinand accepted the proposals. It's clear, though, that he only did so in order to maintain British naval support in the face of the French threat. In 1815, however, when Napoleon's brother-in-law Joachim Murat lost control of Naples, the king was free to go back to his favourite city. His first act after his return was to abolish Bentinck's Sicilian constitution. Instead, he united his two territories into a single political entity, the 'Kingdom of the Two Sicilies', which he insisted he would rule according to the historic Bourbon values of absolute monarchy.

Of all the mistakes Ferdinand made during his long, turbulent reign, this was the most severe. The king had vastly underestimated the popularity of Bentinck's reforms among Sicilians. Thanks to the British, the island's bourgeoisie, powerless though they were, had seen a possibility for obtaining greater political influence, and, as such, were incentivised to fight for new rights. What Ferdinand had failed to understand, though, was that much of the island's nobility had also been persuaded by Bentinck's vision. In the face of the revolutionary climate, many of the established families saw the implementation of a heavily regulated new parliamentary system as the most viable means of holding on to power. Despite the increasing frequency of their rebellions, the Sicilian people had not, before this point, proposed to overthrow the Bourbons themselves. By building a shared interest among these previously divided camps, however, the British inadvertently formed the basis for a revolution.

Following Ferdinand's announcement, groups of Sicilian liberals began to meet, inspired by a secret society of republican, anti-papal forces on the Italian mainland known as the *carbonari* (coal burners). Initially they limited their demands to calling for a return to, and full implementation of, the 1812 constitution. In 1820, in Naples, a group of these *carbonari* organised riots and even attempted to assassinate the king. Fearing for his life, Ferdinand conceded a few constitutional points which, while falling short of Bentinck's proposals, was enough to quell the immediate revolt.

In Sicily, however, the liberals instead worked to build a standing army. Over several months at the start of the decade, the rebels purchased over 14,000 muskets, enough to pose a serious threat to the Bourbon administration. Their hope was that, by doing so, they could intimidate Ferdinand into honouring his pledge to the British. Instead, learning of their initiative, Ferdinand cut off the water supply to Palermo. This immoderate, gratuitous move killed hundreds of islanders indiscriminately during the hot summer months, and caused large numbers of the island's urban poor to abandon their historic loyalty to the Bourbons. More and more working-class citizens began to

gravitate towards the liberal ranks, and as they did so the movement's leaders began to realise that calls for a constitution were
no longer enough. Instead they set their sights on full political
independence.

It took two decades for the liberals to organise the funds and
weapons for their planned uprising. Their decision to wait,
though, proved percipient. The rebels chose 12 January 1848,
the day of the new king Ferdinand II's birthday, as their moment
to strike. They planned the affair meticulously in advance. In
the days leading up to the anticipated revolt, the liberals sent
criers across the countryside to attract volunteers. In the cities,
meanwhile, activists circulated posters and fliers calling on the
population to find weapons of their own:

> Sicilians! The time for prayer has passed, protest is useless, the pleas,
> the peaceful demonstrations. Ferdinand has broken everything. And
> we, a freely born people, reduced to chains and living in misery, still
> dare to stand up for our legitimate rights. Take up arms, children of
> Sicily! Our power is everywhere: the people united will be the end of
> the king. On the dawn of the 12 January, a new glorious epoch of uni-
> versal regeneration will begin. Palermo will welcome however many
> armed Sicilians present themselves to support the common cause, to
> establish reforms and institutions appropriate for the progress of this
> century … Unity, order, obedience to leaders, respect for property.
> Any theft will be considered a betrayal to the nation and punished as
> such. He who is lacking will be provided for in the aftermath. With
> these principles in mind heaven will not fail to reward our just under-
> taking. Sicilians, to arms![6]

The tone of this message, calling as it did for both violence
and restraint, was rather ambiguous. Unsurprisingly, the revolt

was characterised overwhelmingly by the former. In the late morning on the allotted day, groups of armed rebels began to launch attacks against the Bourbon barracks in Palermo. They were met by a large crowd of citizens, who set fire to banks and shops and then erected barricades around La Kalsa, the old Arab neighbourhood, to defend themselves. The monarchy had long been preparing for such an uprising. The numbers that turned out that day, though, were far larger than they had anticipated. The protesters paid little heed to their leaders' calls to uphold propriety. Over the following week they broke into the prisons, cut the telegraph communication with the mainland, and set fire to the royal administrative buildings, eradicating all records of debts that were owed to the crown. Looting was widespread across the countryside. Even in small towns like Trapani, which had virtually no history of revolutionary activity, bandits, such as the infamous Maria Testadilana, kidnapped and executed local landowners. The uprising spread quickly, from the west to the east of the island, in a pattern reminiscent of the War of the Vespers in 1282. On 26 January, after two weeks of intense fighting, Ferdinand's troops were forced to retreat to Naples. The Sicilians, against all odds, had won their independence.

The liberal activists worked fast to re-establish order. On 2 February they formed a revolutionary government which aimed to implement a new constitutional framework for the fledgling state. Their main reference point remained William Bentinck's text, which they adopted in full with a few minor alterations. At the head of the government was Ruggero Settimo, an admiral who had previously fought alongside Bentinck to defend Malta from incursions by Napoleonic forces. He and his supporters quickly made the decision that they would need to work with members of the nobility in order to restore order. They formed a 'national guard', mainly comprised of defectors from the Bourbon army, who rounded up those that had disobeyed Settimo's orders against violent looting. Hundreds of bandits and peasant groups were arrested and dozens were killed. On 18 March the government organised elections, in which all 'literate members' of the population were permitted to vote. As a result of this process, the Sicilian elite came to be split between a majority moderate faction, which sought to establish a constitutional monarchy, and a radical republican minority that was pushing for a fully secular state and a more dramatic redistribution of resources. This rather significant schism undermined the government's attempts at international diplomacy from the outset. When Settimo had helped plan the revolution, he had counted on winning support from his British allies. In the event, the Royal Navy insisted on remaining neutral, and instead elected to play the role of mediator between Sicily and Naples. Keen to demonstrate the legitimacy of the new nation, Settimo bypassed the republican opposition entirely and desperately led an effort to find a king, hoping that if the Sicilians could entice a lord from Genoa or elsewhere in Northern Italy to govern, the British might offer up their military support. Ultimately, however, he failed to find a suitable candidate. Radical members of the government began to clash ever more violently with the monarchists and by the summer the state was paralysed, and incapable of implementing legislation.

In autumn 1848, observing the deadlock in Palermo, the Bourbon forces set out on a counter-offensive to take back the island. Under the command of a particularly ruthless general named Carlo Filangieri, they began by bombarding Messina and Catania, inflicting such damage that newspapers across Europe awarded Ferdinand a new epithet: 'the bomber king'.

Both cities fell within a matter of days. The capital resisted a little longer, until May 1849 when the nobility finally retreated to their country estates and announced that they would no longer support the amateurish government. As Settimo and his supporters fled to Malta, the Bourbon fleet once again pummelled the city centre with heavy artillery, and, on re-establishing control, imposed a night-time curfew and prohibited all public gatherings. Filangieri ordered a permanent unit of soldiers to patrol the streets, banned all dissemination of pro-democratic literature, and frequently turned to torture as a means of exacting intelligence from suspects accused of conspiracy. The Sicilians had failed in their attempt at self-determination. The severity with which the Neapolitans reclaimed the island, though, proved a grave miscalculation, and, as we shall see, served only to fan the flames of a larger and more powerful nationalist movement on the Italian mainland.

6

A Revolution Betrayed (1860–1891)

Italian Unification, the Origins of the Mafia, the Paradoxes of Liberalism

The Sicilian insurrection should be aided, not in Sicily alone, but wherever her enemies may be met ... Our war cry will always be, 'Italy and VICTOR EMANUEL!' I hope even at this juncture the Italian banner will be borne out unscathed.

Giuseppe Garibaldi, *The London Times*, 5 May 1860

The mafia is neither a sect nor an association, and has neither rules nor statutes. The Mafioso is not a robber or a brigand ... The Mafioso is simply a brave man, someone who will put up with no provocation; and in that sense, every man needs to be, indeed has to be, a Mafioso. The mafia is a certain consciousness of one's own being.

Giuseppe Pitrè, folklorist, 1889

The story of the Risorgimento, and the subsequent unification of Italy, has been told so often, and in so many guises, that its legend has become just as important as historical fact. Typically, historians have tended to see the movement as a project of popular liberation. More recently, however, revisionist authors, like the journalist Pino Aprile, have reinterpreted unification as a quasi-imperial mission, planned by the Savoy monarchy in the north to colonise the southern regions for their own benefit.[1] Seen from Sicily, these are not the irreconcilable positions that they might first appear to be.

It would be difficult to deny the promise of Italian nationalism in the context of the mid-nineteenth century. From Venice to Palermo, many of the leading figures were motivated by a strong desire to free the peninsula and islands from 'foreign occupation'. For the southerners, the main opponents were the Bourbons. Other future Italians, however, were more concerned with launching an assault against the Austro-Hungarian Empire, which controlled much of the land in what is now the country's north-east. Following the failed revolution of 1848 those in favour of national unification began to talk increasingly about Sicily as a place where the idea of a new state might flourish. By 1860 this was a question of global significance. Around the world, intellectuals were presenting Sicily's struggle as being somehow emblematic of a broader campaign for popular democracy. On 17 May that year Karl Marx published an article in the *New York Daily Tribune*, in which he explicitly called for international intervention. In it he described the plight of the Sicilian people not only as the most desperate of the age, but of any time and place:

> Throughout the history of the human race no land and no people have suffered so terribly from slavery, from foreign conquests and oppressions, and none have struggled so irrepressibly for emancipation as Sicily and the Sicilians ... Sicily now bleeds again [and yet no one has] a word to say of the massacres in the Sicilian cities. No

voice raises the cry of indignation throughout Europe. No ruler and no Parliament proclaims outlawry against the bloodthirsty idiot of Naples. Louis Napoleon, alone … may perhaps stop the butcher in his work of destruction. England will howl about perfidy, will spout fire and flames against Napoleonic treachery and ambition; but the Neapolitans and the Sicilians must eventually be gainers, even under a Murat or any other new ruler. Any change must be for the better.[2]

Unbeknown to Marx, on 11 May, a week before his article was published, the revolutionary Italian nationalist Giuseppe Garibaldi had landed in Marsala, on Sicily's westernmost point. He was accompanied by just over 1,000 men, often known as the 'red shirts' on account of their uniforms. These were doctors, intellectuals, businesspeople and workers, the majority hailing from what were at that time the impoverished towns and cities of Lombardy, in and around Milan. The group had set out from Genoa to liberate the island in the name of the Savoy king Vittorio Emanuele, ruler of Sardinia-Piedmont. They were also supported by the Action Party, a republican organisation with close links to the *carbonari*, which had embraced Italian unification hoping that it would undermine the political power of the Papacy, to which they were particularly opposed. The ideological makeup of Garibaldi's men was diverse. The red shirts included federalists, republicans, socialists, liberals, Christians and atheists in their ranks. There were forty-five Sicilians among them, including the anthropologist Giuseppe Pitrè and, most importantly, the political theorist Francesco Crispi, who would later go on to govern Italy itself as prime minister.

On paper, there was no chance that the thousand volunteers would be able to defeat Sicily's large Bourbon garrisons. Yet the group was more powerful than it seemed. For one thing they had the element of surprise. On 15 May Garibaldi's troops won their first major skirmish at Calatafimi, a small town near the Greek ruins of Segesta, defeating a battalion of Neapolitan soldiers twice their size. More importantly they were more confident of international support than the revolutionaries had been in 1848. Unlike Settimo, Garibaldi was a celebrity, well known across the world for his military achievements in South America where he had fought in various conflicts, including the Uruguayan Civil War. In the years building up to his expedition, the general had worked tirelessly to build popular support among the European bourgeoisie. In Britain alone he raised around £30,000 in public donations towards the Italian nationalist cause, including from well-known figures such as Charles Dickens and Florence Nightingale. Much of this support was motivated by a genuine desire to assist the people of Southern Italy in their fight against the Bourbons. British donors, though, had other reasons to back the expedition. Like the leaders of the Risorgimento, they too were concerned about the possibility of France or Austria–Hungary obtaining too much power in central Europe. A unified Italy was, as they saw it, the most convenient means of blocking that possibility.

On 27 May, then, as the red shirts entered Palermo, Garibaldi was sure of victory. The city's population, which had heard in advance of his arrival, turned against the Bourbon forces and emptied out their dwindling stockpiles of grenades and other heavy explosives. The rebels, though, were outnumbered. In the first two days of the fighting, Neapolitan soldiers killed over 600 citizens and, once again, bombarded Palermo's port districts from the sea. This time, however, in marked contrast to 1848, British ships began to move towards the Sicilian capital. With the prospect of an Italian state now appearing viable, they shifted their political alliance. On 30 May, just three days after the assault began, the Bourbon commander, Ferdinando Lanza, presented an armistice to Garibaldi, giving him effective control over the island.

Sicily's working classes venerated Garibaldi as a saint-like figure. The peasants spread rumours that he was the reincarnation of the Archangel Michael, and, despite the general's own rather vocal anti-Catholicism, crowds of devotees implored him to baptise their children. Other popular legends maintained that he was immune to disease, and impervious to gunfire. Garibaldi was also popular among the bourgeoisie, who, on the whole, backed unification hoping that it would provide them with a chance to obtain positions in a future parliament. Despite this, however, the Sicilians did not join Garibaldi's revolutionary army in significant numbers, and while the red shirts' ranks did grow over the next months, this was largely thanks to reinforcements from the north. One reason for this was the provincial character of the Sicilian working class. If cities like Catania had cultivated small Jacobin groups, most of the popular uprisings of the nineteenth century had been sustained by a rather simplistic narrative which pitched the poor against the rich. Rural workers, in particular, had no real sense of what a nationalist cause itself would mean.

The extent of this problem became particularly clear in August 1860 when, on hearing of the red shirt victory in Palermo, the local peasantry in Bronte, a small town near Catania, prepared for their own liberation by setting fire to the estates of the landowners. The ruling families here were not, however, Bourbons, but members of the British nobility, the heirs of Lord Nelson. Garibaldi was by most accounts genuinely concerned with the Sicilians' wellbeing. Nevertheless, he was unable to permit this kind of attack against properties that belonged to his most important foreign allies. He therefore sent Nino Bixio, one of his closest friends, to quell the revolt. The red shirt troops attacked and killed dozens of rioters and quickly returned the land to the British. Bixio arrested 150 rebels in the aftermath, executing five of them.[3]

Despite the limited nationalist consciousness on the part of the Sicilian working class, many pro-Italian artists worked to present the Risorgimento as a spontaneous movement that the islanders had self-consciously willed through their actions in 1848. Painters like Michele Rapisardi and Erulo Eroli created canvases depicting the Vespers, that great revolution of the thirteenth century, as a Sicilian precedent to Italian unification, as if the island itself had been the prime mover. Other artists worked on vast melodramatic battle scenes, inspired by French revolutionary landscapes. Filippo Liardo's 1862 painting *Sepoltura Garibaldina* ('red shirt burial'), stands out among the mass of rather banal pieces. The work shows a semi-dilapidated house during what seems to be the immediate aftermath of the insurrection in Palermo. In the foreground is a closed coffin with a red cap on top, symbolising the spirit of the new Italian people. Above this object are two mourning women, each holding extinguished candles, their eyes closed in grief and reverence. At the back of the scene, just visible through the rear window, a *tricolore* flag blows in the wind. On the surface this is a rather simplistic piece of Italian propaganda. Among Sicilians, though, it had quite a particular resonance. Liardo wasn't just trumpeting here, he was imploring his audience to think beyond the provincial reality of bandits and vendettas, to embrace a new national reality. The painting itself is technically impressive. Its message, though, sits rather uneasily with the events at Bronte. Beyond its artistic merits, the canvas is perhaps more important as an example of how differently bourgeois liberals and working people experienced unification, and, by extension, the class divisions that would undermine the Italian project from its very beginning.

The new Italy would require new Italians. What this meant in practice, though, was far from evident: the geographical boundaries of the national territory were in many respects arbitrary, and the cultural and societal differences within that area enormous. In 1860, just 10 percent of the Italian population actually spoke the language, and each region had its own legal system and currency (Sicily's was called the 'onza'). While Garibaldi continued his journey up the peninsula, taking control of Naples in September 1860, the liberals worked to develop a model of what the new state would actually look like. Once again, they settled on a model inspired by William Bentinck. Italy would be a constitutional monarchy with a strong parliamentary dimension. There would be two chambers: one, the Senate, would be appointed; the other, the Chamber of Deputies, would be elected. Trade, meanwhile, was to follow *laissez faire* principles, with limited regulation, and the political power of the church was to be significantly curtailed. In October 1860 the Garibaldians organised a plebiscite, asking the Sicilians if they wanted to be part of a 'single' and 'indivisible' constitutional monarchy led by Vittorio Emanuele. There were 432,053 votes in favour, and 667 against. The results were similar across the peninsula. Despite the fact that suffrage was limited to literate males, and there was still little sense of national community, the state itself was beginning to take shape.

This was by no means a straightforward process. As early as March 1861, when Vittorio Emanuele was proclaimed king of Italy – supported by the prime minister, the Count of

Cavour – the nationalists were beginning to divide into more polarised factions. Garibaldi had been instrumental in defeating the Bourbons. Post-unification, however, as he continued to offer proposals for wealth redistribution, and to give speeches about international revolution, the Savoy monarch began to see him as a threat to the fragile new order. With the Kingdom of the Two Sicilies now vanquished, Vittorio Emanuele relieved the general of his services. Sicily's nationalists were particularly frustrated by this move. Many of the island's liberals, most notably the economist Francesco Ferrara, had been attracted to the Italian project not as an end in itself but as part of a longer-term strategy to liberate the southern peoples, and as a prelude to self-government.[4] Garibaldi's deposition made it clear that this was not going to be the case. There were other warning signs. When he was crowned king, Vittorio Emanuele insisted on maintaining his title 'the second' (of Savoy), rather than presenting himself as 'the first' monarch of Italy. This was a controversial move and only vindicated the arguments of the many republicans who suggested the rest of the country had simply been placed under his dominion, like any other foreign conquest.

The Italian government's first policy decisions did little to assuage the concerns of Sicily's increasingly jaded nationalists. Despite protests from the parliament, Vittorio Emanuele maintained direct power over the military and much of the justice system following unification. In order to fund the new nation's campaigns against Austria in the north, in what is now Veneto and Trentino, Cavour increased taxes across the peninsula. More gravely still, he introduced mandatory conscription, something he considered necessary in order to raise a large standing army that would be capable of securing the new borders. Sicilians were particularly opposed to this measure. Under the Bourbons, the

islanders had been exempted from military service on the basis
that King Ferdinand had deemed them too untrustworthy to be
allocated arms. Now, suddenly, thousands were being called up
to fight for a country they had no real understanding of. One
popular anecdote holds that the peasants around Catania didn't
even know what 'Italia' was, and that well into the 1870s many
thought it referred not to a country but to the wife of the king
(who they imagined to be called 'Talia'). Ferrara, in particular, began to speak out openly against this policy, arguing that
sending these individuals to fight in an unknown land, against
an enemy which posed them no immediate threat, would compromise the moral integrity of the state from its very beginning.

His concerns were soon vindicated. The issue of conscription did indeed turn much of Sicily's working class against the
Piedmontese. Across the old Bourbon territories, protesters tore
the Savoy crest out of the *tricolore* on public buildings while hundreds of men self-mutilated, or fled to the hills, to escape the
draft. In 1862, horrified by these scenes, Garibaldi returned to
Sicily to recruit volunteers with a plan to march to Rome in the
name of the Italian people and redeem the project of unification from what he saw as its distortion by Cavour and the new
government. This time the Sicilians were enthusiastic. While the
mission failed – and Rome remained independent of the new
nation until 1871 when it was made capital – hundreds signed up
to follow their charismatic leader. In response to this, the Piedmontese, like the Bourbons before them, declared martial law
across the south of Italy. Cavour sent a Savoy general named
Giuseppe Govone to the island from Turin to whittle out the
draft-dodgers. His methods, however, were so brutal, and his
contempt for the islanders so great, that the prime minister was
forced to recall him. In fact, Govone's approach was not just

excessive, it was entirely counterproductive. Between 1860 and 1864, armed robbery and attacks on property rose exponentially in both Sicily and Naples. As a result, the Italian government was forced to divert 100,000 soldiers – more than half of the standing army – to Southern Italy, and away from the front-lines against Austria–Hungary.[5] Even Francesco Crispi, Sicily's most important Italian nationalist, conceded that things were not going according to plan. During his election campaign in 1865 he promised to abolish conscription, increase salaries, reduce bureaucracy and provide a new series of loans to help the poorer classes.[6] These suggestions, though, were too little too late. A new, more organised, group had begun to take advantage of the chaos: their name, it later emerged, was Cosa Nostra.

There is no way of telling for certain when and how the Sicilian mafia came into being. At the time of the unification, many Sicilians balked at the notion of unified criminal families, arguing the word 'mafia' was in fact a slander that northerners had invented to make excuses for their own political ineptitude. There are, however, a number of early sources that demonstrate a more organised criminal culture began to develop in direct correspondence with the Italian nationalist movement. In 1864 a Palermitan politician named Niccolò Turrisi Colonna published a study called 'Public Order in Sicily', in which he detailed the emergence of a complex criminal structure on the island. While he does not mention the mafia by name, the report describes a 'sect of thieves' with 'ties across the whole island' which both 'protects and is protected' by the peasantry and urban workers alike.[7] This is the first written record that suggests Sicily's bandit groups and *gabellotti* were beginning to act in alliance, as a single organ. We can glimpse further elements of this evolution through a mutation in the manner by which the islanders began to protest. In 1866, several thousand Palermitans returned to the streets to express their apparent opposition to the Italian government. In the previous decades, as in 1848, the urban poor had tended to take advantage of these opportunities to loot shops and businesses. This time, however, the protesters only damaged two private properties. Instead, they targeted banks, government buildings and, in particular, carabinieri barracks. Armed groups even singled out individual police officers, stripping and mutilating them. Antonio Starabba, the mayor of Palermo, was one of the first to note something strange about the character of this rebellion. The organisers, he wrote, were not representatives of political factions, they were groups of gangs who had begun to 'act in agreement with one another', like 'a kind of government'. They seemed to 'know everything' and had begun to use Palermo's main prison, the infamous Ucciardone, as their base.[8] This was not just a riot, he claimed, it was an assault against the state itself.

The emphasis on intimidation might make it seem like the early mafia was an anti-Italian force. If anything, though, the opposite is true. While the nineteenth-century mafiosi were interested in attacking and manipulating certain aspects of the governing apparatus – the police and prison systems – their main goal was to establish a position of economic and political influence *within* the new nation. Their displays of violence were not, in this sense, protests against liberal capitalism, but part of a broader, more consolidated effort to profit from the power vacuum that unification opened up. One of the first things Garibaldi promised the peasants when he landed in Palermo was that he would give away large portions of land which were, at that point, owned by the nobility and church. After 1861, however, the Italian state decided that these properties would *not* in fact be given away, but sold off at auction. With this in mind, the mafia's use of force was most likely symptomatic of their broader effort to intimidate other incumbent local powers in order to secure properties for themselves. Neither was this confined to Palermo. Newspaper reports from 1871, detailing a series of violent incidents in the lemon groves around the city, demonstrate the organisation moved quickly to take control of agricultural production. The nature of these attacks was diverse. In some instances, the mafia made alliances with established landowners, sabotaging competition for whoever paid the highest price; in others they took direct control of the farms, and enforced rackets on nearby smallholds. Through these and other means, the organisation quickly obtained an enormous influence over one of the island's most valuable exports, and, in the process, the politicians and businesses that so depended on that trade.

Apologists for Cosa Nostra like to present the organisation as if it were the expression of a deep, almost mythological aspect of Sicily's anti-colonial identity. This early history, though, paints quite a different picture. The mafia was not born from some abstract 'spirit' of foreign oppression, but from specific material conditions: it was a direct consequence of top-down imposition of *laissez faire* economics on a territory where the justice system had rarely been respected. John Dickie, one of the world's most esteemed historians of Cosa Nostra and other organised crime groups, has described the early mafia as representing a 'hellish parody of the capitalist economy', and it would be difficult to put it any better.[9] Garibaldi had hoped that, through the market, the peasants might be liberated from generations of poverty and servitude. In lieu of a strong state, however, criminal groups easily intervened in this process, siphoning profits for their own benefit.

By doing so, they helped set the island on a path of underdevelopment that would damage the livelihoods of working people for decades to come.

In the last decades of the nineteenth century, Italy's new ruling class was particularly preoccupied with finding an origin story for the Risorgimento. Since the sixteenth century, the country's inhabitants had obtained a reputation for being weak, lazy and, as it was considered at the time, 'un-masculine'. Northern Europeans referred to Italy by names like 'the land of the dead' or 'the land of sleep', and mocked its fragmented, provincial character. Politicians from all the major parties were eager to disprove these stereotypes. One of the tasks they took particularly seriously was that of finding an ancient precedent for the 'Italian spirit'. Over time, particularly during the fascist era, this came to take the form of a romanticised fantasy of the Roman Republic, with a disproportionate emphasis on militarism. In the nineteenth century, though, this was not such an obvious choice. While apparently glorious, Rome's history, as is well known, was equally characterised by decadence, corruption and betrayal; and many involved in the Risorgimento challenged the wisdom of identifying too closely with that particular narrative. Instead, some scholars suggested that it was in fact the Etruscans, from central Italy, that were the primogenitors of the Italian people. Christians, like Giuseppe Mazzini, looked to the church as a source of unity. Others, mainly leftwing republicans, sought to find more recent reference points in Renaissance city-states.

Sicily – with its esoteric, cosmopolitan, Mediterranean history – presented other options. The island did, after all, have some claim to greatness. By the early nineteenth century, archaeologists like Antonio Salinas had begun to uncover new ruins at sites including Taormina, Segesta, Tindari, Mozia and, most spectacularly of all, the Valley of Temples in Agrigento. Italians had long lived beside and admired Roman remains. Scholars around the world, though, were particularly struck by the 'pure' Greek, and Punic-Phoenician, heritage that was beginning to surface in Sicily. The island's medieval history – particularly that of the Arab-Norman period – also provided it with a certain importance. In 1854, in the aftermath of the failed independence movement, Michele Amari, a Palermitan nationalist, published the first full-length Italian-language history of Muslim Sicily in which he presented the emirate, and specifically its legal and administrative system, as constituting one of the pinnacles of civilisation. This was the first time since Spanish rule began that an Italian scholar had so openly and extensively celebrated the achievements of Islam in Europe. While Amari refrained from expressing his argument in quite these terms, he was nevertheless one of the few figures to suggest that Italy's future identity should be conceived in relation to its long history of intermixing with the cultures of the southern Mediterranean.

The majority of nationalists turned away from this line of thinking. To most intellectuals on the mainland, in powerful cities like Turin, Milan and Florence, Sicily's hybridity rendered it too 'mongrel' to represent a national story. As these circular debates went on, some supporters of the Risorgimento became tired of backward-looking nostalgia and, instead, sought to embrace an entirely new 'European' modernity of the kind that was taking root in France, and Paris in particular. Francesco Lojacono, a Palermo-born nationalist painter who had participated in Garibaldi's Expedition of the Thousand, played a particularly important role in importing such ideas to the island. Lojacono had little time for debates about esoteric ancient heritage. He was, above all, a technician who longed to valorise his island, not by appeal to baroque and neoclassical fantasy, but by depicting its immediate, everyday beauty. Lojacono's early work is mainly taken up with war scenes, with muskets, flags and other revolutionary subjects. Following the unification, though, he shifted his style to focus on landscapes. While he did paint some romantic representations of temples and castles, he was more interested in the background details; in gnarled olive trees and peasants in unkempt fields, surrounded by cacti. He worked on the same hills again and again, experimenting to capture different lights, seasons and figures. One of his most celebrated works, *After the Rain* (1884), shows a simple muddy path, and two riders in the distance, their backs to the viewer. To contemporary eyes this might look straightforward. In fact, it was a quietly revolutionary piece: the angle was far wider than was conventional at the time, and it exhibited a new, almost photographic perspective. The subject, too, marked a departure from the effort to evoke any grand ideals from the past. It was, as he put it, an attempt to depict the world simply as it was, free from idealism.

This 'realist' turn, as it became known, was even more pronounced in literature. Before 1861 the Bourbons had censored translated works by authors such as Balzac and Flaubert which expressed similar sentiments. Following unification, however, a number of Sicilian writers attempted to develop their own response to this continental movement, which they named *verismo*. The Catanian author Luigi Capuana's novel *Giacinta* (1879), sometimes considered the Mediterranean's answer to *Madame Bovary* (1856), was the first Italian example of this current. The book narrates the struggle of a woman against the violent, conservative and patriarchal society in which she has been brought up. The reader follows the protagonist through her life, from her rape as a young girl at the hands of the family servant, to her unhappy marriage with a local count and a failed romantic affair with a fraudulent bank clerk who abandons her after the death of their bastard child. At the end of the novel, as in so many works of this genre, the protagonist commits suicide. Contemporary audiences found this shockingly direct. In the seventeenth and eighteenth centuries most fiction writers had, with a few exceptions, been required to produce literature that had a moralistic, patriarchal function. An author's social role was primarily that of offering a reassuring narrative to reinforce religious propaganda. Capuana's work rejected these assumptions. Rather than offering a didactic frame, or diegetic explanation, as was conventional, Capuana instead adopted an 'impersonal' stance: 'showing' events rather than offering judgement. The novel's narrator rigorously describes small details, from objects to clothes to body language, in a way that the author himself provocatively likened to a scientist looking to diagnose an 'illness'. As the first Italian to pioneer such an approach, Capuana played an important role in reshaping the national novel, which had formerly been an object of light entertainment, into a space for serious social critique.

Most Italian realist authors congregated in Milan, which was, and remains, Italy's literary capital. Nevertheless, the scene was disproportionately represented by southerners. Alongside Capuana, the Neapolitan Matilde Serao and the Catanian Federico De Roberto played important roles in the city's movement, writing novels and journalism critical of the hypocrisies of both the old nobility as well as the modern bourgeoisie. Yet it was another Catanian, Giovanni Verga, that perfected this new form of literary science. While Verga too spent most of his life in Milan, the majority of his books are set in eastern Sicily, among the lowest classes of farmers and poor tradespeople. His story collections *The Life of the Fields* (1880) and *Little Novels of Sicily* (1883) are filled with simple but detailed descriptions of local festivals, vendettas and romances, all of which, like Capuana, he presents in detached, forensic terms. In one particularly insightful story, 'Malaria', Verga documents the spread of that then-widespread disease among the Sicilian peasantry, from the processes of transmission to its effects on the body. This unique mix of journalism, storytelling, poetry, history and scientific writing was deemed so accurate by his contemporaries that physicians published extracts in textbooks to help medical students better understand the condition. Thanks in part to D. H. Lawrence, who enthusiastically championed the artistic value of Verga's stories, and translated them into English, the author's work is still widely read, and remains a vital testimony to the realities of working-class life in the nineteenth century.

The Risorgimento in Sicily was a complex and paradoxical process. On one hand, figures like Capuana or Verga would not have had the freedom to author books such as these under the Bourbons. On the other, their work served overwhelmingly to highlight the serious failings of the new Italian state. Many Garibaldians, these authors included, put great stock in the parliament, which they hoped would strive to better the lives of the working classes. In reality, the political parties spent most of their time arguing about minor factional disputes and, as a result, most Italians quickly came to see them as self-interested cliques, profiting at the expense of the people as a whole. The nobility, for their part, were similarly disillusioned, though for different reasons. Initially, the ruling families had hoped they would be able to hold onto power by obtaining influential roles in the new institutions. In reality, they found themselves confined to the margins, unable to compete with the increasingly prosperous bourgeoisie.

Tomasi di Lampedusa's novel *The Leopard* (1958) dramatises this transformation to great effect. It remains one of the most important documents for understanding how these different class interests interrelated in the context of the new Italian project. The book follows Prince Don Fabrizio, the eldest representative of the Salina family from the west of Sicily. This character is also known by the nickname 'the Leopard', both on account of his family crest, and his intransigence in the face of Garibaldi's arrival in Sicily. The action is split between the family's various estates in Palermo and Donnafugata, in the island's south-east, in the weeks following the landing in Marsala. Most of the book is taken up with the Leopard's philosophical ruminations about the deep forces of Sicilian culture, and what he repeatedly presents as the 'incomprehensible' nature of power and life on the island. As the novel begins, the Leopard's nephew, Tancredi, a pro-Italian liberal, is preparing to marry a bourgeoise girl named Angelica. Their wedding hangs over the subsequent events as a symbol of the ascendency of a new middle class, and the slow decline of the nobility. Tancredi reveals that he has signed up to join the red shirts and professes to his uncle that he believes in the vision of a united Italy. When the Leopard politely questions that decision, his nephew responds with a statement that, by now, has become a kind of manifesto for extreme conservatism: 'if we want things to stay as they are, things will have to change.'[10]

Critics often present *The Leopard* as a historical novel, focusing, for example, on its descriptions of costumes and lavish foodstuffs as evidence of how Sicily's ruling class refused to face up to their moment of decline. Read in more symbolic terms, however, the novel also functions as an allegory about Sicilian culture more generally, and the difficulty Italian nationalists encountered in attempting to *decode* the strangeness of the island's history. For di Lampedusa, Garibaldianism is less a question of politics than the collision of two temporalities: one, Siculo-Mediterranean, based on ritual, repetition and unquestionable forms of hierarchy; the other European Italian, and, as a consequence, linear and teleological, based on progress, change and, by implication, democracy. This fundamental, quasi-metaphysical, distance between the Sicilian nobility and Garibaldians becomes particularly clear in one scene, in which the Leopard is given the 'honour' of being invited by Chevalley, a diplomat from Piedmont, to become a senator in the new Italian government. While the Leopard mulls over the image of what a senator is, ruminating on old tales about Cicero, Chevalley insists on the importance of modernity and the need for new economic thinking. The Leopard fails to understand the argument – or at least feigns to do so – and instead proposes his own, more fatalistic, account of the events of 1860:

I have strong doubts whether the new kingdom will have many gifts for us in its luggage. All Sicilian self-expression, even the most violent, is really wish fulfilment; our sensuality is a hankering for oblivion, our shooting and knifing a hankering for death; our languor, our exotic ices, a hankering for voluptuous immobility, that is for death again; our meditative air is that of a void wanting to scrutinise the enigmas of Nirvana. From that comes the power among us of certain people, of those who are half awake: that is the cause of the well known time lag of a century in our artistic and intellectual life; novelties attract us only when they are dead, incapable of arousing vital currents; from that comes the extraordinary phenomenon of the constant formation of myths which would be venerable if they were really ancient, but which are really nothing but sinister attempts to plunge us back into a past that attracts us only because it is dead.[11]

Chevalley, an ardent patriot, struggles to hide his exasperation with the Leopard's stubbornness. 'Prince,' he asks incredulously, 'do you seriously refuse to do all in your physical power to alleviate, to attempt to remedy the state of physical squalor, of blind moral misery in which this people of yours lies?'[12] Don Fabrizio, though, ignores his guest's concerns and instead continues his diatribe, using the opportunity to cast his now infamous judgement of the Sicilian character:

> You're a gentleman, Chevalley, and I consider it a privilege to have met you; you are right in all you say; your only mistake was saying 'the Sicilians must want to improve' … the Sicilians never want to improve for the simple reason that they think themselves perfect; their vanity is stronger than their misery, every invasion by outsiders, whether so by origin or, if Sicilian, by independence of spirit, upsets their illusion of achieved perfection, risks disturbing their satisfied waiting for nothing; having been trampled on by a dozen different peoples, they think they have an imperial past which gives them the right to a grand funeral.[13]

What's so striking about this passage is how little it actually pertains to the real emotional and cultural life of the Sicilian people. At no point in Verga's fiction, for example, do the working-class islanders entertain this kind of vainglorious sentiment. The Leopard's judgement, and one suspects the character himself knows as much, is not so much a judgement about the Sicilians as a whole as it is an act of self-criticism; an evaluation of the nobility's own insecurities as it faces up to its possible disintegration. In one particularly revealing quip Chevalley changes tack and presents the Risorgimento as an attempt to lift a spell from the island. This short aside cuts right to the core of the novel. Throughout *The Leopard*, the reader observes both this magic and the attempt to demystify it, through Don Fabrizio's eyes. Sicily, he says, is a 'landscape which knows no mean between sensuous sag and hellish drought; which is never petty, never ordinary, never relaxed, as should be a country made for rational beings to live in'.[14] The interior is a desert that is 'comfortless and irrational, with no lines that the mind could grasp'.[15] It's clear, though, that the prince himself is perfectly at home in this hallucinatory world. When he proclaims that the Sicilian summer is 'as long and glum as a Russian winter', he is rather guilefully using his rhetorical skills to exaggerate the island's most alien characteristics and counteract the idea that it might, in fact, be susceptible to democratic change.[16] The more Chevalley argues the case that the Risorgimento must break the nobility's spell over the island, the more Don Fabrizio appeals to poetic language to reconstruct the façade of Sicilian exceptionalism.

Today, many people's first engagement with *The Leopard* comes through Luchino Visconti's 1963 film adaptation. It's a powerful piece of cinema. But while Visconti captures the social themes of di Lampedusa's novel well, he misses some of these deeper connotations of the narrative. This book itself is not by any means a work of realism; it is an allegory about the collapse of a particular kind of fantasy version of Sicilian culture. The author continually evokes a vast array of gothic tropes, from ghostly rooms to haunted houses, to reinforce this theme. At one point, Don Fabrizio even imagines himself, quite explicitly, embalmed in the Capuchin crypt in Palermo, reflecting that he 'would look magnificent on that wall'.[17] This passage, in which the lead character likens himself to a kind of zombie, is one of the defining moments of this novel. The identity of the Risorgimento is entirely reliant on its claim to represent a definitive split with the past. The Leopard's version of Sicily rejects this, to the point of rejecting death itself. It's only at the very close of the book that the tables are turned and Don Fabrizio finally comes to understand that his family, and his class, really are coming to a definitive end. Having spent most of the narrative engaged in rhetorical games, the prince finally gives up in a monologue that is, for all its pomposity, rather tragic: 'He had said that the Salina would always remain the Salina. He had been wrong. The last Salina was himself. That fellow Garibaldi, that bearded Vulcan had won after all.'[18]

For the real-life victors the result did not seem so certain. By the 1870s even the most idealistic Tancredis and Chevalleys who had supported the Risorgimento were beginning to be afflicted by a profound pessimism. In a parliamentary report from 1876, Romualdo Bonfadini, a journalist and statesman from Lombardy, tries to convince his anxious colleagues, and at points it seems even himself, that unification has been a positive thing for Sicily. He points to urbanisation, to the construction of new public offices and medical clinics, to the expansion of ports and creation of more state jobs as evidence of the new government's benevolence. He celebrates developments in freedom of employment and residence, and the emergence of 20,000 new landowners as tangible successes (though, notably, he neglects to mention the mafia). While he does admit that the problem of crime was 'perplexing' – an understatement given that, by now, Palermo's homicide rate was around ten times higher than that of

Milan – the majority of people, he confidently concludes, enjoy a similar quality of life to those in Tuscany or Emilia Romagna.[19]

For all its achievements, the Italian administration was hardly in a position to boast. On the contrary, by the 1870s Sicily's economy was in dire straits. Under the Bourbons, wealth had been distributed in a highly unequal fashion. It's often forgotten, though, that the royal vaults themselves were surprisingly full. While the majority of islanders had lived in poverty, the Kingdom of the Two Sicilies was, in terms of its gold reserves, one of the richest in pre-unification Italy, far wealthier in fact than Piedmont or Veneto.[20] After 1861 this trend was inverted. As part of the national economic strategy, the Italian state developed a model based on a strict geographical separation: the north, with the notable exception of Emilia Romagna, was to be organised towards industrial production; the south, Sicily included, to agriculture. To facilitate this plan, much of the gold that had previously been kept in Naples and Palermo was redistributed to Piedmont, Lombardy, Emilia Romagna and Tuscany, where the government subsequently built a dense network of railway lines. While the state did commission around 300 km of new tracks in Sicily, a fairly large number in proportion to the population size, this was a far cry short of the 2,090 km in the north-west. Similarly, while the island's traditional exports of citrus, salt, wine and fish were fairly stable, only a small handful of families were able to establish a foothold in new and expanding fields, such as shipping and financial services.

This one-dimensional approach to managing the Sicilian economy had disastrous consequences. In the 1880s America began to dramatically increase domestic production of two of the island's most important exports: sulphur and grain. As a result, Sicily's landowners were forced to sell these goods at significantly reduced prices and, just as they had in previous centuries, they increased local taxes, fees and rents on the peasantry to cover their loss of revenue. Between 1888 and 1890, following a series of poor harvests, thousands of islanders struggled to put food on the table, and received virtually no assistance from the government.

The Sicilians could not and did not stand by while the state so flagrantly disregarded their well-being. Instead, they organised themselves, as a matter of necessity, into what some historians, most notably Eric Hobsbawm, have labelled Europe's first and most influential modern social movement: the *Fasci dei lavoratori*.[21] The word 'fasci' comes from the Italian word for 'bundle', and refers to the 'bringing together' of different social groups from urban and rural communities within a unified working-class struggle. The first Fascio was founded in Catania on 1 May 1891 when industrial workers, tradespeople and guild members gathered to form a mutual aid organisation to distribute food and clothes to those who had suffered most as a result of the agricultural crisis. The initiative quickly spread to Messina, where the organisation had an explicit Marxist character, and later to Palermo, where membership was open to democratic reformists and others, including monarchists and Catholics who were critical of the state. From the very beginning the leaders of the movement were insistent that the Fasci were addressing issues that were not just local, and which were, in fact, symptomatic of an urgent international need to better the lot of working people. Many of the key figures, including the accountant and playwright Rosario Garibaldi Bosco, played an instrumental role in founding the national Partito dei Lavoratori in Genoa in 1892, which the next year branded itself as the PSI, the Italian Socialist Party.

Thanks to its strong and broadly diffused organisational hubs, the Fasci spread quickly across Sicily. By January 1893 collectives had begun to appear in the island's smallest towns and villages. In the countryside, where less than 15 percent of the population were literate, participants in the movement generally expressed their grievances and demands by appeal to religious icons.[22] During demonstrations, for example, while some participants would chant secular Marxist rhetoric about the need for radical redistribution, others would wield figures of saints and sing patriotic songs. Sometimes these influences even fused in an unlikely manner. Hundreds in the ranks carried crucifixes and candles while, at the same time, arguing that a rich and corrupt clergy had co-opted the fundamental truth of the faith, and that Jesus was an archetype for socialism. The composition of the cells was similarly diverse. Adolfo Rossi, a journalist who covered the revolts for the Roman newspaper *La Tribuna*, was particularly struck by the extensive female participation. Women, he reported, not only filled the ranks, rejecting their 'usual' position in the background, they were leaders too. Girls as young as fifteen years old were on the frontlines of the movement.[23]

The single factor that enabled the Fasci to contain such a diverse political constituency within their ranks was the strength of their internal democratic process. Each of the bundles decided their policy proposals and direct actions based on a popular majority vote. As a result, in some parts of the island the participants called for highly specific reforms: in the area around Agrigento, for example, the group was particularly concerned with addressing a local imbalance in the tax system which meant that lowly animals owned by peasants, like donkeys, were taxed at higher rates than cows, which tended to be owned by wealthier landowners. At the same time, the Fasci made more general proposals for the reform and reorganisation of the economic system. In the large cities the leaders highlighted the need for higher wages, lower rents and a pension plan. In the towns of the north-west, the Fasci was an openly anti-mafia movement. In the summer of 1893 the local peasants in Corleone organised a strike in which they demanded legal recognition in a trade union and burnt crops that belonged to mafia landowners. In the nearby town of Caltavuturo, the citizens rose up against the local government, which had been accepting bribes from known criminals. Arguably, the most radical manifestation of the Fasci took root in the Piana degli Albanesi, just outside of Palermo, where those involved set up a series of agricultural cooperatives and worked them collectively, sharing all profits evenly among the community. This action, in particular, was more than just a protest; it represented a new model of economic production that was entirely at odds with Italy's modern capitalism.

Ultimately the Fasci faltered not because of their internal weaknesses, but because the Italian state recognised the danger they represented to the 'normal' functioning of the economy. In winter 1893, tens of thousands of peasants took to the streets in eastern Sicily to call on the government to codify a reform to labour law which would provide 'guaranteed constitutional rights' for those working on agrarian contracts.[24] They were joined by labourers from the sulphur mines, who were protesting for better conditions following a spike of poisonings that had killed several of the young workers. By this point the Fasci had grown to encompass as many as 300,000 people and were organised into 177 groups across Sicily.[25] With cities and countryside, peasants and industrial workers unified to this degree, the government in Rome could no longer ignore the movement. On 3 January 1894 the prime minister, Francesco Crispi, Sicily's one-time arch-Garibaldian, declared a 'state of siege' on the island, and sent soldiers down from the capital to dismantle the collectives. Government forces executed over a hundred people that winter. Thousands more were arrested.

Activist groups on the mainland organised solidarity initiatives to show support for the Sicilians. Notably, anarchist collectives in Carrara, in the Tuscan hills, began their own small-scale insurrection in which they called for the release of the political prisoners. Ultimately, however, their gesture proved futile and only encouraged Crispi to further tighten censorship and limit the circulation of socialist materials across Italy. In spring 1894 the central committee of the Fasci in Palermo were put on trial and prosecuted for inciting revolution and armed conspiracy. The courts delivered sentences of up to eighteen years to the movement's leaders. While some small groups continued to struggle on, and the villages of the Piana degli Albanesi continued to live in collective farms, the Fasci as a movement was broken. The result, declared Crispi, was a victory for democracy and public order. Those who had participated in the uprisings, though, were well aware of the truth. The real beneficiaries of this clamp-down were not the Sicilian people, but the criminal landowners and their associates in the mafia.

Crispi's uncompromising response successfully halted the development of socialism in Sicily. At the same time, though, the prime minister had made it impossible for large parts of the working class to live at all. Between 1901 and 1913 over a million Sicilians, approximately 25 percent of the population, were forced to leave the island.[26] The majority of these emigrants hailed from the island's interior and small villages along the southern coast. Many of them headed north to cities like

Turin, to work in iron and steel factories, and, starting in 1900, to produce automobiles for Fiat. While the populations of Palermo and Catania continued to increase, many intellectuals chose to leave the cities, preferring to work in the comparatively open metropolitan centres of Rome and Milan.

For some Sicilian emigrants the United States was the destination of choice. This is hardly surprising. At the turn of the century a whole chorus of adverts, postcards, travel journalism and literature were being produced across Italy, proselytising the 'American dream'. National newspapers were running regular headlines like 'Your Destiny Is in Your Own Hands' and 'How to Become a Millionaire in the United States' featuring stories of people who, having failed to thrive in Europe, had gone on to live prosperous lives across the Atlantic.[27] Many disillusioned socialists, including several leaders of the Fasci, also headed to America, attracted by the country's apparent emphasis on liberty and freedom of expression. Most of them made their journey using a prepaid ticket which US banks sent to them directly, and which were, very often, brokered via mafia contacts. Once they arrived, the brokers that had paid the costs of transit would typically help the new arrival to find a job, requesting a large fee in the process. As a result of this arrangement the vast majority of Sicilian emigrants began their new lives in serious debt.

Most Italians arrived in America via Ellis Island and congregated in New York City. In 1900 more than 150,000 individuals arrived in the metropolis from Italy, and it's estimated that around one-third of these were from Sicily.[28] Many of those new arrivals worked in construction jobs and were tasked with developing the urban area of Manhattan, including the skyscrapers around Wall Street. Southern Italians were considered unskilled and, in most cases, worked the 'sweating system' which implied maximum hours for lowest pay. Other northern Italians, who often had better-paid jobs, discriminated against their compatriots, even describing them as a dirty, feral 'underclass'. In general, the southern Italians settled in the Lower East Side. Once there, however, they soon found that the conditions were not as luxurious as the Italian newspaper reports had suggested. There were no hospitals in the vicinity of the most crowded neighbourhoods and very few schools. Given that most Sicilians could not even speak Italian, let alone English, these communities were inevitably ghettoised.

Still, life in New York did have its advantages. Taxes were relatively low, a novelty if not necessarily a blessing under the circumstances, and with the city growing rapidly, those fortunate enough to have arrived in the country with some money saved had many opportunities to open businesses. Sicilians thrived in a range of areas, as barbers, tailors, fruit sellers and artisans. Women, in particular, benefitted from this new entrepreneurial culture. While in Sicily most were still confined to the home, in America they were free to work, and, indeed, they often had to in order to help cover the high cost of living. The journey itself provided opportunities for emancipation. It was not uncommon for women to travel alone to America, to meet family members that had already established lives there. Rumours began to abound on either side of the Atlantic about lovers who had met one another on the boats and fled their obligations in order to start new lives. It's difficult to grasp the actual scale of a phenomenon like this, and one suspects that it is more a case of literary fantasy than reality. What's certain is that this wave of emigration prompted the birth of a new stereotype, that of the 'American Girl': a sporty, athletic, hedonistic, carefree, sexually promiscuous individual who had escaped the oppressions of conservative Catholic society to find fortune in the New World.

Once in America, Sicilians struggled to shake off their reputation for violence and criminality. The Lower East Side was not only poor, it was often dangerous. Gangs had been active in New York since at least the 1840s, and Irish and Jewish organisations like the Forty Thieves and Shirt Tails were particularly powerful. In the early twentieth century, Sicilians were mainly involved with the Black Hand, which was not so much an 'organisation' as a system of extortion, punctuated with occasional kidnappings. The Black Hand mainly targeted successful northern Italian emigrants, though they did, on occasion, force poorer migrants to pay for protection. Cosa Nostra also began to expand their American activities around this time, though these were, for the moment, largely confined to the southern states, and New Orleans in particular. Many Italian Americans would have been aware of the Matranga family, for example, who ran a ring of bars and brothels in that city. Throughout the 1880s, this mafia clan fought openly with the rival Provenzanos over who would have control of the local fruit monopoly. This was, in fact, one of the first signs that the mafia was taking root in a serious manner in America. In 1890, when one of the Matranga members shot dead a police investigator named David Hennessey, the local population began to speculate that the mafia had been involved. Investigators arrested nineteen individuals, but they never did find the killer. In the meantime, though, some members of the community were so angry they stormed the jail and lynched the defendants. Unfortunately for Sicily's emigrants, this was just the first in a string of similar violent episodes that would taint their reputation even here, in their supposed land of liberty.

7

A Modernist Dystopia (1891–1943)

Political Corruption, Fascism and Futurism, a Colonial Administration

For fifty years our politicians have worked to create the illusion that there is such a thing as a uniform Italy. The regions were supposed to disappear into the nation, dialects into literary languages. Sicily is the region that has most actively resisted this breaking down of history and freedom. On numerous occasions Sicily has shown itself to be more than a region, and to have a national character of its own.

Antonio Gramsci, *Avanti!*, 1918

At the end of the nineteenth century, as tens of thousands of Sicilians grappled with extreme poverty, Palermo's bourgeoisie were enjoying a period of unprecedented prosperity. Much of this can be seen in the flurry of commerce that surrounded a single event. In 1891 the Sicilian capital hosted the Italian Expo, an international showcase of the newest technological and cultural innovations from around the world. Francesco Crispi, who had successfully led the bid on the city's behalf, was optimistic about the possible benefits for the island. Previous editions of the

Expo had taken place in Florence and Milan, two cities that were already well regarded across continental Europe. By championing Palermo, the Italian prime minister hoped to spearhead a new regional plan for modernisation that he imagined would benefit the south and, in the process, contribute to a more favourable international image for his homeland.[1]

On the surface the event was a success. More than 1.2 million visitors came to visit Palermo from London, Paris, Berlin and beyond. Reviews of the programme, which included displays of the latest motorcars and gliders as well as photography demonstrations and cinematic projections, were overwhelmingly positive. The main shows took place in a large arena which was separated from the rest of the city centre by huge concrete walls. Inside, the exhibitors set up their stalls in a series of faux Arab-Norman pavilions designed by the architect Ernesto Basile to appeal to nineteenth-century Europeans' exotic, orientalist fantasies about the Mediterranean. The investment in this project, though, was about far more than a few kitsch models. The Expo had a profound and long-lasting impact on the city's geography. Since the Arab occupation, Palermo had developed largely according to its medieval street plan, around narrow, winding allies, with the cathedral at its centre. During the final years of Bourbon rule, however, the central districts had declined significantly. Years of revolt and revolution had torn holes in the buildings. With the city's population now approaching 300,000, the housing supply had been pushed to its limit. A string of Italian governments had tried and failed to find a solution to these issues since the 1860s. During the Expo, however, Crispi found an excuse to authorise funding for a new district, one which would allow the island's growing middle class to enjoy the space and light of a modern European city.

To do this, the Palermitan administration approved construction of a 'second city centre' a kilometre to the north of the old town. Today this corresponds roughly to the area between two of the city's most iconic buildings: the neoclassical Teatro Massimo, and Teatro Politeama Garibaldi. During the Expo, the Politeama in particular became a popular meeting point for the bourgeoisie. Its surrounding square, named after Ruggero Settimo, the head of Sicily's short-lived independent government, became the city's most important public space, and was home to cafés, bars, ice-cream parlours and kiosks selling drinks, tobacco and newspapers. Palermo's wealthiest families scrambled to purchase properties on the nearby Viale della Libertà, which, in turn, developed a reputation for its literary salons and poetry schools. Most of these villas were later destroyed by the mafia during the city's post-war construction boom, and have since been replaced by tower blocks, but in the late nineteenth and early twentieth century, this road, flanked by the city's English garden, was home to a series of elegant art nouveau buildings stretching all the way to the seaside suburb of Mondello. Sicily's rulers had long dismissed this area as an uninhabitable marshland – as its Arab name, Marsâ 'at Tin (Port of Mud), captures. Following the Expo, however, the city council ordered that the land be drained to make way for a new sand beach. Over the next twenty years, teams of builders transformed Mondello from a malarial bog into Sicily's first coastal resort, an exclusive entertainment complex, complete with fish restaurants and lidos. Nowadays, by contrast, the area is an overcrowded, concrete-ridden place, filled with pubs and restaurants. Only its iconic yellow pier remains as a testament to Palermo's short-lived belle époque.

While international visitors were impressed by these outward displays of wealth, the effect was largely illusory. The Sicilian bourgeoisie was larger than it had been at the time of unification, but it remained less influential than the equivalent class in France or Northern Italy. Few of the islanders could actually afford this lifestyle. Most of the families that purchased property on the Viale della Libertà, for example, did so using cheap money that the state made available through loans in order to enhance the show. While the Expo was a triumph, the economic foundations on which it was built were shaky to say the least. This was far from just a Sicilian problem. In 1892, a government whistleblower revealed that the Banca Romana, one of the country's biggest banks, had been duplicating notes since the late 1880s to provide funds for construction projects across Italy, and even distributing interest-free loans to political parties and journalists. In the aftermath of these revelations, Crispi's successor, Giovanni Giolitti, arrested several bureaucrats and liquidated the institution in an effort to keep things quiet. Nevertheless, this was a major scandal that would undermine Italy's institutions for years to come. In Palermo, journalists began to investigate the numerous discrepancies within the municipality's public finances. Crispi's government had dramatically increased public spending in Sicily in order to fund the Expo. In the years following the event, though, independent investigators began to discover that many of these payments had been vastly disproportionate to their corresponding projects, and others had not been accounted for at all. A small group of particularly dedicated journalists suggested that the mafia might have intervened to pocket this money themselves, but the government, and much of the public, treated these accusations as pure speculation.

At the start of 1893 a shocking murder forced the state to take these claims more seriously. On 1 February a well-known right-wing politician named Emanuele Notarbartolo was killed in

mysterious circumstances when returning home to Palermo by
night train from the nearby town of Termini Imerese. Notarbartolo, a prominent member of the nobility, had served a number
of important roles, including as mayor of Palermo and director
of the Bank of Sicily. In the months preceding his death, he had
been investigating allegations of corruption against a man named
Don Raffaele Palizzolo, a figure who was similarly well known
in high society and who, in the run-up to the Expo, had been
openly distributing state construction contracts to his friends
and family. During his time as mayor Notarbartolo had already
begun to investigate these nepotistic rings. By the winter of that
year, however, he had begun to identify a circle of Cosa Nostra
affiliates who were directly involved in mediating the loans that
Palizzolo was distributing via the Bank of Sicily. Palizzolo's associates made various threats against Notarbartolo. In 1882 he was
actually kidnapped by masked men and his family were forced
to pay a sizeable ransom for his release. Despite this, however,
Notarbartolo continued to dig deeper. That February night, as he
settled down to work in his empty first-class carriage, preparing
to release his findings, two men approached with knives drawn.
A railway engineer found his body on the tracks the next morning, punctured by twenty-seven stab wounds.

It didn't take the police long to find the killers. The culprits
were two low-paid workers, Matteo Filippello and Giuseppe
Fontana, both of whom were associated with mafia families
in Villabate. What their contemporaries found most striking,
though, was how well connected these men were with figures
high up in Sicilian society. Before these events Italians had
spoken about the mafia as a euphemism for a vague, anarchic-
seeming aspect of Sicily's character. After this assassination,
however, the media began to ask more serious questions about

the actual structure of Cosa Nostra. In 1899 Paolo Valera, a journalist and author, published a brave novel, *The Notarbartolo Murder: A Mafia Crime*, which, while ostensibly a fictional work, was one of the first public-facing texts to accuse members of Sicily's financial elite of having orchestrated the murder. The real Palizzolo, though, was a powerful man. By fabricating alibis and bribing officials, the boss succeeded in delaying his trial for almost a decade. It wasn't until 1902 that he was convicted in a court in Bologna. As in so many mafia trials, though, this was not the end of the story. Palizzolo appealed, and, after two years, during which witnesses mysteriously vanished along with vital evidence, another jury in Florence overturned the verdict. These events were a historic failure of the justice system. But they also threw the mafia into the open. Shortly after Notarbartolo's murder, Ermanno Sangiorgi, a Palermo-based detective, began interviewing people in the hill-towns around the capital, asking them what they knew about Cosa Nostra. His report confirmed what others had speculated about in the 1860s. The mafia, he discovered, was not just a gang, it was a unified world, which, despite familial divisions and tensions, was structured around a single logic, and even had its own ranking system.[2] Thanks to help from a number of informants, Sangiorgi ordered hundreds of arrests. In the end, though, as had been the case with Palizzolo, only thirty-two of these individuals were convicted, and several were later acquitted on technicalities.

As the case against Palizzolo heated up, dozens of prominent mafiosi moved from Sicily to America. These figures were not by any means in exile. They were actively engaged in developing new trans-Atlantic business opportunities for Cosa Nostra, in collaboration with the Matrangas and other families. On 12 March 1909 the increasing degree of coordination between clans on the two sides of the ocean became clear when the mafia claimed their second high-profile victim: Joseph Petrosino, an Italian-American police investigator from New York. The circumstances around this killing were even more sensational than that of Notarbartolo. Throughout the first decade of the twentieth century Petrosino had been investigating a man named Cascio Ferro (later known as Don Vito) who, at the time, was in charge of a Black Hand counterfeiting ring between Sicily and America. In 1903 Petrosino had Ferro arrested on suspicion of murder, but the courts concluded there was insufficient evidence to begin a serious trial. Ferro returned to Palermo, where in the coming years he rose up the ranks of the local mafia. Petrosino, though, was convinced of his guilt, and for six years continued to pursue the case from afar. And so, in 1909, the policeman set out on a 'secret mission' to Sicily, to investigate some new leads. Shortly after arriving in Palermo he received a tip-off from an anonymous source who claimed they could help with the case. When Petrosino arrived at the rendezvous point in Piazza Marina, however, he was met by two of Ferro's associates who shot him dead at point-blank range in front of the old Inquisition headquarters. Coming shortly on the back of the Notarbartolo case, this event signified a serious escalation of mafia violence. In the 1860s the organisation had been an occult force, indistinguishable from parts of the post-unification bourgeoisie. By assassinating an American policeman on Italian soil, however, Cosa Nostra was sending a message: it was no longer just a 'band of criminals' but an autonomous globe-spanning institution that was sufficiently embedded in the state to break the law without any serious fear of reprisal.

With the notable exception of the financial sector, the Italian economy was in a relatively healthy state at the start of the twentieth century. For a brief period, between 1902 and 1908, the country enjoyed massive economic growth, largely thanks to the proliferation of new medium-sized rubber, chemical, metal-work and textile factories in and around Piedmont. One might think this would serve to consolidate the liberal government's rule. In fact, the reverse was true. The inequality with which these profits were distributed – overwhelmingly benefitting the bourgeoisie in the north – fuelled a significant popular back-lash against *laissez faire* economics. The socialist party, the PSI, was the most vocal in demanding a full-scale system change, arguing that nationalisation and redistribution of this new-found wealth would provide the basis for a fairer, more unified and more prosperous country. In the nineteenth century the radical left had largely been a grassroots movement. By the national elections of 1913, however, they had transformed into a formi-dable parliamentary force, with 25 percent of the public vote, and seventy-nine seats in the Chamber of Deputies. Following this result, many liberals began to defect to their ranks. Other members of the intelligentsia, generally wealthier figures, like the novelist Enrico Corradini and poet Gabriele D'Annunzio, resisted this turn. These men, instead, began to define them-selves as nationalists. Like the PSI, this group professed to be pro-proletarian and anti-individualist. Unlike the left, however, its adherents were sceptical of democracy, and keen to champion the moral benefits of war.

When conflict broke out in Europe in 1914 after a young Yugo-slav anti-imperialist named Gavrilo Princip assassinated Franz Ferdinand, the heir to the Austro-Hungarian throne, the Italian government initially announced that the country would remain neutral, reasoning that the population was too politically divided to fight. The PSI supported this decision on the basis that conflict would undermine democratic class struggle. The nationalists, though, were vehemently pro-war. That winter, they and other conservative factions organised interventionist rallies across the Italian mainland, drumming up protests against the government that attracted thousands to the streets. On 16 May 1915, at the peak of this fervour, over 200,000 people converged in Rome's Piazza del Popolo demanding the country take up arms, once again, against the Austrians. Observing the large crowds, the king, Victor Emmanuel III, made the decision to bypass parliament and declared that the country would indeed intervene, on the side of Britain and France. His decision, while constitutionally valid, was ill-advised. Despite the sizeable nationalist rallies only a few thousand volunteers actually signed up to join the army. As a result, while the Italian ranks were larger than the Austrian-German forces, they were comprised, on the whole, of poorly trained conscripts. Most of the war took place in the Alps in the north-east of Italy along the border of what is now Slovenia. The winter temperatures were freezing and, as a result of the last-minute decision to intervene, the government struggled to provide adequate rations to the front line. From the very beginning, the campaign was plagued by high levels of desertion. Indeed, more Italians were executed by their own generals in the conflict than any other of the participating armies.

Sicilians did all they could to avoid the draft. As the Italian recruiters made their rounds in the small villages of the interior, hundreds of men fled to the refuge of the Nebrodi mountains, where, following in the footsteps of previous generations, they formed armed bands. These groups were quite different to the bandits that had previously thrived on the island. Since the eighteenth century, Sicily's brigands had, with some exceptions, been opportunistic individuals who had sought to take advantage of the historically weak power of the state for their own benefit. During the war, though, increasing numbers of men adopted this lifestyle as a conscious form of political disobedience. As the conflict raged in the Alps, the draft-dodgers raided the island's farms, stealing cattle and horses. They did this in order to survive, but it was also an act of protest. Some of the groups burnt crops and, on several occasions, vandalised police stations and local government buildings. Between 1916 and 1918 the Sicilian countryside was transformed into a small-scale war zone itself as the draft-dodgers clashed with the mafia, who stepped in to protect the rural landowners. Despite these Wild West-like scenes, 500,000 Sicilians were forced to serve on the front line, and around 10 percent died in the conflict. Of the roughly 650,000 Italians who lost their lives during the war, around 50,000 came from the island.[3]

Somewhat remarkably, given these scenes of domestic unrest and the amateurishness of the armed forces, the Italians were victorious. In November 1918, the Austro-German forces surrendered, conceding land in what is now South Tirol, Trentino and Friuli Venezia Giulia. The human and political cost of this, though, was enormous. In the build-up to the war, the nationalists had argued that by bringing together young men from different backgrounds, who spoke different dialects, the conflict would serve to complete the unfinished job of unification. If anything, the opposite proved true. In 1918, as soldiers began to return home, Italy's economy entered into freefall. Over 2 million citizens found themselves unemployed in the aftermath, and high rates of inflation pushed the price of basic goods far beyond what most people could afford. To make matters worse, the unrest in Sicily and other parts of the south had severely damaged the national food supply, and grain and meat shortages were endemic across the peninsula. In Northern Italy, in Turin and Milan, thousands joined grassroots communist unions, and organised strikes in the industrial centres to demand pay raises and welfare reforms. Across the Po Valley, in Emilia Romagna, socialists took direct control over the local administration, and created a dense network of cooperatives and peasant unions. In Sicily, returning soldiers attempted to convince the island's bandit groups to establish land occupations of their own, but these efforts were largely unsuccessful. Across the country as a whole, support for socialism rose to a historic high. In the elections of 1919 the PSI won 32 percent of the public vote, and 156 seats in parliament.

In reality, of course, it was a quite different type of politics that profited from the post-war crisis. In 1919, a militant journalist named Benito Mussolini founded a new reactionary social movement, the *Fasci di combattimento*, the precursor to the Fascist Party, which ultimately blocked the ascendency of the left. This was an unexpected move. In the first decades of the twentieth century, Mussolini had himself been involved in revolutionary socialist circles, and had even edited the PSI's newspaper, *Avanti!* He was expelled in 1914 in the lead-up to the war due to his support for intervention. In the years that followed, Mussolini began to criticise what he saw as the fundamental failures of Marxism. Class struggle, he argued, was a divisive dogma, which would prevent the party from taking, and, more importantly, maintaining, power. More generally, he argued, the philosophical basis of communism was too materialistic, too lacking in spiritual or cultural, force, to bring a nation as fragmented as Italy together. As such, in theory at least, fascism was an attempt to provide a synthesis between the pre-war currents of socialism and nationalism. What actually distinguished this new force, though, was its casual use of violence. From their very inception, Mussolini's most militant supporters – the blackshirt 'squadristi' – began attacking trade unionists and activists who, on an arbitrary basis, they deemed 'anti-Italian'. The fascists travelled to left-wing rallies, often drunk and high on cocaine, to assault demonstrators with guns, knives and their own trademark club, the *manganello*. Most Italians, including many nationalists, were shocked by this thuggish behaviour. In 1921, however, when an offshoot of PSI supporters formed their own communist party, the PCI, an influential minority of wealthy landowners began to donate money to Mussolini's faction, hoping that fascism might protect them from the threat of what they perceived to be a near-imminent Bolshevik-style revolution.

From this moment on, as socialist and communist groups fought among one another about how best to claim power, Mussolini's new party, bolstered by support from the middle class, began to gain headway in the north. In the south, however, where the bourgeoisie was smaller, the movement enjoyed little in the way of popular support. The fascists won no Sicilian seats in the elections of 1919 and 1921 and there was still no party newspaper on the island. On 28 October 1922, when 25,000 of Mussolini's blackshirt supporters marched on Rome to demand representation in parliament, there were fewer than one hundred Sicilians among them. Nevertheless, despite this fragmented support, the king, Victor Emmanuel, responded to the march on Rome by giving Mussolini permission to form a government, hoping that by doing so, he might at least pacify the movement's more violent tendencies. In Sicily, where local politics was, despite the war, still dominated by mafia families associated with the older liberal and conservative factions, this had little immediate impact.

It was not until 1924, two years into Mussolini's term as prime minister, that fascism began to make its first serious inroads on the island. That summer Mussolini set out personally on the first of two tours he would take to Sicily. He was shocked, above all, by the open criminality of the political class. One incident in particular stood out. During a visit to the villages of the Piana degli Albanesi, near Palermo, he was met by Francesco Cuccia, a known Cosa Nostra boss. As Mussolini stepped out of his car, protected by a police escort, the mayor turned to greet him. The security forces could stay where they were, quipped the mayor. He, by which he meant the mafia, would make sure the prime minister was safe. This was an ill-judged remark to say the least. Mussolini was furious that a representative of the state could be so blasé and indeed arrogant about advertising their own delinguency. The mafia, he decided, was the emblem of all that was wrong with Sicily. On returning to Rome he delivered a speech to the Italian people promising that his new government would not only stand up to the organisation but would wipe it out for good.

In June 1924 Mussolini authorised Italy's first major policing operation against Cosa Nostra. At the head of the campaign was Cesare Mori, a renowned officer from Lombardy who, in the aftermath of the war, had achieved some modest success in rounding up bandits in Sicily. Mori was a conservative monarchist who, in the years leading up to the march on Rome, had opposed the fascists on account of their excessive violence. He therefore accepted Mussolini's offer with particular enthusiasm, seeing it as a chance to atone for what, by now, he considered to be a mistake, and to demonstrate his loyalty to the ascendant party. Mori was not naïve. He understood that his real task was not, in fact, to tackle Costa Nostra as a whole, but to clean up the political administration. He started by arresting small gangs of brigands, socialists and anarchists in the province of Trapani, in the west of Sicily, as well as low-level mafia affiliates. Parallel to this, though, he quietly found excuses to arrest a number of liberal and nationalist politicians that opposed Mussolini. In October 1925, amid this general climate of censorship and oppression, the prime minister banned all opposition parties, formally transforming Italy into a dictatorship. Impressed by Mori's loyalty, he promoted the police chief to the role of prefect in Palermo, awarding him, in the process, new powers to bypass all decisions made by the local council. Mori was now free to confront Cosa Nostra with every tool at his disposal, without fear of compromising the interests of the island's political and financial elite.

Between 1925 and 1929 Mori commanded a full-scale paramilitary operation against the mafia. It remains to this day one of the most forceful attempts to challenge the organisation. The campaign began in earnest in Gangi, a small inland town just south of Palermo. On 1 January 1926 Mori cut off the electricity and water supply and ordered his men to move into the houses of men that, according to his informants, belonged to criminal families. For over a week the police tortured members of the local population, including children, in an effort to draw their suspects out from hiding. Finally, after ten days, Mori's men discovered a series of tunnels under the main square which led to a small cave where their targets had been concealing themselves throughout the occupation. The prefect arrested the men and locked them in cages, and, after a token trial, they were sentenced to decades in prison. Over the next four years the state arrested over 11,000 individuals using methods similar to these. Among them were high-profile criminals, including Cascio Ferro, the boss who had ordered the assassination of the American policeman, Joe Petrosino. Despite Mori's brutal tactics, and his flagrant disregard for judicial norms, the international media were impressed by his capacity to deliver results. The *New York Times* published a series of approving features about 'The Iron Prefect' and in 1928 *The Times* of London even went as far as to call him 'a superman'.[4]

Mori's campaign certainly destabilised organised crime in Sicily. The idea that it totally destroyed Cosa Nostra, however, is clearly nonsense. Mori himself acknowledged in his memoirs that in June 1929, when he was removed from his duties, the mafia still occupied important positions of influence in places like Agrigento. Even in Palermo itself, low-level criminals continued to openly run fruit and vegetable monopolies in the markets of Ballarò and Vucciria. From Mussolini's perspective, however, these were mere technicalities. The mafia, he insisted, had been defeated. All that was left now for Sicily, in the dictator's mind, was to engender a more passionate and affirmative support for the regime. Giovanni Gentile, the Sicilian-born philosopher and fascist education minister, was particularly enthusiastic about this task. The problem with the islanders, he argued, was their innate scepticism towards abstract ideas. They were in the grip of a profound 'anti-romanticism' that prevented them from engaging with the realities of the modern world.[5] Gentile altered the Italian curriculum to present patriotic history as a form of metaphysical destiny. There's little evidence, though, that this approach had any serious effect in Sicily. For one thing, the rate of absenteeism in the island's schools was so high at the time that the education system was a limited way of spreading propaganda. More fundamentally, though, much of the local population simply refused to engage with the new fascist state. In the final months of his campaign Mori had tried to galvanise some excitement around the regime by ordering local municipalities to hoist more Italian flags and propaganda posters. When he returned to check on proceedings, however, he found that these objects had been defaced, or, more often, that the local authorities had simply taken them down after a few days.

Ultimately, it was thanks to the church that fascism was able to establish deeper roots in Sicilian society. This is a highly complex issue. In principle the Vatican was hostile to the very idea of the Italian nation-state. For the first seventy years of the unified country, popes had habitually come to speak of themselves as 'prisoners' of a political project that had 'stolen' their land and power. They had even forbidden the faithful from participating in the political system at all, and had implored them not to vote in elections. After the war, however, Catholic attitudes began to soften. In the nineteenth century, the clergy had opposed the liberal state on the basis that it was immoral and disrespectful of Christian values. The rise of socialism, though, which included individuals who did not simply wish to limit the church, but desired its total abolition, posed an even greater threat. In reality Mussolini was himself a militant atheist, and had written tracts against Catholicism in his youth. Nevertheless, after years of living in a liberal society, governed by many anti-clerical politicians, some Christians and conservatives were attracted to fascism's emphasis on family values and hierarchy, and its disdain for democracy. By the mid-1920s influential members of the clergy began to moot the possibility of an alliance. Initially the dictator was reluctant to engage in dialogue. After establishing the regime, however, he resigned himself to the fact that winning church support would be vital to maintaining power. In 1929 he therefore approached Pope Pius XI with an offer. He would recognise the Vatican as an independent state and provide generous reparations for the actions of previous Italian governments, on the sole condition that the institution provide an explicit endorsement of fascism. After a short debate, the papal authorities agreed. On 11 February the various parties signed the Lateran Treaty, thereby cementing a new political alliance between the church and state.

This diplomatic agreement had immediate implications on everyday life and worship in Sicily. Catholic masses began to be accompanied by blackshirt rallies, and religious holidays, including saint-day celebrations, were merged with secular events. The two actors even began to synergise around certain policies. Since coming to power Mussolini had become convinced of the need to increase the national population in order to maintain what he referred to as 'racial purity'. Among other measures he approved financial benefits for large families, introduced a new tax that discriminated against unmarried men and inaugurated a government campaign against contraception. These moves were particularly popular among the Sicilian clergy. While tensions occasionally came to a head – as, for example, in 1931 when Mussolini closed the Catholic-run Boy Scouts, in order to attract recruits for his own youth movement – this collaboration was largely fruitful. For Sicily's practising Christians this was not, then, a huge change. Many believers simply came to see the new state as the augmentation of a religion they had followed for centuries. While the Sicilians were not particularly fond of fascism, the regime succeeded, in this way, to establish a forced consensus that far surpassed anything that previous Italian governments had managed to achieve.

Fascism was, in essence, a far-right movement propped up by conservative factions. Yet it was not only that. In Sicily, as on

the mainland, a minority of the regime's most vocal supporters were young, literate urban-dwellers, many of whom were
highly critical of the government's pandering to what they saw
as outdated institutions, including the church. Chief among this
strand of right-wing agitators were the futurists, a heterodox,
heretical band of provocateurs who defined themselves less by
their deference to the state than by their belief in the prospect of
an imminent technological utopia. The most famous of all was
Filippo Tommaso Marinetti, who in 1909 published the famous
'Manifesto of Futurism', which pledged to obliterate the old world
of libraries and museums and replace them with 'energy and fear-
lessness', 'courage, boldness, and rebelliousness', and, most of all,
'speed, war and technology'.[6] The movement was mainly centred
in Milan, where it served as the leading expression of Italian mod-
ernism. Perhaps surprisingly, though, given the island's relatively
provincial culture, Sicily also played a role in its development. It
was in fact a Palermitan poet and journalist named Federico De
Maria who founded one of Italy's first avant-garde magazines, *La
Fronda*, in 1905. Marinetti was a regular contributor and, together
with Sicilian intellectuals such as Lauria Minutilla and Federico
Pipitone, he wrote several poems and essays about velocity, vital-
ity and electricity. These were some of his first drafts of ideas that
would later form the basis of futurism.

After the war many young Sicilians came to see Marinetti's
movement, and more tentatively fascism itself, as offering the
best chance of their individual liberation. Today this seems like
a contradiction in terms. Some artists, however, were attracted to
the sheer novelty of the ideology, and what they saw as its stated
break with the 'boring' high-cultured canonical tradition that was
still being perpetuated by the nobility. Futurism was fascism's
revolutionary core, and, like most avant-garde movements, it

was profoundly paradoxical. While on the one hand it was fuelled by machismo, it also provided women with their first opportunities to make a serious impact on the art world. Adele Gloria, for example, a futurist poet, painter, photographer, sculptor, dancer and clothes designer from Catania, produced a series of works in the 1930s that criticised the corruption and moral hypocrisy of the island's nobility and bourgeoisie. Her most important work was a sound poem named *FF. SS. '89' Direttissimo* – a reference to a new high-speed train connecting Catania and Rome – which was heavily influenced by the Russian avant-garde. Despite supporting Mussolini, Gloria considered herself a feminist, and was a militant defender of women's rights to work, fight and enjoy a free sex life. She, and other young futurists, contributed to a whole network of independent magazines like *La Balʒa futurista* and *Pickwick*, which connected them to the metropolitan debates that were taking place in Milan. Some artists from the east of Sicily even penned their own futurist manifesto which called on the government to repurpose the ancient Greek theatre at Syracuse in order to host experimental works. They were, as they put it, 'against all forms of ancient revivalism' and deplored audiences 'sitting with their butts on the ground for hours and hours to hear about how Agamemnon cheated on his wife'.[7]

In 1927, inspired by this abundant youthful energy, Marinetti chose Sicily to host Italy's national futurist conference. This was the island's most high-profile artistic event since the 1891 Expo. On this occasion, though, there was not an Arab-Norman pavilion in sight. Instead, the main proceedings took place in Palermo's then newly inaugurated Excelsior Supercinema. The conference itself, which had a mandatory blackshirt dress code, was an important opportunity for Sicilian artists to show off their talents to key figures from the mainland. Among the main protagonists were Giovanni Varvaro, who developed a series of 'speed paintings', Vittorio Corona, who focused on cubist experimentation, and Giulio D'Anna, an early pioneer of *aeropittura* (landscape pictures, depicted from the sky). Perhaps the most important of the attendees, though, was Pippo Rizzo, sometimes known as 'the Picasso of Palermo'. Rizzo's work, more than any of his contemporaries', sought to impose a particularly Sicilian stamp on the fascist-futurist aesthetic. Rizzo's best paintings, such as *Sails in the Wind* (1925) and *Return* (1928) combine the angular, fragmented collage techniques of the northern modernists, with a warmer Mediterranean naturalism of the kind Francesco Lojacono had pioneered in the years following the unification. While he painted cars and planes, Rizzo was equally concerned with landscape, folklore and the realities of rural life. He even painted carnival floats, frescos and peasant carts. His fellow fascists were rather dismissive of this aspect of his work. While the state encouraged folk traditions insofar as they prevented Italians from valorising other foreign cultures, some politicians were concerned that they might also serve to undermine national unity. To be completely clear: Rizzo was a fascist who complied, seemingly uncritically, with the strictures of the regime. His anti-elitism, and respect for Sicilian working-class history, however, are a unique and rather refreshing counterbalance to some of the more toxic, alienating aspects of Italian culture in the '20s and '30s.

While most Sicilian artists embraced fascism, it's important to challenge the widely held assumption that all of the island's cultural practitioners were active and willing proponents of every aspect of far-right ideology. After all, censorship was rife under the regime, and the secret police, OVRA, were watching artists particularly closely for any sign of dissent. Those who did not openly support the state – such as the Palermitan dialect poet Ignazio Buttitta or the painter Renato Guttuso – were threatened with prison time. Even those who did join the party and seemingly admired the regime managed to call certain aspects of its rather flimsy philosophy into question. Luigi Pirandello, the Nobel Prize–winning author and by far the most famous of all Sicily's modernists, spent much of his life traversing these boundaries, usually in rather awkward fashion. In his early years, the author was inspired by the nineteenth-century realists and was a committed reformist. His 1913 novel, *The Old and the Young*, was, in fact, a work of unashamed leftist propaganda which celebrated the heroic struggle of the Fasci against the island's noble landowners. Following the war, however, Pirandello declared himself 'apolitical', which in practice meant switching his allegiance to Mussolini's insurrection. Around the same time, during which the author was suffering from a severe nervous breakdown, his style shifted to become more introspective, more philosophically and psychologically probing. The heroic peasants and revolutionaries of his early work were replaced, quite suddenly, by strange archetypal figures and allegorical, meta-theatrical plot lines. In his most famous work, *Six Characters in Search of an Author* (1921), the writer rejects storytelling altogether and instead presents his audience with an empty stage in which the boundaries between the actors and their roles break down. In this work, as in his later novels, Pirandello challenged the idea that we have any authentic Self behind our social personas. All social life, he began to argue, is a form of performance, of theatre.

It's difficult to square this nihilistic worldview with the author's apparent adherence to fascism. The strange proximity between the two positions, though, is particularly clear in *Henry*

IV (1922), a mock-historical drama in which Pirandello both pokes fun at, and tacitly endorses, authoritarian leadership. The preamble to the play tells the story of a wealthy man who fell off his horse during a carnival procession, during which he had been tasked with performing the role of the eleventh-century German king Henry IV. On waking, the audience learns, this man experienced a kind of delusion, and came to believe himself to really be the monarch in question. The action itself takes place twenty years after these events in 'Henry's court', an elaborate fiction that the man's relatives have created to ensure his peace of mind. For the first forty minutes or so, the audience has the impression of a genuine medieval court drama in which 'Henry' plays the role of an archetypal tyrant, bellowing orders to his knights, servants and counsellors and attending to administrative tasks.

In act two, however, this reality is turned on its head. As the court packs up for the day, the mad king finds himself 'alone' in a room with two particularly dim-witted courtiers. Bored and frustrated, he reveals a shocking secret to both them and to the audience. He has long been aware, he confesses, that he is not Henry IV. In fact, he has consciously chosen to play along with the illusion, because he prefers this fictional world to so-called reality. One might reasonably expect the courtiers to storm out at this point. Instead, as the other characters return to the stage, the actors continue to play their roles while the sadistic monarch watches them squirm. At the end of the play, Henry finally passes judgement on the cast and the audience: '*You* are fools!' he bellows. 'You should have known how to create a fantasy for yourselves, not to act one for me ... I can perform the madman to perfection, here; and I do it perfectly calmly, I'm only sorry for you people that live your madness so agitatedly, without knowing it or seeing it.'[8]

At first it might seem rather surprising that this work ever got past the regime's censors. While Pirandello insisted his play had nothing to do with contemporary politics, his portrayal of this charismatic leader as, essentially, a malicious maniac ruling over a horde of fools, does seem rather provocative. In fact, Mussolini and Gentile not only enjoyed the play, they considered it among the author's best works. This fact arguably cuts to the core of fascist ideology. Pirandello's meditation on the collapse of metaphysical foundations does, initially, seem incompatible with the regime's emphasis on strong national, racial and gender identities. At the same time, though, by suggesting that all identity is performative, Pirandello undermines the very basis on which one might level opposition to fascism's egregious abuses of power. There is, in the author's world, no foundation from which to build a better society, only a chaos of primitive power games and deranged forms of self-deception. There are no heroes in *Henry IV*. Neither the monarch nor his subjects are capable of developing authentic or genuinely autonomous identities. This message is clearly anti-democratic. At the same time, though, the play asks questions that fundamentally undermine fascism itself: how, Pirandello seems to want to ask, might the regime deliver on its promises if its grand narratives are based on nothing but hot air? How can any such political venture avoid collapsing into mindless violence? Tellingly, nowhere in his work does he provide a serious answer to these questions.

The Great Depression marked a turning point in the development of Italian fascism. In the years leading up to 1929 Mussolini had presided over what was, in many respects, a liberal market economy. In the pre-dictatorship era the fascist government had attempted to tackle the post-war deficit by privatising dozens of industries that had previously been under state control, including the telephone network, motorways and some metalworks. This decision rendered Italy vulnerable to the effects of the global economic downturn. When the depression hit, all sectors that relied on access to global markets, such as automobiles and textiles, came to a standstill. Sicily, which was entirely dependent on exporting corn and wheat, was hit particularly hard. Mussolini responded to this undeniable setback by completely redrafting the country's economic model. In 1930 he introduced protectionist measures and established a 'corporatist', state-capitalist system, which was comprised of government-affiliated companies that were required to meet centrally planned production targets in steel, oil and other primary goods. Historians often point out that by the end of the decade, the fascist state controlled more of the national economy than any country in the world after the Soviet Union. This corporatist system, though, was concentrated in the north. In the south, precisely where deflationary energies had most damaged livelihoods, and where welfare was most urgently needed, Mussolini proved himself unable to act. Instead, he chose to build an empire.

This was not, by any means, a new proposal. In the years following unification Italy's liberal government had engaged in a series of foreign expeditions in Africa, and won territories in Eritrea, Southern Somalia and Libya. These colonies, though, had not provided the nation with significant economic, political or military capital. In the 1930s, as part of his larger totalitarian vision, Mussolini began a concerted effort to better exploit these existing assets. This was an exceptionally violent process. In 1932 Italian forces imprisoned as many as 40,000 Libyan civilians in concentration camps in the desert during their effort to reinforce their military presence in Benghazi. There are countless other examples. The main focus of fascist-era policy, though, was Ethiopia. In 1895, under Francesco Crispi, the Italians had tried and failed to take control of the mineral-rich country. In light of the depression, however, as Britain and France struggled to maintain control over some of their own African territories, Mussolini became obsessed with fulfilling that aborted mission. Ignoring the structural weaknesses in the domestic economy, the dictator was possessed by the desire to prove to the other Western powers that fascism had strengthened Italy, and that it could not be sidelined on the global stage.

In 1935 the fascists went to great lengths to galvanise popular support for the proposed mission to Ethiopia. That summer in Catania the city's residents were celebrating the centenary of the death of Vincenzo Bellini, the city's most esteemed composer. To mark the occasion the government organised a huge festival in June and July which invited the citizens to enjoy free performances of patriotic operas like *Norma* and *La Sonnambula*. The musical events were interspersed with pro-imperial speeches. Prominent Sicilian fascists described how their fellow islanders could, by setting out across the sea to 'save' the African people from tyrannical rule by the emperor Haile Selassie, rediscover their 'lost' identity as a militarily strong Mediterranean power. To further sweeten the pill, the government in Rome promised new lands for Sicilian farmers, claiming that, post-conquest, the islanders would be able to emigrate and live more prosperous lives as colonial landowners in Africa. Mussolini allocated vast sums to Sicilian architects who constructed monuments – in a new rationalist style – which attempted to re-frame the fascist state as a new kind of Roman Empire, of which Sicily had, of course, been the first province. The most iconic construction of all was Palermo's post office, a huge concrete temple with a colonnade of ten thirty-metre-high pillars, which towers over the surrounding nineteenth-century villas to this day. This onslaught of propaganda proved successful. On 3 October 1935, when Mussolini formally declared war on Ethiopia, support for fascism in Sicily was at its peak. Huge, spontaneous rallies took place across the island. The working class, who until this point had quietly resigned themselves to domination under fascism, were suddenly enthused by the prospect of escaping their poor, underdeveloped homeland.

The expedition itself was a catastrophic failure. Instead of bolstering the regime, the Ethiopian campaign was one of the decisive factors in its eventual collapse. In principle, the mission should have been straightforward. The fascist army was far better equipped than the African forces and twice as large. Despite these advantages, though, the Italians struggled to move supplies around the unfamiliar territory. The Ethiopian soldiers took advantage of this and succeeded in organising several highly effective guerrilla strikes against the invaders. In December 1935, the defending forces put forward a particularly strong counter-offensive in the mountains near Gondar to the north of the country, which virtually halted the Italians' progress. Mussolini escalated his propaganda campaign and called on all patriotic citizens to donate their precious metals, such as wedding rings and other jewellery, so that they could be melted down into gold bars or simple armaments to assist the war effort. Thousands responded to this call, including Pirandello who is thought to have sent his Nobel Prize medal to the country's foundries. Ultimately, however, the government turned to more drastic measures to resolve the impasse. Furious at the lack of progress, Mussolini gave permission to Pietro Badoglio, the general in charge of the operation, to make use of illegal chemical weapons in order to turn the tide. And so, on 26 December, the Italian army began deploying mustard gas and arsenic shells on the frontline. The African forces were quickly neutralised, but at considerable cost. These substances polluted acres of farmland and forest and contaminated lakes and rivers. Organisations from the League of Nations to Amnesty International have protested these war crimes for decades. Remarkably, though, it was not until 1995 that the Italian government officially acknowledged these events ever took place.

On 9 May 1936 Mussolini declared Ethiopia the capital of a new colonial territory, 'Italian East Africa'. In reality the fascists never entirely subjugated the country. The local population continued to fight back, and conducted a series of bomb attacks against their new rulers throughout the years of occupation. The country eventually won its independence in 1943. Even during these seven years, though, Italian power was never exactly stable. Mussolini was insistent, for example, that Italians should govern the new territory on their own terms, without assistance from the existing Ethiopian leaders. This was a brazenly arrogant move. The occupying forces had little knowledge of Ethiopia's complex cultural history, and as a result, when tensions broke out among local tribes, as they frequently did, they had no idea how to mediate the disputes. The Italian officers quickly obtained a reputation for lechery and for their heavy use of drink and drugs. In the build-up to the war, the colonial soldiers had invented a whole genre of propaganda songs, like 'Faccetta Nera' (Pretty Black Face) and 'Africanina', (Little African), in which they had fantasised about abducting exotic-seeming women. Unsurprisingly, post-conquest, this sentiment translated into real abuses. The Italians conducted terrible acts of sexual violence against their colonial subjects. Many in the fascist state objected to these actions too, not on moral grounds, or not primarily so, but because they undermined what they saw as a pragmatic need to keep the races separate. In 1937 Mussolini introduced discrimination laws to prevent excessive mixing between white and black people. There's little evidence, though, that the colonial officers paid heed to these rules.

In 1935 the fascists had made huge efforts to make Sicilians feel part of the colonial mission. In the years that followed, however, the islanders became scapegoats for its failures. In 1938 a magazine called *The Defence of the Race* began to circulate in Italy, and played an important role in popularising Aryan ideas of white supremacy in the country. While the publication had a relatively small distribution, its readers were influential intellectuals, many of whom held prominent positions in major universities. Later that year they pressured Mussolini to introduce explicit laws, 'for the protection of racial prestige' which, before all else, served to strip the Jewish population of their rights to participate in any aspect of public life. Many of those who contributed to this magazine were convinced that the 'racial impurity' and 'mixed blood' of southern Italians had played a decisive role in the chaos of the Ethiopian campaign. According to so-called 'race scientists' like Giulio Cogni, the Neapolitans, Calabrians and Sicilians had, in preceding centuries, bred too closely with Africans and Arabs. As a result, they had become too connected to 'primitive peoples' and could not therefore be considered Italians at all.[9] While versions of these arguments had been doing the rounds since the time of unification, they only grew in popularity and ferocity in the aftermath of the colonial mission.

To make matters worse, Sicilians faced further economic marginalisation within Italy. The single factor that had enthused the islanders about the Ethiopian campaign was the possibility that it might provide them with a means of breaking free from their servile existence. As it turned out, due to the administrative chaos in the colony and the fallout from the chemical weapons, only a few thousand Italians migrated at all and only a few hundred of these were Sicilians. While the state continued to commission large-scale monuments celebrating the triumph of those who had died building the empire, the islanders were forced, once again, to confront their seemingly inescapable poverty. It's difficult to get a sense of what this meant in practice due to the intensity of censorship at the time. One report, though, by an anonymous colonial journalist paints a rather grim picture:

> Every time a steamship arrives from Africa the people of Messina come out and play music on cylinder pianos, hand-organs, guitars and mandolins for the returning passengers. There are hawkers, priests, friars and nuns … above all there is a crowd of people in rags begging. They are asking for bread, clothes, money, cigarettes, anything. To fetch a pack of cigarettes, children will throw themselves into the sea … how much better if those billions could instead have been devoted to the totalitarian regeneration of Sicily, which is a potential earthly paradise waiting to become a real paradise and richly productive, if only every strip of its coastal, interior or mountain land could be given the water that it lacks. Italy would have on its doorstep that agricultural and non-agricultural wealth that it is going in search of so far away with its risky enterprise.[10]

The author wrote this paragraph in a private notebook which was never published. One suspects, though, that many Sicilian fascists shared this sentiment. While Mussolini continued to engage in foreign expeditions in the latter years of his rule, sending a mission to support the Francoists in the Spanish Civil War, even he saw the need to invest more directly in Sicily. In 1937 the dictator made his second, and final, tour of the island. He was pleased by the rationalist buildings, and the progress that had been made in tackling the mafia. The extent of poverty among the peasantry, though, was worse than he had been expecting. On his previous visit, the dictator had only observed the relatively prosperous north-west of the island. In the south, however, he encountered starving people, many of whom were living in stone huts devoid of even basic sanitation. During a stop in the Val di Noto, near the new provincial capital of Ragusa, the dictator gave an impromptu speech in which he promised to 'save Sicily from the rural village'. The fields, he promised, would soon double their yield, the peasants 'would be happy to live on the land they work on' and Sicily would become 'one of the most fertile districts in the world'.[11]

In 1940 the fascist state formed a new organisation named ECLS (Ente di colonizzazione del latifondo siciliano) which was tasked with organising an 'agricultural revolution' on the island. The acronym though, and the word 'colonisation' in particular, was revealing. Sicily was no longer Italian, or not really. It was rapidly becoming a subaltern, sub-national territory; a mirror to Ethiopia within the country's own borders. The architects in charge of ECLS worked to design and build a series of new towns across Sicily's rural interior. Each of these new settlements was based around a uniform model, with a central agora that was home to a town hall and church, a post office, medical facility, school, carabinieri barracks, and recreation area.[12] These were not towns in any ordinary sense of that word. The houses, for example, were separated into individual units and dispersed evenly around the hillsides, quite far from the central square. The architects argued that this arrangement provided privacy for the residents. In reality, they planned this system around the model of a panopticon, to make it easier to police the local population and minimise the risk of social unrest. The regime constructed thirty of these conurbations, most of which were clustered around the centre of the island. Today, the vast majority of these places, like Borgo Lupo, Borgo Schirò and Borgo Baccarato, lie abandoned, the populations having been forced to leave due to a lack of infrastructure or employment opportunities. These ghost towns have left a scar on the island. As the Sicilian historian Rosario Mangiameli has recently argued, these structures were nothing other than 'open air prisons', designed to encourage forced labour. In a just world, he insists, they would have 'no place in the island's peasant history'.[13]

In 1939 Nazi Germany invaded Poland thereby marking the start of the Second World War. By this point, though, Italy's fascist regime was already on the verge of collapse. The country had spent the equivalent of a year's national income during the Ethiopian war and, as a result of this vast expense, the lira had devalued by half. Inflation, which had been out of control for most of the fascist period, increased dramatically. The country's use of chemical weapons had marginalised it from the League of Nations, and following his intervention in Spain Mussolini had little option but to side with Hitler. It was clear, however, that the regime's days were numbered. One can get a sense of the melancholia that marked the end of fascism in Sicily in a mural which the artist Mario Sironi designed for Messina train station on the eve of Italy's entry to the war. The foreground shows Mussolini, surrounded by a throng of peasants, soldiers and blackshirts. Behind these figures, though, are emblems of the island's past: ancient Greek nymphs dancing in Agrigento's Valley of Temples; Norman knights riding into the distance.

Presumably Sironi conceived this work to inspire nationalist sentiment among the users of the railway station. Yet it was too late for that. While the actual collapse of fascism would be external, provoked by American intervention in the war, the regime's ideology was already becoming unstuck in Sicily. The mural is closed to the public today. If you peer through the waiting room gates, though, you can just make out the fantasy backdrop, with its classical ruins and fairy tale castles. Even on its own terms this looks less like a model of the future than a tacky nostalgic trinket: an appropriately ugly eulogy to fascism's failed experiment on the island.

8
The Return of the Mafia (1943–2013)

The American Connection, Concrete
Cathedrals, Bunga Bunga

*[Sicily] has a long and unhappy history that has left it primitive and
undeveloped with many relics of a highly civilised past ... two houses
out of three are without drinking water laid on, and only about half have
sanitation ... The native, living as he does in primitive conditions, has
become immune from many diseases which British soldiers are likely to
contract. The insanitary condition of the island is one of its best defences
against an invader.*

A Soldier's Guide to Sicily, publication
distributed to Allied troops in spring 1943

Sicily played a marginal role in the first years of the Second
World War. Between 1940 and 1942 its main function was to
provide air support to Italian naval vessels in the Mediterranean
that were engaged in attacks against British Malta. Mussolini did
station 300,000 soldiers to the island, but the government was
too concerned with coordinating land campaigns in Africa and
Yugoslavia to dedicate serious reinforcements to what they saw

as a relatively peripheral site. The Allied generals quickly identified Sicily as a weak point in the Axis strategy. In January 1943, at a meeting in Casablanca, Winston Churchill and Franklin D. Roosevelt agreed to launch an offensive named 'Operation Husky', which was to serve as a practice run for the later D-Day landings in France. In theory the attack was supposed to be limited to military bases, roads and train lines. In practice, starting in May that year, the Allies began a project of intensive carpet bombing over Sicily's major cities, including Palermo and Messina, which prepared the way for a full-scale ground invasion. Heavy bombers dropped their payloads indiscriminately, destroying churches, schools and numerous historic buildings. What little loyalty the islanders still had for the regime seems to have quickly collapsed. On 10 July, as British and American paratroopers landed on the beaches near to Syracuse, the majority of the fascist army retreated back home. For just over a week, the Allies pushed north, fighting off small groups of Nazi squads. On 22 July they drove into Palermo where an apparently jubilant civilian population welcomed them as 'liberators' and decorated their homes with the star-spangled banner. When the festivities died down the city's Anglican church organised a mass: not for the Sicilian dead, but for the Americans who had been killed during the offensive.

Sicily's enthusiastic capitulation to the Allied forces remains a point of contention to this day. One might think that Italians would see this in favourable terms, as evidence of the local population's long-standing ambivalence towards fascism. More often, though, mainlanders point to this fact as further evidence that the island is populated by cowards and cheats. The Sicilians, so the argument often goes, could not profess to be heroes, like, say, the communist partisans who fought fascism in the Alps. They were, at best, the passive occupants of a place where Italy lost the war. This is a rather simplistic version of events. In fact, months before the Allied landing large numbers of islanders had themselves been preparing to rise up against the government which they felt had abandoned them. In 1942, groups of disaffected monarchists, liberals and socialists came together to form their own autonomist party, MIS, which had a single demand: the right to form a Sicilian nation-state with full independence from Italy. The movement's supporters rallied behind the Trinacria, a symbol formed of a Medusa head adorned by three wheat stalks and three female legs, each of which refers to a different cape at the island's extremities. By choosing this particular figure, which was of ancient Greek origin, the movement's leaders were attempting to reclaim some aspect of the island's pre-modern heritage, and, in doing so, to obliterate the memory of centuries of colonial-style rule. While MIS never succeeded in its overall objective, the Trinacria has served as the island's regional flag since 2000.

Technically speaking this kind of activity was illegal. One of the first things the British and Americans did after setting up a provisional government in Palermo was to ban all political parties. MIS, though, was an exception to this. Few of the Allied soldiers and bureaucrats could understand Italian, let alone the island's various dialects. The occupying forces were therefore entirely dependent upon the movement's educated and apparently anti-fascist leaders in order to maintain control. As part of the same strategy the Americans also released hundreds of prisoners, reasoning that these individuals would be similarly opposed to any efforts to regroup on the part of the far right. What they failed to realise, however, was that many of the incarcerated were in fact mafia affiliates that Mori had arrested during his campaigns twenty years previously. By attempting to block the return of fascism the Allies inadvertently provided Cosa Nostra with a chance to rebuild. In September 1943 the provisional government made the particularly egregious error of appointing a mafia boss and major benefactor of MIS named Tasca Bordonaro to be the first post-fascist mayor of Palermo. Over the next months he used his position to orchestrate Cosa Nostra's return to power in the city. Similar scenes took place across the island. In Mussomeli, an isolated inland town, Giuseppe Genco Russo, another boss who had been arrested in the '20s, bribed his way into a position in local government which he used to establish a series of new drug-smuggling routes between the island and North Africa. The most powerful of all was Calogero Vizzini, whom the Allies appointed as mayor of Villalba, a small town near Caltanisetta, an important hub for agricultural and sulphur production in the very centre of the island. In the months following the invasion, Vizzini came to dominate the black market, selling foodstuffs and basic medicine to the local population. By the end of the war the Americans were so reliant on his services that they made him an honorary colonel in the US military.

For most Sicilians, life in occupied Sicily was even more precarious than it had been under the regime. In addition to food shortages, an outbreak of malaria spread across the island in the winter of 1943, killing and hospitalising thousands. Amid the chaos, a new generation of brigands and highwaymen came to prominence while making a small fortune by looting mafia and military stockpiles and reselling them to the local population. Chief among these individuals was Salvatore Giuliano, a devout Sicilian nationalist who was pro-American to the extent that he sent a letter to President Truman pledging his allegiance to the country, and even participated in a breakaway faction of MIS, numbering more than 40,000, that campaigned for Sicily to become the forty-ninth of the United States.[1] Giuliano quickly won a reputation among the islanders for being a kind of modern-day Robin Hood, a romantic folk hero who would steal from the wealthiest to distribute fairly among the poor. In reality Giuliano's ambitions were intimately linked to the interests of Sicily's larger cartels. In 1944 he volunteered to command EVIS, a mafia-funded armed wing of the independence movement, and led a series of terrorist attacks against Italian state targets. To some degree these actions were a genuine expression of the islanders' resentment against the old fascist elite. There's no escaping the fact, however, that the main purpose of this guerrilla organisation was to assist the old Cosa Nostra families in their efforts to regain positions of influence.

The blurring of boundaries between banditry, mafia and social movements was the single defining characteristic of Sicily's post-war politics. This became particularly clear following 25 April 1945, when the Italian resistance on the mainland formally declared the end of Mussolini's rule. Faced with MIS and its associated movements, the Italian king, Umberto II, understood that if he was to prevent Sicily from seceding he would have to offer the islanders some tangible benefits. On 15 May 1946, with this in mind, he therefore declared Sicily an 'autonomous' region of Italy, a status it maintains to this day. In practice this decision means that the islanders have the right to their own elected president, to call their own parliament and to take their own decisions about key budgetary issues including urban planning, tourism and the allocation of state jobs. Seen in context, this move had potential to aid the island's return to democracy. By putting this structure in place at a time in which the state itself was in such fragile health, however, Umberto in fact opened the door for figures like Russo and Vizzini to infiltrate the structures of the autonomous region from its very beginning. While most Sicilians welcomed Umberto's decision, it was too late for the king at a national level. On 2 June 1946 the Italian government organised a referendum on the future of the country. Voters were asked to choose between the monarchy and a new republican state. In Sicily, 64 percent of residents voted in defence of Umberto. Most Italians, particularly those in the central and northern regions, voted overwhelmingly for the republic.

Historians often point to this discrepancy as evidence that Sicilians were anchored in the political right following the war. In reality, this argument is rather anachronistic. While some reactionary groups did thrive in the 1940s, the post-conflict years, if anything, served to reanimate the previously suppressed socialist tradition. Many individuals that the Allies released from prison had previously been involved in the activities of the PSI and PCI. In 1944, for example, Sicilian politicians and trade unionists including Pio La Torre and Girolamo Li Causi were free to organise a militant communist-affiliated campaign against mafia bosses in which they mobilised workers to take direct control of the land on the south of the island in territory controlled by Vizzini. Itinerant bands of older socialists that had been forced into hiding during the regime, began to tour the island, organising talks, concerts and rallies, while newspapers that had been banned returned to circulation. These were not marginal activities. In fact, the scale of organisation was so vast that the Sicilian left obtained a level of institutional influence that exceeded that of the 1910s.

In April 1947 Sicily had its first local elections as an autonomous region. The results were surprising to all involved. The independence movement, pacified by Umberto's concessions, won just 8.8 percent. The centre-right conservatives won 20.5 percent. The

Blocco del Popolo, an alliance of socialist and communist groups, were the clear winners with 30.4 percent of the vote.

For a brief moment, thousands of Sicilians began to hope that, after decades of false promises under fascism, life for the island's working classes might finally improve. Unfortunately, this was not the case. On 1 May 1947, just weeks after the result, the PCI organised a party at Portella della Ginestra, just outside of Palermo, to celebrate their historic victory and, more generally, mark the fact that the first free vote since the collapse of the regime had passed without violence. This was the first significant workers' day celebration since 1923. It was not a militant rally. Most of the crowd was made up of families who had gathered to eat picnics together and listen to a brass band. Around ten o'clock in the morning just as the speeches began, a volley of machine-gun fire hit the crowd from the nearby foothills. Eleven people were killed and twenty-seven injured.

Yet this was not the end of it. In the months that followed, a series of other smaller, more targeted attacks took place across the island. On 24 December, at Canicattì, an important wine producing town, another anonymous group opened fire on a crowd of agricultural workers who had been planning a protest. Twenty people were killed. Throughout the winter of 1948 several prominent leftist leaders were assassinated, including Epifanio Li Puma, a socialist intellectual, and Placido Rizzotto, a partisan and prominent labour activist. These were not just attacks against socialism. They were clearly mafia-led attempts to rig the political system in favour of the centre-right parties. Unfortunately for all democratically minded Sicilians, the strategy worked. In the national elections of April 1948 the centre-right jumped to 48 percent of the vote and support for the Communist Party collapsed across the island.

One final detail helps explain the severity of the problems the left would face in years to come. In the months following the massacre at Portella della Ginestra, a story was published in the local media which suggested that Salvatore Giuliano, the legendary bandit, had played a leading role in organising the attacks. Since its origins the PCI had tried to discourage the working class from idolising these figures and to instead organise their own forms of collective action. Giuliano, though, was so loved among the island's peasantry that many simply refused to believe that he had been involved. In 1950 the plot thickened when the police found Giuliano dead, face-down, with two gunshots in his back in the small town of Castelvetrano. Initially the officers themselves tried to take credit for this, claiming that they'd killed him in a firefight. Later evidence, though, revealed that this was not the case. In 1952, during a trial of the bandit's associates, a man named Gaspare Pisciotta confirmed that Giuliano himself had ordered the attack at Portella della Ginestra, and that several politicians from the ranks of the centre right, including the minister of the interior Mario Scelba, had also been involved in the plot. Pisciotta went on to claim that he himself had killed Giuliano, his ex-boss, on their orders, to cover up the evidence.

It's impossible to establish much concrete information about these allegations, and historians have since called many aspects of Pisciotta's account into question. One sentence from his testimony, though, stands out in particular: 'We were one body,' he remarked. 'Bandits, police and mafia, like Father, Son and Holy Ghost.'[2] Journalists at the time disregarded these rather prosaic comments as the ramblings of a deranged criminal. Subsequent events, though, have cast some doubt over these conclusions. In February 1954, two years into his incarceration in Palermo's Ucciardone prison, Pisciotta died after consuming a large dose of strychnine which someone had mixed into his morning coffee. The culprit has never been identified.

The collapse of fascism in Italy was a long, slow process. For decades, well into the 1970s, small-scale vendettas continued to break out across the peninsula and islands between those nostalgic for the regime and those who had led the resistance against it. Unlike the 1920s, though, the state succeeded in containing both of these energies by appealing to a new and, as we shall see, incredibly resilient, centrist paradigm. The most important representatives of this political tendency were the Christian Democrats (DC), a hybrid party which combined elements of social conservatism with economic liberalism. On the one hand, the party promoted Catholic values, defending, for example, the ideal of the nuclear family. On the other, many of the members were pro–free trade, and happy to endorse certain aspects of American consumer culture. In the north of Italy, the communist PCI provided an almost constant opposition to this.[3] In the south, though, things were different. The combined power of mafia groups and the church continued to undermine efforts at working-class organisation. In fact, after the 1948 elections, the institutional left was virtually absent in Sicily. The DC would win every single regional election, and almost all the presidencies, until 1996.

During their many years of governing, the DC presided over a catastrophic mismanagement of Sicily's economy. While some local politicians enacted measures that helped the island – such as breaking up the island's largest agricultural estates into smaller units – the party's internal culture was so obscure, and so corrupt, that most of these interventions were severely limited or failed altogether. A good illustration of this is Alcide De Gasperi's *cassa per il mezzogiorno*, a £1.2 billion fund which the then prime minister allocated in 1950 to build new motorways, dams, drainage systems, and some limited industrial projects in Southern Italy.[4] In theory this was a sound proposal. In Sicily, though, as in other mainland cities like Naples, mafia groups easily intervened. Historians have estimated that criminal contractors succeeded in siphoning off as much as a third of the fund, typically by bribing officials to win state projects, then producing rushed, poor-quality jobs, and finding ways to pocket the surplus.[5] The consequences of this are visible to this day in the hundreds of half-constructed hospitals, housing estates and factories that are spread across Southern Italy. Local people, rather poetically, call these 'cathedrals in the desert'. While this makes them sound like holy sites, they've actually had a devastating impact on both the economy and politics of the south. Perhaps the greatest indicator of this is that despite fifty years of planning, and the fact that the Strait of Messina is just 3 km at its narrowest point, there is still no bridge between Sicily and the peninsula.

During the DC years a broader culture of nepotism and clientelism began to take root in Sicily and indeed much of Italy. Responsibility for this goes far beyond any single individual. Amintore Fanfani, though, deserves more blame than most. Starting in the 1950s the then labour minister, who would go on to serve five terms as prime minister, enacted a series of reforms which were designed to increase the DC's control over the economy. Specifically, Fanfani authorised the creation of public sector 'firms', which were owned directly by the party, and which controlled, among other things, welfare, utilities and parts of the housing stock. Defenders of this system argue that it protected these vital public services from speculative market forces. In reality, the firms enabled the government in Rome to directly appoint top jobs to 'trusted men' across the country who then took on the role of distributing favours to those closest to the party. Palermo, in particular, suffered greatly as a result of this. In the late 1950s Fanfani appointed one of his acolytes, Giovanni Gioia, to be the DC's provincial secretary for Sicily. Between 1959 and 1963 Gioia worked together with two known mafiosi, Salvo Lima, who was the city's mayor, and Vito Ciancimino, who was in charge of the Office of Public Works, to deal out construction contracts to Cosa Nostra. This was a remarkably transparent process: in these years the city council openly granted 80 per cent of the available tenders to just five individuals.[6] Only a minority of those that received the funds had any experience in construction. Instead, mafia builders simply demolished huge parts of the city's historic architecture and hired their own firms to build cheap, modern tower blocks which they then harnessed as a means of exploiting the rental economy. This process razed much of the city's historical architecture to the ground, including most of the nineteenth-century Liberty villas around Politeama. Locals today refer to this moment as 'the Sack of Palermo' on account of the destruction it caused.

This process was not confined to the capital. Throughout the 1960s a flurry of similar unregulated, speculative investments spread across the island. With the development of commercial air travel, in particular, Cosa Nostra sought to find opportunities to profit from Europe's growing tourist industry. Starting in Cape Lilibeo, in south-west Sicily, where the weather is warm most of the year round, the mafia invested in hotels, beach houses and resorts. While some of the structures were inhabited, serving as seasonal homes for wealthy businesspeople, they were, on the whole, opportunities for money laundering, and as such were more often left empty as real estate investments rather than managed as businesses.

This diversion of funds was not only illegal, it often had dangerous consequences. On 19 July 1966 several of these cheaply built apartment buildings collapsed during a landslide and crumbled down a hill just metres from the Greek ruins at Agrigento. Fortunately, no one was killed. International observers, though, were shocked to see news footage of plaster and concrete hurtling towards one of the world's most important archaeological sites. In August that year the PCI led a small social movement to challenge 'illegal building' but this was little more than a token gesture. The uncomfortable truth is that, by the 1960s, many Sicilians had become reliant on the DC's clientelist system in order to survive, and the possibility of disrupting this seemed to pose a direct threat to their own personal interests. This failure to act had a corrosive effect on Sicily's civil society. In the past the islanders had been able to blame natural and political disasters on foreign powers. This time, though, as the mafia destroyed the island's heritage and polluted its environment, the inhabitants had nobody else to point their fingers at. Quietly, without fanfare, support for separatism collapsed almost entirely.[7]

Cosa Nostra's other main source of revenue in the post-war years was the drug trade. In the '50s and '60s, Sicily became one of the central nodes in the movement of heroin and cocaine between North Africa, Europe and the Americas. This industry brought an unprecedented amount of wealth into the hands of the island's ruling families. As the mafia's profits increased, the organisation was forced to reform its internal protocols in an effort to reduce infighting between factions. At the start of 1958, following several meetings with the American mob in Palermo's Hotel Delle Palme, Cosa Nostra's bosses decided to form the Sicilian Mafia Commission. The purpose of this institution was to limit the use of violence against state targets, to enforce the codes of silence and to regulate territorial boundaries between clans. Those assembled appointed a leader, Salvatore Greco, whose job was not to govern the organisation, but to ensure balance among the parties. On paper Cosa Nostra was more unified than it had ever been. In reality, however, the peace was more fragile than it seemed. In 1962, following a dispute about a stolen shipment of heroin, a group of second-tier bosses attempted to take control of the structure. Leaders of various clans, most notably the La Barbera brothers, organised drive-by shootings which were targeted, on the whole, at members of the Greco clan who in turn were forced to retaliate. This conflict, which some historians call the 'First Mafia War' killed dozens of individuals, almost all of whom were associated in some way or another with Cosa Nostra. The peak of the violence took place on 30 June 1963 when a group of seven police officers, and their military escort, died as they attempted to defuse a car bomb in Ciaculli, a suburb of Palermo. The government could not afford to turn a blind eye to these events. In the aftermath the carabinieri arrested over 1,000 suspected mafiosi in an attempt to weed out the most violent of the low-level hitmen. The majority of the bosses managed to escape into hiding. Greco himself fled to Venezuela where, until his death in 1978, he continued to coordinate the trans-Atlantic drug trade.

Throughout these violent years the PCI continued to lead the opposition to the DC-mafia hegemony. In 1968, as in much of Europe, thousands took to the streets in Sicily calling for radical social change. The mobilisations on the island had begun the previous December when students at Catania university organised an occupation to protest against the poor quality of the island's educational facilities. Many of the students were members or affiliates of the Communist Party and they organised events using its cultural infrastructure, most notably through social centres such as the Casa del Popolo, and the newspaper *l'Unità*. They set up occupations which had an explicit Marxist-internationalist character and, over the coming years, mobilised to confront what they called the 'neofascism' of the local politicians and university barons. Beyond the student movement the PCI's political leaders were focused on attacking the DC's foreign policy, which was staunchly pro-NATO. On 24 March, tens of thousands of students and workers gathered in Catania to participate in an enormous anti-Vietnam protest. A few weeks later, a militant group marched on, and attacked, the US naval base at Sigonella, just outside of the city limits.

The most important events of that year, though, took place in the west of the island. On 14 January a series of powerful earthquakes hit the Belice valley, 30 km south of Palermo, destroying the towns of Gibellina, Poggioreale and Salaparuta. While the DC debated among themselves about how to fund the aid mission, students in the capital mobilised quickly to form mutual aid groups and tenants' unions through which they were able to provide housing and supplies for thousands of refugees. The PCI supported these activities through demonstrations and strikes, marching under the slogan 'bureaucracy kills more than earthquakes'. As so often in Sicily's history, the state responded to these provocations with violence. On 2 December the island's police murdered two trade union activists, Angelo Sigona and Giuseppe Scibilia, in what was clearly an act of intimidation. The mafia, unsurprisingly, took advantage of this opportunity to unleash their own aggression against emerging social movements. In 1970 a Cosa Nostra member 'disappeared': Mauro De Mauro, a correspondent with the island's most important left-wing newspaper, *L'Ora*. Two years later, they shot his colleague

Giovanni Spampinato dead while he was investigating a story about corruption in the south-eastern province of Ragusa. As in the 1940s, this violence proved effective. In 1967 the PCI had won 21.3 percent of the vote in Sicily. By 1971, this dropped to a historic low of 12.5 percent.

Despite the electoral fragility of the Communist Party the events of 1968 did have a significant impact on Sicilian society. Much of this was the result of pressure from left-wing groups on the mainland. In 1974, for example, thanks in part to a long-term PCI-led campaign, Italians voted in a referendum to approve the right to divorce. While the majority of Sicilians voted against the motion, they nevertheless won that right. Two years later, in 1978, despite intense opposition from the DC base, the government approved a bill to legalise abortion. The fact that this move was possible during a moment in which the Christian Democrats were in power is an important indicator of how deeply the protests of the previous decade had challenged the ruling orthodoxy. In Sicily, as in the rest of Italy, a young, educated middle class was developing which, while economically precarious, was organising itself to demand, and enact, social change. In the following years some of the '60s youth movements evolved into 'autonomist Marxist groups': anarchist-inspired organisations that spoke out against bourgeois family values, religion and the 'cult of work'. Feminism was the most creative and interesting current to emerge in these years by some way. Throughout the 1970s Italian women put forward various original arguments, such as the call for wages for housework and other forms of domestic unpaid labour, which, arguably, remain radical necessities to this day.

Another of the most important and often overlooked campaigns in Sicily at the time was the islanders' struggle for homosexual rights. For most of the twentieth century, and indeed long before that, the combination of Catholicism, mafia and lingering aspects of fascist machismo, had facilitated an appallingly homophobic culture in Sicily. The island's history is filled with hate crime against gay people. One particularly horrendous event took place on 31 October 1980 in Giarre, a small town outside of Catania, when a right-wing activist killed two young lovers, the twenty-five-year-old Giorgio Agatino Giammona and fifteen-year-old Antonio Galatola. In the wake of those events the islanders stood up, for the first time, to confront this. That winter, in light of the double homicide, a collection of activist organisations opened a dedicated gay social centre in Palermo to protect LGBT rights. It was the first such space anywhere in Italy.

This confluence of new social energies shattered the foundations of post-war politics. Across the country the left began to fragment into dozens of extra-parliamentary movements, each with their own specific identity-based agendas. This pluralism had some positive aspects, in that it fuelled a diversity of creative demands, and connected politics more intimately with people's lives. It also accelerated the fragmentation of the communist movement. In 1976, as part of the effort to force progressive measures through parliament, the leader of the PCI Enrico Berlinguer proposed a 'historic compromise' with the centre-right. This was, it must be recognised, the very same logic that led to the victories regarding the divorce and abortion laws. Nevertheless, many Italian communists were vehemently opposed to Catholicism; to some the idea of making an agreement with the DC marked the end of the PCI's claim to represent left-wing politics at all. In response to this, even as the party won 34 percent of the national vote, Marxist-inspired terror groups like the Red Brigades and Prima Linea escalated a campaign of armed struggle across the peninsula, conducting attacks against 'imperialist multi-nationalists', including judges, politicians, police officers and university lecturers. Neo-fascist groups, with similarly melodramatic names like Ordine Nuovo and Avanguardia Nazionale, took advantage of this violent turn in order to organise attacks of their own which were generally bloodier and more indiscriminate. They then blamed the violence on the radical left. In March 1978 these tensions came to a head when militants associated with the Red Brigades kidnapped a prominent DC politician, Aldo Moro, and, after two months of moving him between apartments, dumped his body in the centre of Rome, riddled with bullets. The individuals that murdered Moro believed that their actions might stimulate a revolution. In fact they only served to solidify the pact between the communists and Christian Democrats. In the months that followed, the PCI and DC worked together to organise a generalised clamp-down in which they arrested all left-wing figures that even vaguely broke with the orthodoxy of the establishment line.

These events seemed miles away to Sicilian socialists. Most left-wing activists on the island were struggling to confront the more immediate reality that, if the movement was to have any hope of success, it would have to find a way of defeating the mafia. One young man, Giuseppe 'Peppino' Impastato, pushed this logic to its extreme. Born in 1948 in Cinisi, a small town in the west of the island, Peppino turned against Cosa Nostra at the age of just fifteen when his uncle was killed by a car bomb in the First Mafia War. In the following years, as a teenager, he gravitated towards Marxism and, in 1968, organised a protest against plans for a new runway at Palermo's airport, which proposed to expropriate rural workers from their land. The PCI, fearful of upsetting the project's developers over what they saw as a minor issue, refused to support the venture. Disillusioned by this lack of solidarity, Peppino, like many others of his generation, became increasingly attracted to autonomist politics. In the early '70s he set up a pirate radio station, Aut, where he broadcast shows about art, music and politics. In contrast to similar stations, though, which limited themselves to debates and cultural programming, Aut also transmitted its own investigative journalism, and broke regular news stories about a local Cosa Nostra boss, Gaetano Badalamenti, and his ties to the local authorities. Peppino received several death threats for this work. Despite this in 1978, at the height of the Moro affair, he decided to candidate himself for a minor leftist party called 'Proletarian Democracy' hoping to confront this corruption from inside the political system. On 9 May, in response to this, Badalamenti's men made good on their word. They abducted the young activist, tied his body to the train tracks on the outskirts of Cinisi, and blew him to pieces with a homemade bomb. By killing Peppino the mafia hoped to silence his campaign. In the end, however, they only served to amplify his voice. Two days later, when the local population went to the polls, they came together to defy this violence and elected the murdered man into the council. While the circumstances were tragic, Peppino did not die in vain. This was Sicily's first collective victory against mafia intimidation.[8]

Cosa Nostra is an organisation that thrives in moments of political crisis. It's perhaps unsurprising then that, looked at as a whole, the 1970s proved a godsend for the organisation. Over the course of that decade the state was so concerned with policing protests and armed uprisings that it neglected to confront organised crime. Successive Italian governments dodged their own complicity in the deaths of individuals like Peppino, arguing that, as an autonomous region, Sicily was supposed to confront such matters on its own. Given the close links between the mafia and the local administration, of course, this argument was naïve at best. In the latter part of the decade, Cosa Nostra continued to increase their business ventures in the drug and arms trades virtually unhindered. Once again this was accompanied by a surge in violence. Historians estimate that between 1978 and 1983 – a period sometimes known as the 'Second Mafia War' – organised crime families killed between 500 and 1,000 people in Sicily, including children. Unlike the '60s, however, this period also saw a marked escalation of attacks against state targets. On 6 January 1980 a mafia assassin shot dead the Sicilian president Piersanti Mattarella, a prominent Christian Democrat, while he was driving to church with his family shortly after he'd announced a project to tackle corruption inside the DC. On 3 September 1982, when the Italian government reluctantly sent reinforcements to the island to deal with the situation, the mafia assassinated Palermo's head of police, Carlo Alberto dalla Chiesa, in response.

Throughout the 1980s Sicilians experienced a further shrinking of their already limited civic space. This was particularly the case from 1983 when Totò Riina, head of the Corleonesi mafia, fought off rival claimants to establish himself as Cosa Nostra's 'boss of bosses'. For the next decade he governed the organisation as a virtual dictator. Unlike Salvatore Greco, Riina was particularly concerned with exploiting the mafia's local power. He increased the protection money (*pizzo*) across the island and ordered his men to ensure that anyone who didn't pay up would face the consequences. The mafia assaulted hundreds of individuals and burnt homes and businesses in accordance with this new rule. In Palermo's Zen 2 development, a peripheral area known, unfortunately, for its absence of schools, green spaces and other services, the mafia purchased apartments and distributed them to the local population at low rents. There were catches to this of course. Cosa Nostra controlled the gas, electricity and water supplies, and charged huge amounts for these services that far exceeded what the residents could afford. As a result, in the years after signing their contracts, many of the new renters were forced to become foot soldiers for the mafia in order to keep their homes. In the post-war years the mafia had largely treated Sicilian cities as transit points through which to pass drugs. Starting in the '80s, Riina worked to build larger local markets alongside the export business. Across the island, in districts like Giostra in Messina and San Giuliano in Trapani, Cosa Nostra began to seek out new recruits, and concentrated their efforts on attacking rival small-time dealers. Librino, a satellite town outside of Catania, is a particularly grim monument to this transition. Modernist architects designed the complex in the late '60s as a utopian social housing project. By the 1990s, however, it was falling to pieces, and its economic activity was almost entirely taken over by arms and drug trafficking.

In response to these problems the Italian media began to present Sicily as a fear-ridden, backward-looking place. Newspapers earnestly compared the situation on the island to that in Beirut (which at the time was at war with Israel) and it became tacitly acceptable, on much of the peninsula, to offer racist slurs against Sicilians.[9] Yet something strange happened in parallel to this. Despite the terrible realities on which these stereotypes were based, international observers, particularly in America, began to look at Sicily in surprisingly favourable terms. To some extent this might be said to have begun as early as 1972 when Francis Ford Coppola released his film adaptation of *The Godfather*.

The plot, it's true, is concerned with murders and racketeering. Nevertheless, the on-screen version of the island is that of a Mediterranean paradise, where despite the gang violence life is essentially comfortable. The Cosa Nostra of Coppola's world is not made up by thugs like Riina. Their leader is the charismatic and charming Don Vito, who rules over his organisation according to codes of honour and respect. By the '80s a whole industry of copycat books and films – most notably Michael Cimino's *The Sicilian* (1987) – was beginning to develop, which was blind to Sicily's decrepit tower blocks and concrete-covered beaches, instead treating the mafia as a kind of folklore which was as much a part of the island's identity as its vineyards and olive groves. This 'Sicilian fever' reached its apex in 1988 when Giuseppe Tornatore produced the island's first domestic box-office hit, *Cinema Paradiso*. The film's sentimental, cliché-ridden plot lines about emigration, vendettas and old silent movies, have aged rather poorly. At the time, though, audiences and critics alike celebrated the work as a near-perfect piece of escapism; a fitting antidote to modern industrialised metropolitan society.

Luxury businesses proved particularly effective at exploiting Sicily's new-found cultural mystique. In 1987, Dolce & Gabbana decided to use the island as the backdrop for their fall–winter catalogue, reasoning that its crumbling houses and old palazzi would provide a sophisticated 'old-world beauty' that would help present their clothes in a new light. The campaign was an enormous success and many other businesses sought to imitate it in years to come. Some Sicilian towns attempted to rebrand themselves as high-end tourist destinations. Developers in Portorosa, near Messina, built a swanky new boat club, hoping to entice the business of an elite yacht-owning clientele. Taormina, a small town with a remarkable view of Etna, which had been a tourist resort since Roman times, reinvented itself as a flagship destination for wealthy customers. The wine sector similarly flourished as global consumers began to acquire a taste for the island's unique volcanic whites such as Grillo and Etna Bianco. The greatest success story of all was Nero d'Avola. Historically, producers had exported this dark ruby red to France and Northern Italy, where it was used to provide colour to intensify more dilute blends. From the late '80s, however, some of the world's most important oenologists, such as Giacomo Tachis, began to write admiringly of its qualities. By the end of the decade, sommeliers around the world were following suit and today wine writers consider it among Italy's most prestigious 'noble' varieties.

The overall economic impact of this growth in high-end consumer goods provided few benefits to the Sicilian population as a whole. Cosa Nostra had a large stake in many of these industries and, as a result, the bosses pocketed a considerable portion of these profits. While violent crime rates began to dip slightly at the end of the '80s, in part as a result of this economic diversification, many tourist companies and hotel chains continued to see Sicily as too dangerous a destination to invest in. Life did improve, in some respects, for the majority of islanders, though this was less a consequence of structural changes to the economy than a new availability of credit. In the '80s, as national growth began to decline, the Italian government devalued the lira and loosened restrictions on the banking sector's ability to distribute loans. This was a key moment in Italy's economic history and, arguably, marked the origin of the country's spiralling national debt which plagues it to this day. While the state did not meaningfully tackle issues of poor public services and housing, this 'cheap money' did have the important effect of giving the islanders access to consumer goods in a manner typical of a western European territory. In 1990 Southern Italy's GDP was around half that of the north. For the first time in Sicily's history, though, the majority of islanders were able to purchase cars, TVs and fridges on a scale that vaguely approximated residents on the mainland.

This apparent affluence helped encourage an unprecedented wave of immigration towards the island. Since records began, in the aftermath of unification, Sicily had been a land characterised by the mass emigration of the local population. Towards the end of the '80s, though, this trend began to reverse as people from North Africa and Eastern Europe started to arrive. Many of these individuals were fleeing persecution and conflict of some kind. Most were looking to work, and enjoy the benefits of consumer capitalism that were lacking in their countries of origin. According to official figures, Sicily's foreign workforce rose from 14,700 to 67,000 over the course of the '80s, an increase of 352 percent. Considering the number of undocumented workers, though, the number is likely to be far higher than that. Most of these people found work cultivating tomatoes and other fruit and vegetables in the south of the island where the local landowners were more than happy to welcome them. These individuals tended to accept low pay and, unlike the local Sicilians, they were seen as less likely to mobilise into trade unions. Conditions were, and remain, inhuman in much of the island's agricultural sector. Slave labour practices are widespread, and for decades, reports of sexual assault, torture and imprisonment have surfaced on an almost weekly basis. This issue remains perhaps the most significant struggle for civil rights campaigners on the island.

Still, despite these harsh realities, migration has also proved beneficial both for some of the people who have arrived on the island, and for Sicily more generally. The communities are giving new life to places that might otherwise have been left abandoned. Take the port of Mazara del Vallo for example. Starting in the late 1970s small groups of Tunisian families began to move across the Mediterranean to make homes in the city. This was the first time since the twelfth century that a significant number of people from the Maghreb had settled in Sicily. While some migrants worked in the fields, many of these individuals began to set up businesses as independent fishermen catching bream and bass, and, more importantly, the local delicacy of *gamberi rossi* (red prawns) which are in fact some of the most valuable on earth. There's no denying these individuals have transformed the city for the better. When the migrants first moved in, many of the central neighbourhoods – including the historic Kasbah, which was bombed heavily during the war – were empty. Now this area is filled with restaurants, shisha bars, community centres and a mosque. Local artists have created placards and painted tiles which are spread across the entire city that depict the Aghlabid invasion and the years of conflict and coexistence with the Normans. While many of the migrants that arrived in Sicily in the '80s faced poverty and exploitation, places like Mazara are an equally important part of these peoples' story. The Kasbah is a powerful testimony to how, even in the darkest moments of Sicily's history, communities have succeeded in building a better future for themselves.

On 23 May 1992 Giovanni Falcone, one of Italy's most esteemed judges and prosecuting magistrates, was killed by a bomb when his convoy was targeted by members of Cosa Nostra on the motorway near Palermo Airport. The operation was meticulously planned. The assassins placed 400 kilos of explosives in advance under the tarmac and detonated the device from a nearby hillside by remote control. The attack wasn't just a practical hit, it was a theatrical performance, designed to undermine the very notion of justice on the island. Two months later, on 19 July, the mafia placed a second, related bomb in the car of one of Falcone's close associates, Paolo Borsellino. The device, which detonated outside his mother's house on a Sunday afternoon, killed him and five of his bodyguards. There had, as we've seen, been dozens of similar murders in the years leading up to these attacks. The assassinations of Falcone and Borsellino, though, were different. These were two of the highest-profile anti-mafia investigators in Italy, with important political connections in Rome. Their deaths would mark a turning point in the state's attitude towards Cosa Nostra, and, according to some rather optimistic voices, the start of a slow decline of mafia power on the island.

At the time of their murders Falcone and Borsellino had been following vital evidence that linked Cosa Nostra's activities to some of Italy's most prominent businesses and political lobby groups. The pair were well prepared in their research. In 1986, at the tail end of the Second Mafia War, they had helped lead one of the most important investigations into Cosa Nostra, in a series of legal cases known as the Maxi trials. The process itself did little to destabilise the mafia's daily operations under Riina. Nevertheless, the proceedings were a major intelligence leak for the organisation. Unlike previous approaches to tackling the organisation, which had been largely based on intimidation, Falcone and Borsellino emphasised the importance of talking and negotiating with those who had been involved in criminal activities. They were also the first magistrates to offer meaningful state protection to insiders willing to speak out about how the mafia works. As a result, informers like Tommaso Buscetta and Salvatore Contorno came forward, and offered unprecedented information about the internal hierarchies, codes and procedures used by Cosa Nostra as a whole. By the early '90s, thanks to leads provided by these sources, the pair of magistrates had begun to map the mafia's financial and political connections, and detail specific money-laundering scams.[10]

It's no coincidence that Falcone and Borsellino were killed when they were. In February 1992, three months before the former's death, the Italian judiciary had launched the largest anti-corruption movement in the republic's history: *mani pulite*. This public inquiry began when the national police caught Mario Chiesa, a prominent socialist politician, flushing thirty million lire of cash kickbacks down his toilet (about £15,000). In the months that followed, the investigators discovered that dozens of individuals from all the major political parties were involved in similar activities, and that the culture of bribery and payoffs was effectively present in all areas of Italian politics. The government – at the time a frail placeholding coalition – was facing the wrath of much of the Italian public. The media were in uproar, both about the assassinations themselves, and the scale of state corruption. With anti-political sentiment at a breaking point among the population as a whole, the prime minister, Giuliano Amato, decided that a direct assault against Cosa Nostra would provide an opportunity to demonstrate to the electorate that the state was genuinely working to clean up the system. On 25 July 1992 he therefore ordered 7,000 soldiers to Palermo, placing the Sicilian capital under what was, effectively, martial law. This was the first full-scale military operation against the mafia since the fascist era. That summer and autumn the police and armed forces worked together to arrest hundreds of mafiosi. Many of them agreed to share information with the state. This tactic yielded immediate results. On 15 January 1993 carabinieri in Palermo succeeded in arresting Totò Riina himself in his villa outside of the capital. After two decades of searching, the island's most notorious criminal leader was finally put behind bars.

In some respects this was a major victory for the state, though it did create bloody consequences of its own. In the spring and summer of 1993 Cosa Nostra retaliated Riina's arrest by launching a furious terror campaign on the Italian mainland. On 14 May the mafia detonated a bomb in Rome near the house of a journalist named Maurizio Costanzo who had made a joke about the boss on a TV talk show. The device injured twenty-seven passers-by. Cosa Nostra also targeted cultural heritage sites, presumably on the basis that this would weaken both the government's claim to protect the safety of its citizens, and the country's morale as a whole. On 27 May they planted an explosive device outside of Florence's Uffizi Gallery which killed five people. Another bomb exploded in July, in Milan's Via Palestro, killing a further five and heavily damaging two contemporary art museums.

For most of the twentieth century, Sicilians had tended to keep quiet about organised crime. From 1993 on, however, the state required citizens to actively demonstrate that they were against the mob or else face prosecution for collaboration. From the perspective of the government in Rome, this made sense. The reality among the island's population, though, was more complex. Many Sicilians still saw the local administration as effectively indistinguishable from Cosa Nostra. To make things more complicated still, some residents were critical of the anti-mafia itself, viewing this institution as an opportunity for careerist politicians to make a name for themselves. This was by no means a minority opinion. In 1987 Sicily's most respected novelist, Leonardo Sciascia, wrote a piece in the *Corriere della Sera* in which he implicitly accused Borsellino of harbouring fascist sympathies, and of having no ethical investment in tackling crime beyond the advancement of his own career. Sciascia was no supporter of Cosa Nostra. On the contrary, as a socialist he had spent a good deal of his life challenging the organisation's oppression of the working class. More than many other public intellectuals, however, Sciascia felt compelled to defend the argument that the mafia, or so he felt, was not just a criminal organisation with a formal hierarchy, but was the reflection of a deeper rebellious aspect of Sicilian culture. He even offered his own personal confession: 'It pains me to speak against the mafia', he wrote, 'because within me, as in every Sicilian, the residue of mafioso feeling is still alive ... when I struggle against the mafia I'm also struggling with myself; it is like a split, a laceration.'[11]

Sciascia died in 1989, well before Riina's arrest. In the political climate of the early '90s, though, many intellectuals pointed to these lines as evidence of exactly how Cosa Nostra had 'colonised' Sicily's identity and twisted it to the extent that it had become incompatible with democratic values. In the end it was left to another novelist, Andrea Camilleri, to communicate Sicilian scepticism towards the state in a form that was more palatable for the middle classes beyond the island. Camilleri is best known as the author of the Inspector Montalbano novels, which have sold in the millions and been translated into over 120 languages. Most international readers are attracted to these books for the same reason that cinemagoers enjoyed *Cinema Paradiso* in the '80s: these are escapist, fantasy-like tales, which present Sicily in a warm, affectionate light. They are light, easy holiday reads. In an Italian-Sicilian context, however, these works have had a serious social role. Camilleri was the first author to offer a truly affirmative notion of Sicilian identity that celebrated the island-ers' values without sugar-coating the realities of the mafia. The heroes of most Italian police dramas tend to be motivated by a fairly banal, implicitly Catholic, sense of good and evil. Montal-bano, though, is a chaotic figure. Rather than idolising the law itself, the inspector is motivated by an intuitive sense of right and wrong, a 'natural' sense of justice. In *The Shape of Water* (1994), to take just one example, Montalbano spends much of the plot talking with an old friend, a Cosa Nostra sympathiser, who aids him in his investigation. At the novel's close he even allows a vendetta to take place on the basis that it is beyond his remit to intervene. Ethically ambiguous moments like these provided an important counterbalance to the black-and-white moralism that the state was encouraging at the time. More generally, though, the Montalbano stories tend to evoke a far broader range of themes than criminality. They celebrate the island's food and music, its history, landscape and the diversity of the inhabitants. Most importantly of all, Camilleri took the decision to write his books in dialect and, in doing so, proved to the reading public that Sicilian, the language that, albeit in a quite different form, gave birth to the sonnet itself, was every bit as capable of liter-ary expression as the variants of Italian spoken on the mainland.

Camilleri's work has had an important role in redeeming Sicilians from some of the more aggressive stereotypes that have been levelled at them since the '80s. Unfortunately, how-ever, democratic political actors, particularly those on the left, have struggled to translate this fragile civic confidence into a programme for change. In 1991, following the collapse of the Soviet Union, the PCI disbanded and fragmented into a coali-tion of various liberal organisations. The most important of these in Sicily was La Rete, a local party which had a quite specific remit: to tackle corruption within the regional administration. The party organised large-scale peaceful demonstrations against Cosa Nostra. While it gained some influence in local politics as a result, most notably Leoluca Orlando's election to mayor of Palermo as its representative in 1993, it never translated this into national success. Instead it was the Milan-based media mogul Silvio Berlusconi who benefitted most from the changes that were taking place in Italian society. At the start of his political career Berlusconi was an ardent critic of both the DC and PCI. He spoke openly against the mafia, and, somewhat ironically given the scandals that would characterise his career, criticised the corrupt elite of both of the old parties. His main enemies, though, were a mysterious group of magistrates – 'communist prosecutors' as he called them – that he claimed were rigging the *mani pulite* process against innocent people. In 1993 he created a new party, Forza Italia, named after a popular football chant – 'Go Italy!' – to capitalise on the anti-political mood. Cosa Nostra almost certainly supported his candidacy. Journalists have since revealed that several members of Berlusconi's party, such as Marcello Dell'Utri, have worked with the mafia in the past. Some have even claimed he was in direct contact with Riina in prison. The extent of this influence, though, shouldn't be overstated. Berlusconi was not a mafia boss, and his links to the organisation remain mysterious. Indeed, even if the mafia were involved in intimidating citizens to vote for him – as the high-ranking turncoat Antonino Giuffrè has claimed – this does not account for the scale of his popularity.[12] When Berlusconi led a right-wing coalition to victory in the general election of 1994, securing 42 percent of the vote, Sicilians were among his most vocal supporters.

On paper Berlusconi's modest success on the island was improbable. The leader of Forza Italia was, after all, closely linked to the financial and industrial elite in Northern Italy, and throughout his political career he maintained a close relationship with members of the right-wing Lega Nord (which in the '90s and early '00s was a separatist party aiming to 'liberate' the wealthy region of Lombardy and its surrounding area from what its supporters considered the 'vampiric' south). Berlusconi's rhetoric, though, did much to temper the potential toxicity of these alliances. Unlike other politicians, and particularly those in the centre-left in Tuscany and central Italy who have tended to look down rather condescendingly at Sicily, Berlusconi championed the island's Mediterranean identity. When campaigning, he cleverly adopted an almost Montalbano-like persona. He sang traditional southern folk songs and praised the climate, hospitality and cuisine of these often-maligned regions. By subverting the cultural norms that the northern elite had established over centuries, Berlusconi appealed to the anti-institutional aspect of Sicilian culture, and made his opponents look boring and old-fashioned by comparison.

Of course the mogul did have a more tangible weapon in his arsenal: his grip over the media. During his period in office Berlusconi was effectively in control of over 90 percent of the Italian television audience, both through his MediaSet empire and his influence over the state broadcaster RAI. At the time some of his critics labelled this a kind of 'videocracy'. What they often failed to see, however, was that his control over TV was not purely top-down in nature, it was closely linked to a pseudo-democratic revolution that was taking place in Italian society. It's true that Berlusconi relied a good deal on the major networks. What's often forgotten, though, is that he also oversaw an enormous expansion of small local channels which provided citizens with a sense of voice. This form of soft power was particularly effective in the southern regions. Throughout the '90s a whole new network of stations developed in Sicily and Naples in particular. Many of them broadcast music by *neomelodici*, working-class singers who fused traditional Arab-inflected Mediterranean folk with '80s synth pop. These songs often describe the frank realities of living alongside, or as part of, the mafia. Many of the artists have themselves been associated with organised crime groups, and Cosa Nostra still controls many of the record labels, management companies and broadcasting satellites. Most of the *neomelodici* take their aesthetic coordinates from Berlusconi's TV channels, and tend to sport fake tans, sequined bikinis and Botoxed lips. It's easy to laugh at this, as indeed many centre-left supporters did in the late '90s. Doing so, though, neglects to appreciate the sense of genuine ownership that people felt, and still feel, in relation to this cultural scene. Berlusconi did not need to offer concrete policy proposals to Sicilians. Instead he simply shaped the island's mass culture to match the image of his own cavalier persona by cleverly exploiting these decentralised forms of cultural propaganda.

At the dawn of the new millennium the centre-left in central Italy, in Tuscany and Emilia Romagna, posed a constant threat to the prime minister. In the south, by contrast, Forza Italia quickly took up the mantle of postmodern successor of the DC. Indeed, Berlusconi kept control of Sicily for the duration of the first decade of the '00s. As a result it was left to cultural practitioners to offer the only real resistance. Street artists started creating explicitly political works, painting murals on illegally built houses, and defacing mafia-owned properties. Hip-hop musicians, like Stokka and MadBuddy, released albums that attacked the government and neoliberal elite, most notably on *Palermo Centrale* (2001). Authors, like Michele Perriera, turned to science fiction to describe the ecological degradation of the island's rivers and coasts. The most enigmatic of all these figures, though, were two film directors, Daniele Ciprì and Franco Maresco. Throughout Berlusconi's rule the duo began to develop a strange, idiosyncratic art form in which they appropriated tropes from the MediaSet world and twisted them to present a nihilistic, postapocalyptic pastiche of the country. Their most famous works are *Cinico TV* (1992–96), a bizarre black-and-white sketch show inspired by the work of Samuel Beckett, and the feature film *Totò che visse due volte* (1998), which offers a blasphemous retelling of the Gospels and ends with Jesus being abducted by the mafia and melted in an acid bath. Italy's film council actually banned the latter of these works on its release stating that it was an affront to the dignity of 'the Sicilian people, the Italian world, and all of humanity'.[13]

The sheer misanthropy of Ciprì and Maresco's work is a good indicator of the poor health of Sicilian culture at the dawn of the twenty-first century. The political polarisation of the postwar era had been replaced by a profound, widespread sense of fatalism. While Cosa Nostra had moved away from its more overtly violent activities, the organisation still had an influence over much of public life and had settled into a new rhythm of electioneering, bribery and blackmail. Decades, indeed over a century, of living in fear of the organisation had taken their toll on Sicilians. Many islanders saw the idea that politics could transform their lives for the better as a ridiculous proposition. In 2010, the Palermo-born writer and philosopher Fulvio Abbate recorded a YouTube video in which he confessed a perverse wish to see the Sicilian capital blown off the face of the earth by a napalm bomb. While a few outspoken patriots criticised him as being 'anti-Sicilian', thousands of islanders agreed, and the clip went viral. The message was clear. The political left was dead. Berlusconism had blocked all possibility of serious civic action. Progressive change had become impossible. At least, that's how it seemed.

Epilogue
'They Are Our Salvation' (2013–Present)

Nobody, myself included, needs to demonstrate how deeply Mediterranean identity is rooted in Sicily, [the island] was the cradle of grand, rich civilisations, from the westerners and Christians of modern Europe, to those of Islam and Judaism ... Just as Brussels, and to a certain extent Strasburg, represent the heart of European identity so Sicily could be an appropriate place to forge and valorise a Mediterranean identity.

Abraham Yehoshua, novelist, 2017

When I arrived in Sicily I felt immediately at home, there was something about it that reminded me of Africa. There are some parts of Palermo, such as Ballaro market, that seem like Nigeria to me. The cultures all mix there and become something united.

Chris Obehi, Italo-Nigerian migrant and musician, 2020

On 3 October 2013 an overcrowded ship caught fire en route from Libya to Europe and capsized in the Strait of Sicily. More than 350 people were killed. The individuals on board – hailing in the main from Eritrea, Ghana and Somalia – had each paid over 1,000 euros to traffickers to secure their passage. These people, without exception, were fleeing debt, war and poverty. But they were also moving consciously towards something: an idea of peace, of safety, of a roof, of dignity. Deaths in the central Mediterranean had been steadily rising in the years leading up to the events of that autumn. The first major wave of refugees began in 2011, when NATO forces ousted Muammar Gaddafi from power in Libya using Sicily as an airbase. This tragedy, however, stood out among other, smaller, capsizes. Given the size of the death toll, public officials began to talk openly about an urgent, and growing, humanitarian emergency along Europe's southern borders. In a matter of days hundreds of journalists set up camp in the port of Lampedusa, a quiet fishing town on a small island to the south of Sicily. From there they broadcast footage around the world of dead bodies, terrified children and masked figures in white overalls. These were the origins of Europe's so-called 'refugee crisis'.

More than 170,000 individuals made the crossing from North Africa into Sicily in 2014. They arrived at a tense moment. That year, Sicily, like much of Italy, was in the midst of a profound economic crisis. At a regional level, the situation was comparable to that of Greece. Unemployment was at 22 percent, rising to 52 percent among young people, and a third of families were living in a state of poverty. Unsurprisingly the local authorities struggled to cope with this new influx of people. In many cases the refugees were left in limbo. The state placed unaccompanied minors in holding facilities which were lacking in specialised medical staff; older migrants were forced to wait interminably for asylum documents, for permits to stay and work. The scale of this problem, though, and its coincidence with the economic crisis, inaugurated a new era in Italian politics. Initially the government's response seemed promising. In 2013, following the tragedy in the sea around Lampedusa, a centre-left coalition, led by Matteo Renzi, authorised a rescue mission named 'Operation Mare Nostrum', which permitted the Italian coastguard to venture into international waters to assist all boats in difficulty. While this was a small-scale initiative, and other forms of aid were sorely lacking, it nevertheless saved 150,000 lives in 2013–14.[1] The mission, though, was short-lived. EU member states refused to provide further funding to support an operation which, they argued, constituted a 'pull factor' and which would encourage more people to make the treacherous journey.

Over the following years, the European Commission gradually shifted their priorities from the need for 'search and rescue' missions to 'border policing'. In 2014 Operation Mare Nostrum was replaced by an EU Frontex–funded initiative called 'Triton' which obliged the coastguard to limit their rescues to a narrower area of water. Over the next two years, as a result of this, deaths in the central Mediterranean spiked to an all-time high of 7,000 people. Still, some politicians called for a further tightening of borders. On the Italian mainland Matteo Salvini, the head of the Lega, began to demand tougher measures to stop people from setting out on these journeys. He quickly began to rise in the polls. In an effort to appease his growing base the centre-left began to deport hundreds of individuals, but this served little function other than to alienate many of their own supporters. In 2018 the Italians elected Salvini to government where, as a minor coalition partner, he took on the role of interior minister. While he was ousted the following year, during a botched attempt to seize the majority for the Lega, he used his short time in office to order the total closure of all of Italy's ports and, in June that year, forbid any refugees from disembarking on Italian soil.

Throughout these grim developments Sicilians have consistently opposed the callousness of the political class. Despite the limitations imposed by the EU, for example, fishermen based in Sicily's southern ports like Augusta and Pozzallo have continued to rescue people in international waters, and many residents in those towns have taken refugees into their own homes. While around 30 percent of mainland Italians plan to vote for the Lega in the future (as of winter 2020) their support on the island is just 5 percent. Nevertheless, this has not been a peaceful period. In 2014 thousands of Sicilians took to the streets under the banner of *forconi* (the pitchforks), to protest against European austerity measures. The protesters, who were comprised of various precarious peoples, from logistics and factory workers to farmers and the young unemployed, rioted for several months and blocked the island's motorways. One of their main demands was for an Italian exit from the EU. Fascist groups like CasaPound attempted to capitalise on the unrest, blaming the refugees for the economic crisis, but they failed to galvanise considerable support. Instead, 48 percent of Sicilians gravitated towards the Five Star Movement (M5S), a populist 'anti-establishment' force which came to power as part of the 2018 coalition, and which has promised to 'clean up' Italian politics by instigating a 'direct democratic' revolution. This party is problematic to put it mildly. Its parliamentarians have perpetuated various conspiracy theories over the years, in particular those propagated by the global anti-vaccine lobby, and many of its representatives in Rome have close links to the Lega. Nevertheless, the nature of this grassroots movement marks a shift from the Berlusconi years. In the '90s and early '00s, Sicilians were, on the surface, happy to capitulate uncritically with neoliberalism. Today, thousands are actively pledging their support for a force that, in theory if not in practice, has promised to end precarious labour practices, tackle inequality and confront the climate emergency.

The most promising developments in current Sicilian politics, though, are taking place at a local and municipal level. It's here that civil society groups are most successfully integrating the struggle for migrant rights with those of the island's official residents. Leoluca Orlando, the mayor of Palermo, has had an important role in this. In 2014, as refugee boats began to increase in frequency, he decided to demilitarise the city's port and transformed the seafront into an event space which, through a series of talks, concerts and art exhibitions, has been promoting 'cultural dialogue'. As EU leaders argued about pull factors, Orlando made the case that those attempting to close borders should be put on 'a new Nuremberg trial' for the massacre they were condoning. In 2015 Orlando began to argue for the abolition of residency permits across the EU to ensure that economic migrants, who often fail to qualify for asylum, can have access to welfare services. To reinforce this demand his administration introduced a 'Palermo card', a hypothetical document which outlined the holder's moral right to free movement. In recognition of this the local government began granting residency to new arrivals even where they did not fit the criteria determined by the national rules in Rome. Despite the severity of economic crisis, many Palermitans supported this stance. Orlando was re-elected to serve his fifth (non-consecutive) mandate in 2017 with a comfortable majority. Since then he has continued to oppose the rightward turn in Italian politics. He has, among other things, created a bureaucratic loophole which protects migrants' rights to access education and healthcare and which guarantees all people forced to occupy buildings, whether documented or not, access to water and energy. Most dramatically of all, when Salvini made his decision to close the ports in 2018 Orlando simply refused to obey the edict, declaring: 'Palermo in ancient Greek meant "complete port". We have always welcomed rescue boats and vessels who saved lives at sea. We will not stop now.' Other mayors, in Syracuse and Lampedusa, quickly followed suit.

These principled, defiant leaders are helping re-energise Sicily's civil society. After decades of sporadic struggle against Cosa Nostra, the islanders are mobilising, with increasing confidence, to call for democracy, economic justice and the recognition of universal human rights. The best example of this can be seen in Ballarò, Palermo's old Arab souk. For much of the twentieth century this area was a hotbed of mafia activity. Since 2013, however, it has come to develop its own distinctive democratic culture. It's a place where many of the most progressive aspects of Sicilian history – its cosmopolitanism, innovative grassroots movements and hybrid artistic creativity – are re-emerging in the present day. The community itself is remarkably mixed. About 35 percent of Ballarò's residents are of migrant backgrounds and include people from Ghana, Gambia, Nigeria, Somalia, Pakistan, Afghanistan, Bangladesh and Mauritius as well as Romanians, Bulgarians and generations of Sicilians. At least twenty-five languages are regularly spoken in the area. The main businesses are fruit and vegetable stalls, bakeries and street food stands. Thanks to the new influx of migrants, though, the corner shops are, for the first time since Spanish rule, overflowing with African and Middle Eastern ingredients such as aromatised waters, freekeh and manioc. The residents are working together to renovate houses and public spaces. In recent years they've set up barbers and laundrettes, sports facilities and art studios. The area is home to a social centre, Porco Rosso, which, among other activities, assists new arrivals with residency and welfare applications and provides free language lessons. Molti-Volti, a self-described 'Siculo-ethnic' restaurant and co-working space, promotes fusion food and affordable collective dining as a means of encouraging social mixing. Their founders describe the neighbourhood as 'a laboratory' that 'represents all the elements of the future society'.

If Ballarò is anything to go by, Sicily's future might indeed be more tolerant and more ethnically and culturally diverse than any time in its recent past. Whether this will be sustainable in the long term, of course, will depend on whether more powerful political actors can step in to defend the experiment from the threat of criminal violence which, unfortunately, remains a serious problem. In 2016 a mafioso named Emanuele Rubino shot a Gambian student, Yusupha Susso, in the head, not far from the market. Fortunately, Susso survived, though he was left in a temporary coma from which he is still recovering. While the incident itself was horrific, the local community's reaction gives some cause for optimism. In the past, acts like these were commonplace and, in most cases, met with silence. Following the attack against Susso, however, many residents and traders took to the streets to speak out. Some of them went even further. In 2017 ten Bengali shopkeepers and a Tunisian vendor who had previously been handing over protection money to Cosa Nostra refused to make further payments. Supported by a grassroots anti-mafia group called Addiopizzo, these individuals took the brave step of denouncing Rubino to the police along with a number of his associates. In April 2019, thanks to their efforts, the courts condemned Rubino and eight other men who ran rackets in the market to a combined total of sixty years in prison for the crimes of extortion, mafia membership and racial discrimination.[2]

This example alone demonstrates how much the Sicilian capital has changed in the past decade. After centuries of adhering to the tacit law of *omertà*, local residents, both old and new, are working, in dialogue with state institutions, to transform society from the bottom up. In the past decade more than 650,000 refugees have arrived in Sicily. While the vast majority of them have moved on to Northern Italy and other countries to meet family members or find better work prospects, some have put down roots on the island. This is not just limited to Palermo. Across Sicily migrants are transforming the social fabric of the island. In Catania, groups of Gambian citizens are working to renovate the neighbourhood of San Berillo which the local administration had previously abandoned to squalor and decay. In medium-sized cities like Messina, Syracuse and Trapani, migrant-led associations are organising protests against the poor conditions in refugee camps, in an effort to call out mafia involvement in the sector and ensure new arrivals can become active protagonists in shaping the future of life on the island. Across the countryside families are adopting child refugees and, with the assistance of EU funds, are teaching them the skills they will need to contribute to civil society. The very presence of these young Africans and Asians is giving new life to underpopulated parts of the interior that, as a result of generations of emigration, were previously struggling to survive. As one resident of Sutera, a crumbling hillside village, recently put it: 'We have been dealing with integration for 2,000 years ... if then Sutera was the "salvation" for many foreigners, well, guess what? Today, the true salvation of Sutera is the refugees.'[3]

These developments are remarkable in their own right. They're even more profound when considered in the larger arc of this island's history. For centuries Sicilians have struggled to assert their autonomy in the face of Catholic monoculture, Italian nationalism, fascism and organised crime. Now, as a new migrant population begins to establish itself, they have begun to envisage a different kind of society. Inevitably, many people still see Sicily as a frontier between Europe and Africa. The history and present of the island, though, show how limiting this kind of logic is. Throughout its ancient and medieval past, but also during its fraught modernity, Sicily has thrived most when it has looked outward, openly, to the rest of the world.

Despite economic woes, that have now been exacerbated by the outbreak of Covid-19, more and more Sicilians are coming to recognise that accommodation, dialogue and respect for differences will be vital components in building a more peaceful and prosperous future. In Palermo, Leoluca Orlando is about to reach the end of his term and it remains unclear who will step in to continue fighting for cosmopolitan values within the political establishment. His vision of the capital, though, is a powerful testimony to the kind of thinking that the next generation might fruitfully turn to if they are to save the island from repeating the horrors of its recent past. In his own words: 'Palermo is not a European city. It's a Middle Eastern metropolis in Europe. It's not Frankfurt nor Berlin, with all respect to them. We are proud of being Middle Eastern and we are proud of being European. We have experienced the tragic and tiring journey to attain legality against organized crime, and today we want to be the reference point for the effective exercise of civil and social rights. Thanks to migrants we are recovering our history and our harmony.'[4]

Acknowledgements

I began working on this book in 2014 in a tiny flat just off Via Roma in Palermo, where the traffic was so loud it was impossible to sleep. It was there, during some insomniac summer nights, that I started getting clued-up on Sicilian history, slowly at first, and then obsessively. I wouldn't have been there at all if it wasn't for Federico Campagna, whose enthusiasm about the island's culture ignited my own interest. His advice was instrumental in getting this project off the ground. John Merrick did heroic work in decrypting my first drafts and making them more focused and accessible. I'm grateful to him, and to the rest of the team at Verso, for engaging so profoundly with the ideas I set out to communicate.

I wrote most of this book in Florence, where I now live, while taking regular trips back down to Sicily. I was able to do so thanks to the staff at the Palermo town hall and library as well as the organisers of Manifesta12 and BAM, who invited me to cover their respective festivals. I'm indebted to several guides for their tips, but Francesco and Fina from the Mirabilia Arab House in Mazara del Vallo, and Cristiana at La Casa del

Gelsomino in Ragusa, offered particularly fascinating anecdotes about food and folklore that I'm delighted to be able to broadcast more widely.

Over the years several editors have provided me with a platform to test out arguments about cosmopolitanism. En Liang Khong, Georgette Jupe and Marina Benjamin stand out. Many others helped with queries about translation, though Marco Delfiol was my Babel fish. Colleagues at European Alternatives and Krytyka Polityczna helped refine elements of the narrative, as did Dan Hancox, Niki Seth Smith, Ismail Einashe and Marina Warner. Daniel Trilling taught me a great lesson in journalistic ethics during a trip to Augusta's *scuola verde* for refugee children. Paul Ginsborg opened doors to some vital archives, while Anthony Barnett and Judith Herrin offered invaluable guidance on all aspects of the publishing process.

I'm especially grateful to my parents, Ann and Dougal Mackay, for their love and support, Jack Alexandroff and Oliver Rahman for their brotherly comradeship, and Elena Dan, for being such a wonderful travel companion, and putting up with me talking at length about King Roger II over many a dinner. Echoes of our conversations mark every page of this book.

Notes

Introduction

1 Kapka Kassabova, *Border: A Journey to the Centre of Europe*, London: Granta, 2017, p. xviii.

1. The Liquid Continent (800 BC–826 AD)

1 Homer, *The Odyssey*, trans. A. T. Murray, London: Heinemann, 1919, pp. 311–13.

2 In fact, there are traces of even earlier civilisation in Sicily, such as the cave paintings at Addaura, near Palermo, which show sacrificial figures, and which have been dated to approximately 6000 BC. According to some historians, the so-called Stentinello culture – a neolithic society with elaborate burial rituals, active around 4000 BC – was also present in Sicily, and may have built the extraordinary megalithic temples on nearby Malta.

3 It's worth reiterating here that 'Greek', as understood in early antiquity, is a broad cultural and linguistic trope and does not refer to a defined racial group. Neither was this 'Greek' culture confined to peoples with origins in the geographical area of the modern nation-state that goes by that name. The new Aegean colonisers did not impose an external belief system on the other islanders; on the contrary, they developed the stories that we now recognise as 'Greek' together with these groups.

4   Hesiod, *Theogony and Works and Days*, trans. M. L. West, New York: Oxford University Press, 1988, p. 27.

5   See, for example, Ovid, *The Metamorphoses*, trans. Horace Gregory, New York: Viking Press, 1958, p. 73.

6   Pindar, *Olympian Odes, Pythian Odes*, trans. William H. Race, Cambridge: Harvard University Press, 1997, p. 215.

7   Local residents have long maintained that this stream is, in fact, the very same that Arethusa, the aforementioned naiad, used to escape Alpheios's grasp during her flight from the Peloponnese.

8   This term does not, as is commonly understood in modern English, refer only to a 'bad' ruler, but rather to an individual with no hereditary claim to power.

9   Edmund Stewart, *Greek Tragedy on the Move: The Birth of a Panhellenic Art Form c. 500–300 BC*, New York: Oxford University Press, 2017, p. 54.

10   Kathleen Freeman, *Ancilla to the Pre-Socratic Philosophers: A Complete Translation of the Fragments in Diels*, Cambridge: Harvard University Press, 1996, p. 36.

11   James Davidson, *Courtesans and Fishcakes: The Consuming Passions of Classical Athens*, London: HarperCollins, 1997, p. 5.

12   Ibid., p. 5.

13   Plato, *The Platonic Epistles*, trans. J. Harward, Cambridge: Cambridge University Press, 1932, pp. 117–18.

14   Dante Alighieri, *Inferno*, trans. Steve Ellis, London: Vintage, 2007, canto 12, line 17.

15   Just outside of Syracuse there is a limestone cave known by the nickname 'the Ear of Dionysius', where the tyrant apparently ordered all those suspected of conspiracy to be subjected to merciless punishments. Legend maintains that the acoustic served to amplify the individuals' screams such that they could be heard across the ancient city.

16   Plutarch, *Lives*, trans. Bernadotte Perrin, vol. VI, Cambridge: Harvard University Press, 1954, p. 11.

17   The real Gorgias offered some rather nuanced views on political discourse, particularly the importance of paradox. His lost work 'On Nature or the Non-Existent', of which only fragments remain, presents a radically sceptical view of the world, starting with the premise, so often wrongly considered as a 'postmodern' novelty, that 'nothing exists'.

18 Plato, *Gorgias*, trans. Terence Irwin, Oxford: Oxford University Press, 1979, p. 23.

19 Ibid., p. 106.

20 See, for example, Cicero's invective against Verres in Cicero, *Select Orations*, trans. C. D. Yonge, New York: Harper & Brothers, 1877, p. 533.

21 It's thought that in the first and second centuries BC slaves made up to as much as 30 percent of the Sicilian population. In theory these individuals had more rights under Rome than they did in Greek city-states, as from the late Republican era they could potentially become citizens. The intensification of agricultural production, though, clearly placed new, unsustainable demands on those unfortunate enough to belong to this class.

22 Cicero, *Tusculan Disputations*, trans. A. E. Douglas, vol. V, Warminster: Aris & Phillips, 1990, p. 115.

23 The revolt of Boadicea in Britain (60 AD) and the continual rebellion among the Germanic tribes are two important indicators that the *pax romana* was, in fact, more of a propaganda campaign than reality. In the case of Sicily, however, this was indeed a relatively peaceful time.

24 According to this theory, Christianity arrived in Sicily via Syracuse, where Jewish refugees fled to escape persecution in the first century AD. At the time the separation between Christianity and Judaism was rather vague, and many of the arrivals would have seen the Messiah as a renewal of their own faith rather than a radical new rupture. The split between Judaism and Christianity became more pronounced following the refusal of the latter to intervene openly in the Bar Kokhba revolt against the Romans in 132–36.

25 These gruesome stories have captured the imagination of believers far beyond the island. In the seventeenth century in particular, baroque artists, including Lorenzo Lippi and Francisco de Zurbarán, dedicated paintings to St Agatha. Caravaggio, meanwhile, depicted the *Burial of St Lucy* in 1608, emphasising the saint's mother prostrate before her dead daughter. The piece ranks alongside the artist's greatest works.

26 The central nave and two aisles provided a space for a large congregation, and the apse a place to focus on the idea of God. Christian architects often added two chapels on either side, to reflect the symbolism of the Trinity.

2. The Polyglot Kingdom (826–1182)

1   Over the subsequent decades the Arabs used these structures to demark new administrative boundaries: the province around the landing point was, predictably, called Val di Mazara, that around Palermo, Val Demone, and the unruly area that had previously belonged to Syracuse, the Val di Noto. These divisions would continue to influence the island's political life for centuries to come.

2   See: 'Violenze e scene di ferocia durante la conquista?' in Salvatore Tramontana, *L'isola di Allah*, Milano: Einaudi, 2014, pp. 61–67.

3   One of the most emblematic texts that would come from the Arab expansion more generally, is the *summa totius haeresis saracenorum* (anthology of Saracen heresies) written in the twelfth century by the French abbot, and later saint, Pietro di Cluny. The author describes, among other things, how: 'Vomiting forth almost all of the excrement of the old heresies, [Mohammed] denies the trinity ... the plotting of the devil, first spread by Arius, then promoted by this Satan, will be completed by the antichrist, in complete accordance with the intentions of the devil.' Summa 208, as quoted in Alberto Ferreiro, ed., *The Devil Heresy and Witchcraft in the Middle Ages*, Boston: Brill, 1998, p. 359.

4   For Theodosius's full account see Lancia Di Brolo and Domenico Gaspare, *Storia della Chiesa in Sicilia*, Palermo: Lao, 1880, p. 250.

5   Quoted from the Arabic and French in *A Companion to Medieval Palermo: The History of a Mediterranean City from 600 to 1500*, Leiden and Boston: Brill, 2013, p. 57.

6   Di Brolo and Gaspare, *Storia della Chiesa in Sicilia*, p. 250.

7   An unsubstantiated urban legend maintains that the popular street food, *Pani ca meusa* (spleen sandwiches fried in lard), can be traced to the Jewish community's taste for kosher offcuts. Whatever the truth of this, while non-Muslims were forced to pay higher taxes, all religious groups were free to trade and shared some degree of prosperity.

8   Evidence of this building's tenth-century function is evident in a marble pillar just to the left of the building's entrance which is inscribed with Arabic verse from the seventh surah of the Qur'an.

9   The technological innovations that were taking place in Baghdad contributed directly to the island's development. The expansion of industry, for example, including hemp, cotton silk and paper, was made possible

by the introduction of a new kind of automated crank. Similarly, water-wheels improved crop yields and helped with the rearing of animals.

10   Amato di Montecassino, a Benedictine monk, provides a rather bleaker account of old people 'dying like animals', the young vanishing 'suddenly' and children passing away unbaptised, as 'pagans'. See: 'Colture estensive e pane quotidiano' in Tramontana, *L'isola di Allah*, pp. 137–43.

11   Perhaps the best emblem of this is the *cassata*, a marzipan cheesecake which some attribute to the Arabs despite the fact that no recipe for this dish exists before the seventeenth century. While many delicacies, like *caponata*, deep-fried aubergines, bear some similarity to plates served in the Middle East, the versions people consume today have little to do with those from the early medieval period and were more likely developed under later Spanish rule.

12   Every summer in San Vito Lo Capo, a beach resort to the west of Palermo, chefs from Sicily, North Africa and the Middle East come together to participate in the Mediterranean's largest couscous festival. The most popular dish among the islanders themselves is *couscous alla trapanese* in which the grains are drowned in an aromatic seafood stock and topped with fried fish.

13   Sadly, many today continue to emphasise the crusader aspect of the Norman conquest. A good example is the Palio degli Normani, a jousting tournament based around a historical re-enactment of Roger and Robert's initial conquest of the island, which takes place in August each year in the small town of Piazza Armerina. Vast crowds cheer as Christian 'knights', i.e., athletes from the various neighbourhoods, compete to see who can best 'attack' a series of immobile wooden planks which are dressed up as 'Saracen warriors'.

14   Ibn Hamdis, 'Versi sulla terra perduta' in *Poeti arabi di Sicilia*, Messina: Mesogea, 2005, p. 35, translation my own.

15   Quoted in Hubert Houben, *Roger II of Sicily: A Ruler between East and West*, trans. Graham A. Loud and Diane Milburn, Cambridge: Cambridge University Press, 2002, p. 55.

16   These were replaced in the king's late reign by a silver coin, the *ducalis*, which was, in turn, based on models from Constantinople.

17   See: Charles Burnett's essay 'Reading the Sciences' in *The European Book in the Twelfth Century*, ed. Erik Kwakkel and Rodney Thomson, Cambridge: Cambridge University Press, 2018, p. 268.

18 Roger and Al-Idrisi also presented their results in the form of a large silver planisphere. Unfortunately, though, this was lost in subsequent decades; most likely melted down into currency. Nevertheless, the fact that the *Book of Roger* itself is constructed around a 'curved' framing suggests a primitive understanding of gravity.

19 Ibid., p. 17.

20 Quoted in *From Arabye to Engelond: Medieval Studies in Honour of Mahmoud Manzalaoui*, ed. A. E. Christa Canitz and Gernot R. Weiland, Ottawa: University of Ottawa Press, 1999, p. 16.

21 Ahmed Djebbar, 'Philosophy and Science in Islam: A Fruitful Cohabitation', in *Arab Muslim Civilization in the Mirror of the Universal*, Paris: UNESCO, 2010, p. 257.

22 Ibn Qalāqis, *Splendori e misteri di Sicilia*, trans. Adalgisa De Simone, Messina: Rubbettino, 1996, pp. 88–91.

23 Muhammed Ibn Ahmad Ibn Jubayr, *The Travels of Ibn Jubayr*, trans. R. J. C. Broadhurst, London: Jonathan Cape, 1952, pp. 179–80.

24 Near the city walls there was an entertainment district which hosted jousting tournaments and a zoo boasting an exotic aviary. At the time this was considered the triumph of a city which was at the very peak of its prosperity. In Ibn Jubayr's words: 'Over esplanades, through doors, and across royal courts they lead us, gazing at the towering palaces, well-set piazzas and gardens, and the ante-chambers given to officials. All this amazed our eyes and dazzled our minds.' Ibid., pp. 346–7.

25 See: Sulamith Brodbeck, 'Monreale from its Origin to the End of the Middle Ages', in *A Companion to Medieval Palermo: The History of a Mediterranean City from 600 to 1500*, Leiden and Boston: Brill, 2013, p. 386.

3. The Anti-Christ of Palermo (1182–1347)

1 In his essay 'The Artistic Culture of Twelfth-Century Sicily, with a Focus on Palermo', William Tronzo argues that the Normans' architectural feats were 'just' elaborate stylistic experiments and 'not the representation of intrinsic beliefs'. He is by no means alone in holding this belief. See: *Sicily and the Mediterranean: Migration, Exchange, Reinvention*, New York: Palgrave Macmillan, 2015, p. 70.

2 See, for example, David Abulafia, *Frederick II: A Medieval Emperor*, New York: Oxford University Press, 1992.

3   Jacob Burckhardt, *The State as a Work of Art*, London: Penguin, 2010, p. 9.

4   Friedrich Nietzsche, *Beyond Good and Evil*, trans. Walter Kaufmann, New York: Vintage, 1966, p. 112.

5   Friedrich Nietzsche, trans. Judith Norman, 'Ecce Homo: How to Become What You Are', in Aaron Ridley and Judith Norman, eds, *The Anti-Christ, Ecce Homo, Twilight of the Idols and Other Writings*, Cambridge: Cambridge University Press, 2005, p. 127.

6   Giovanni Gentile, *Il Pensiero Italiano Del Rinascimento*, Firenze: Sansoni, 1939, p. 85.

7   Ernst Kantorowicz, *Frederick the Second 1194–1250*, trans. E. O. Lorimer, New York: Frederick Ungar, 1957, p. 27.

8   A few years previously, in 1225, Frederick had married the princess Yolande of Jerusalem in an effort to secure his own claim. Despite the fact that Yolande died following childbirth in April 1228 Frederick continued to present himself as a legitimate king of the city.

9   While there was no siege or military conflict, the proceedings were hardly free from controversy. The nobility of Jerusalem and the leaders of both Islam and Christianity heavily contested Frederick's subsequent rule.

10 This evocative English interpretation is taken from Tony Nardi's reading on the CBC podcast 'The Wonder of the World: Frederick II, Part 1', 30:04, CBC.ca. A written source can be found in William Jones, *The History of the Christian Church from the Birth of Christ to the XVIII Century*, Dover: Trustees of the Freewill Baptist Connection, 1837, p. 291.

11 John Ruskin, *The Complete Works* vol. 21, 'The Pleasures of England', New York: The Kelmscott Society, 1885, p. 180.

12 Much of this text extended and refined premises that Frederick had set up in 1220 in the Assizes of Capua. The full document is available to read in English translation as *The Liber Augustalis or Constitutions of Melfi Promulgated by the Emperor Frederick II for the Kingdom of Sicily in 1231*, trans. James M. Powell, New York: Syracuse University Press, 1971.

13 As with the language itself, it is impossible to identify precisely when such stories developed in the forms we know them today. Most of the modern tales, though, come from research conducted by the anthropologist Giuseppe Pitrè, who travelled across the island in the nineteenth

century to transcribe its oral traditions. See: Giuseppe Pitrè, *Fiabe, novelle e racconti siciliani*, ed. Jack Zipes, Firenze: Donzelli, 2013.

14   See: Salvatore Marrone, *Giufà e Pitrè. Cultura e ironia*, Roma: Aletti, 2016, p. 1.

15   This 'title' was bestowed on Frederick by Matthew Paris, an English historian, in his *Chronica Majora* (1250) where he wrote: 'Obiit insuper stupor mundi Fredericus, die Sanctae Luciae in Apulia.' Quoted in Richard Vaughan, *Matthew Paris*, Cambridge: Cambridge University Press, 1979, p. 60.

16   John of Procida, *Sicily's Rebellion against King Charles*, trans. Louis Mendola, New York: Trinacria, 2015, p. 117.

17   Ibid., p. 135.

4. A Silent Scream (1347–1693)

1   Johannes Nohl, *The Black Death: A Chronicle of the Plague*, trans. C. H. Clarke, Pennsylvania: Westholme Publishing, 2006, p. 19.

2   Ibid., p. 19.

3   The vast majority of Sicily's towns and cities are on the water and, being ports, were particularly vulnerable to both the fleas and vermin that transmitted the plague. For a breakdown of the estimated death toll see: Susan Scott and Christopher J. Duncan, *Biology of Plagues: Evidence from Historical Populations*, Cambridge: Cambridge University Press, 2001, p. 85.

4   Among the most bizarre artefacts of this period are the so-called Drolleries of Trapani, painted by Cecco di Naro, Simone di Corleone and Darenu di Palermoare. These wooden works, showing extraordinary fantastic beasts, are now part of the permanent collection at Palermo's Palazzo Abatellis, where they are displayed alongside *The Triumph of Death*.

5   Henry Charles Lea, *The Inquisition in the Spanish Dependencies*, New York and London: Macmillan, 1922, p. 12.

6   There was one exception to this. As the Ottomans expanded their territories in the Balkans, the Sicilian state agreed to provide a safe haven for a large number of orthodox Albanian refugees. Given that this community's Easter tradition was, and is, conducted in seven languages, and that their musical tradition, a particularly important component

of worship, contains several trance-like dances, with mystical connotations, this policy seems quite remarkable. These diasporic groups,
now known as the Arbëreshë, congregated in the Piana degli Albanesi
around Palermo and would go on to develop their own highly sophisticated literary culture which played a role in the founding of the Albanian
nation-state in 1912.

7   The discovery of these works is a fascinating story in its own right.
In 1906, during routine renovation on the palace, the anthropologist
Giuseppe Pitrè was alerted to the presence of some curious graffiti in
some of the small cell-like rooms, which seemed to date to the time of
the Inquisition. As an expert in Palermo's local history Pitrè deduced
that the imprisoned people must have produced these themselves. Before
he could conduct a full analysis, however, the esteemed scholar passed
away. In WWII further investigation was hampered when the Allied
forces gave a certain Don Totò, a local art dealer, permission to use the
building to house his collection. This rather cantankerous gentleman
only allowed two intellectuals inside to examine the works in detail: the
novelist Leonardo Sciascia, and the photographer Ferdinando Scianna.
In 1977 the pair published their photos and analysis in a book *A Silent
Scream* which, for decades, was the only access that scholars had to the
space. It wasn't until 2002, following Don Totò's death, that the pieces
were fully restored and, ten years later, the cells opened to the public.

8   For a full-length overview see Giuseppe Giarrizzo's analysis in *Cultura e
Economia nella Sicilia del '700*, Caltanissetta and Roma: Salvatore Sciascia, 1992.

9   In Palermo the monks developed their own process of mummification in
which they would chemically embalm bodies, at first those of the order,
and later the general public, so that they might be prepared for Jesus's
second coming. Visitors to the catacombs of the Church of Santa Maria
della Pace can still walk among a series of preserved corpses which are
kitted out in their best Sunday clothes to await the moment when, as
they saw it, 'those who sleep in the dust of the earth shall awake, some
to everlasting life' (Daniel 12:2).

10 For a general overview of magic cults in Southern Italy, see: Ernesto De
Martino, *Sud e Magia*, Milano: Feltrinelli, 2016.

11 Many of these figures were straightforward charlatans. De Simone,
a trader in Palermo, confessed to the police that he didn't believe in

necromancy at all and was simply tricking his customers to make ends meet. After musing on the case, the Inquisition spared De Simone's life, but banned him from the Sicilian territories. For this story, and many others, see: Maria Sofia Messana, *Inquisitori, negromanti e streghe nella Sicilia moderna*, Palermo: Sellerio, 2007, pp. 468–9.

12   The name Beati Paoli itself does not emerge until the eighteenth century. Nevertheless, we can trace prototypes back as early as 1186 in which an anonymous author of the 'chronicle of Fossanova' describes a secret sect called the *vendicosi* which supposedly killed corrupt priests and landowners.

13   Quoted in Francesco Renda, *I Beati Paoli: storia, letteratura e leggenda*, Palermo: Sellerio, 1988, p. 51, translation my own.

14   Leonardo Sciascia, *Nero su Nero*, Milano: Einaudi, 1979, p. 34.

15   Umberto Eco, 'I Beati Paoli e l'ideologia del romanzo popolare' in *Il superuomo di massa. Retorica e ideologia nel romanzo popolare*, Milano: Bompiani, 1998, pp. 69–89.

16   Giorgio Vasari, *The Lives of the Artists*, trans. Julia Bondanella and Peter Bondanella, New York: Oxford University Press, 1991, p. 188.

17   Giorgio Vasari, *Vite de' più eccellenti pittori, scultori e architetti*, vol. 11, Siena: Pazzini Carli e Compagno, 1794, p.114, translation my own.

5. Decadence and Parlour Games (1693–1860)

1   The circumstances behind this dynastic change were fraught to say the least. Over three decades, during the War of the Spanish Succession (1701–14), the War of the Quadruple Alliance (1718–20) and the skirmishes that followed, Sicily passed between various Habsburg and Bourbon factions, and was even, for a brief spell between 1713 and 1720, a possession of the Savoy family. The implications of this were, on the whole, minimal for most of the islanders. Most of the fighting took place on the European mainland, with the notable exception of the Battle of Francavilla (1719), in the east of Sicily, in which Austrian forces killed 2,000 soldiers. The main burden, though, lay on the shoulders of the nobility, who were forced to pay quite large sums of money to a string of temporary rulers, to help fund far-off battles. Their resentment towards this was an important factor in this class's reluctance to engage in civic affairs.

2   Cagliostro was accused of having played a role in the 'Affair of the Diamond Necklace', in which a group of tricksters succeeded in stealing an extraordinarily expensive piece of jewellery from the French queen Marie Antoinette. While the story was discussed across Europe there is no evidence to suggest that the Sicilian was involved in organising the heist.

3   The squire of the Carolingian cycle is still referred to by different names in different parts of the island: in Catania he is called Peppenninu, in Messina, Lillu Scagghiozza and in Palermo he is in fact two people, Nofrio and Virticchio. Similar diversity can be seen in the marionettes which in Catania evolved to become large and heavy with rigid legs, while in Palermo they are leaner and more flexible.

4   This is my own translation of the Italian text, which was itself adapted from the Sicilian spoken word in Domenico Tempio, *La Carestia: Poema epico*, trans. Francesco Belfiore, Canterano: Aracne, 2017, p. 17.

5   See: 'On the Sulphur Trade of Sicily, and the Commercial Relations between that Country and Great Britain', in *Journal of the Statistical Society of London* 2, no. 6, January 1840, pp. 446–57.

6   Francesco Ferrara, *Memorie su la rivoluzione siciliana del 1847 e 1848: Brani di una lettera da Palermo sul movimento avvenuto in quella citta nella fine di novembre 1847*, Roma: Tip. di L. Tonna, 1847, author's translation.

6. A Revolution Betrayed (1860–1891)

1   See, in particular, Pino Aprile, *Terroni: All That Has Been Done to Ensure That the Italians of the South Became "Southerners"*, New York: Bordighera Press, 2011.

2   Karl Marx, 'Sicily and the Sicilians' in the *New York Daily Tribune*, 17 May 1860.

3   For a detailed account of the atrocity at Bronte see: Lucy Riall, *Under the Volcano: Revolution in a Sicilian Town*, New York: Oxford University Press, 2013.

4   Francesco Ferrara, 'Sul giusto modo d'intendere l'annessione della Sicilia all'Italia', in *Opere complete*, ed. Riccardo Faucci, vol. VIII, Roma: Assobanca, 1976.

5   Mario D'Addio, *La giustizia dopo L'unità in Amministrazione della giustizia e poteri di polizia dagli stati preunitari alla caduta della destra*.

Atti di congresso di storia del risorgimento italiano. *Pescara 7'10 novembre 1984*, Roma: Istituto per la storia del Risorgimento italiano, 1986, p. 325.

6   Francesco Crispi, *A' suoi amici di Sicilia Francesco Crispi già deputato al Parlamento*, Florence: G. Barbera, 1865, p. 10. Google Play Books.

7   This is John Dickie's translation from *Cosa Nostra: A History of the Sicilian Mafia*, New York: Palgrave Macmillan, 2004, p. 49.

8   Quoted in John Dickie, *Blood Brotherhoods: The Rise of the Italian Mafias*, London: Sceptre, 2012, pp. 95–96.

9   Dickie, *Cosa Nostra*, p. 58.

10 Tomasi di Lampedusa, *The Leopard*, trans. Guido Waldman, London: Vintage, 2007.

11 Ibid., p. 137.

12 Ibid., p. 140.

13 Ibid., p. 141.

14 Ibid., p. 138.

15 Ibid., p. 76.

16 Ibid., p. 138.

17 Ibid., p. 174.

18 Ibid., p. 190.

19 Archivio Centrale dello stato, 'L'inchiesta sulle condizioni sociali ed economiche della Sicilia 1875–1876', eds S. Carbone and R. Crispo, vol. II, Bologna: 1969.

20 There are several studies that have demonstrated this. The most thorough and authoritative, though, is: 'Anteo D'Angio, 'La Situazione Finanziaria Italiana dal 1796 al 1870', in *Storia d'Italia* vol. II, Torino: De Agostini, 1973, p. 241.

21 See: Eric Hobsbawm, *Primitive Rebels*, Manchester: University of Manchester Press, 1963, p. 93.

22 Giovanni Federico, Alessandro Nuvolari and Michelangelo Vasta, 'The Origins of the Italian Regional Divide: Evidence from Real Waves, 1861–1913. Conference paper, EH-TUNE Economic History Workshop, Siena, 2016, digitised September 2017.

23 See: Adolfo Rossi, *L'agitazione in Sicilia. A proposito delle ultime condanne*, Milano: Max Kantorowicz, 1894, and 'La Situazione in Sicilia: Le notizie giunte finora sull'organizzazione dei Fasci. Le donne', in *La Tribuna*, 8 October 1893.

24   See: 'Partito Socialista Siciliano. Comitato Centrale. Lavoratori della Sicilia!' in *Lotta di Classe*, 13–14 January, 1894, no. 2.

25   The full geography of local groups has been documented by Francesco Renda in his appendix to *I Fasci Siciliani 1892–4*, pp. 339–43. The leadership itself claimed numbers were as high as 300,000 though some historians, such as Santi Fedele, have challenged this. See: Santi Fedele, *I Fasci siciliani dei lavoratori: 1891–1894*, Cosenza: Rubbettino, 1994, p. 225.

26   See: *Emigrazione e storia d'Italia*, ed. Matteo Sanfilippo. Cosenza: Luigi Pellegrini, 2003, p. 157–8.

27   See: 'Come si diventa milionari negli Stati Uniti', *La Domenica del Corriere*, 20 July 1902.

28   See: *Corriere della Sera*, 10 January 1900.

7. A Modernist Dystopia (1891–1943)

1   Romualdo Giuffrida, 'Introduzione', in *Esposizione nazionale Palermo 1891–1892. Catalogo Generale*, Palermo: Accademia Nazionale di Scienze, Lettere e Arti, 1991, p. xiv.

2   See: 'Rapporto Sangiorgi', Archivio Centrale dello Stato, DGPS aa.gg, Atti speciali 1898–1940, b. 1, f. 1.

3   Pierluigi Scolè, 'I morti', in *Dizionario Storico della Prima Guerra Mondiale*, ed. Nicola Labanca, Bari: Laterza, 2014, p. 183.

4   'Editorial' in *The Times* of London, 17 January 1928.

5   Giovanni Gentile, *Che cos'è il fascismo?*, Vallecchi: Firenze, 1925, p. 50.

6   Filippo Tommaso Marinetti, 'The Founding and Manifesto of Futurism', *Le Figaro* Paris, 20 February 1909, in *Futurism: An Anthology*, eds Lawrence Rainey, Christine Poggi and Laura Wittman, New Haven and London: Yale University Press, 2009, p. 51.

7   Guglielmo Janelli, *Utilizziamo il teatro greco di Siracusa. Manifesto dei futuristi siciliani*, Messina: Edizioni della Balza Futurista, 1924, author's translation.

8   Luigi Pirandello, *Sei personaggi in cerca d'autore – Enrico IV*, Milano: Mondadori, 1990, p. 218, author's translation.

9   See, for example, Giulio Cogni, *Il Razzismo*, Milano: Fratelli Bocca, 1937, pp. 212–13.

10   Quoted in Christopher Duggan, *Fascist Voices: An Intimate History of Mussolini's Italy*, London: Vintage, 2013, p. 291.

11 Benito Mussolini, 'Aqua e strade per la Sicilia,' in *Corriere di Alessandria*, 15, no. 83, 24 August 1937, p. 1, author's translation.

12 For a full account of Edoardo Caracciolo's life and work, see *Edoardo Caracciolo. Urbanistica, architettura, storia*, ed. Nicola Giuliano Leone, Milano: FrancoAngeli, 2015.

13 Leandro Perrotta, '14 milioni per i borghi fascisti. Lo storico: "Creati per isolare"', *Focus Sicilia*, 16 September 2019.

8. The Return of the Mafia (1943–2013)

1 This letter was reprinted by his biographer Gavin Maxwell in the book *God Protect Me from My Friends*, London: Pan Books, 1972, p. 18. For information on the party, meanwhile, see: Monte Finkelstein, *Separatism, the Allies and the Mafia: The Struggle for Sicilian Independence*, Pennsylvania: Lehigh University Press, 1998, p. 78.

2 Maxwell, *God Protect Me from My Friends*, p. 193.

3 Thanks to high rates of subscription in regions like Tuscany and Emilia Romagna, the PCI became the largest communist party in Europe. Nevertheless, their power was severely limited by the DC's army of constitutional lawyers. After the war the centre-right repeatedly resisted calls for regional councils, on the basis that this would enable the communists to obtain more direct authority over certain relatively wealthy parts of the country. Eventually, after decades of protest, this system was put in place in 1970. To this day these regions, and their councils, remain some of Italy's strongest democratic institutions, and have often challenged authoritarian or poorly conceived national legislation.

4 In reality even the success stories were problematic. The most emblematic project from this time in Sicily was a huge petrochemical plant in Augusta, a small town just outside of Syracuse. State and private investments helped bring thousands of jobs to an area of the island where, since unification, there had been no significant employers. This decision, though, was made without any local consultation and radically transformed the way of life of an area that had been dedicated to small-scale fishing for centuries. Over decades of activity, the plant has polluted the local environment and contaminated the nearby sea with dangerously high levels of mercury.

5   Giuseppe Galasso, *Il Mezzogiorno: da 'questione' a 'problema aperto'*, P. Lacaita, 2005, p. 396.

6   Dickie, *Cosa Nostra*, p. 224.

7   This phenomenon was already underway throughout the '50s. By the regional elections of 1959, though, the MIS won just 0.1 percent of the vote share, in part, though by no means exclusively, due to the events in Agrigento.

8   For decades, in a manoeuvre typical of the time, the government tried to pass off Peppino's death as a botched left-wing terror attempt, and later as a suicide. In 1979 the Centro Siciliano di Documentazione, which would later adopt Peppino's name, helped organise the first explicitly anti-mafia demonstration. Against all intimidation, it would serve as a vital intellectual resource for raising awareness about, and, in pockets, challenging Cosa Nostra. Remarkably, it wasn't until 2002 that the state formally acknowledged the role of the mafia in the murder, and the courts gave Gaetano Badalamenti, then aged eighty-two, a life sentence.

9   'Terrore mafioso: Palermo come Beirut' in *l'Unità*, 30 July 1983.

10   Nino Di Matteo, a judge who has in many ways inherited the responsibilities of Falcone and Borsellino, is continuing to uncover the extent of what he calls the 'mafia-state'. In his book *Il patto sporco: Il processo Stato-Mafia nel racconto di un suo protagonista* (Milano: Chiarelettere, 2018), he argues that Cosa Nostra has had a pact with government institutions for decades which has, in several cases, resulted in bloodshed.

11   Leonardo Sciascia. 'I professionisti dell'antimafia' in *Corriere della Sera*, 10 January 1987.

12   Philip Willan, 'Mafia Supergrass Fingers Berlusconi', *Guardian*, 12 January 2003.

13   'La motivazione ufficiale: blasfemo e sacrilego', *La Repubblica*, 4 March 1998.

Epilogue

1   International Organization for Migration, 'IOM Applauds Italy's Life-Saving Mare Nostrum Operation: "Not a Migrant Pull Factor"', press release, 31 October 2014.

2   Ismail Einashe, 'How 10 Asian Shopkeepers Took on the Sicilian Mafia

in Palermo and Rebuilt Their Neighbourhood' in *South China Morning Post*, 2 January 2019, and 'The Bangladeshi Shopkeepers Who Took on Sicily's Cosa Nostra Mafia', in *The Sunday Times*, 1 December 2019.

3   Lorenzo Tondo, '"They Are Our Salvation": The Sicilian Town Revived by Refugees', *Guardian*, 19 March 2018.

4   Giuseppe Caccia, 'From the Centre of the Mediterranean: "Freedom of Movement as a Human Right"', PoliticalCritique.org, 9 June 2017.

Bibliography

Abbate, Fulvio. *La peste bis*. Milano: Bompiani, 1996.

Abulafia, David. *Frederick II: A Medieval Emperor*. New York: Oxford University Press, 1992.

———. *The Great Sea: A Human History of the Mediterranean*. New York: Oxford University Press, 2011.

Abu-Munshar, Maher Y. 'Sultan al-Kamil, Emperor Frederick II and the Submission of Jerusalem' in *International Journal of Social Science and Humanity* 3, no. 5, September 2013.

Adler, Nathan Marcus. *The Itinerary of Benjamin of Tudela*. London: Oxford University Press, 1907.

Ahmed, Ali Jimale. 'Incantations' in *Mediterranean: Migrant crossings*. New York: Upset Press, 2017.

Alajmo, Roberto. *L'arte di annacarsi: un viaggio in Sicilia*. Bari: Laterza, 2012.

Alighieri, Dante. *Inferno*, trans. Steve Ellis. London: Vintage, 2007.

———. *The Divine Comedy:* vol. II, *Purgatory*, trans. Mark Musa. London: Penguin, 1985.

Amari, Michele. *History of the War of the Sicilian Vespers* vol. I, trans. Francis Egerton Ellesmere. London: Richard Bentley, 1850.

———. *Racconto popolare del Vespro siciliano*. Palermo: Sellerio, 1987.

Amato (di Montecassino). *The History of the Normans*, trans. Prescott N. Dunbar. Woodbridge: Boydell Press, 2004.

Ames, Christine Caldwell. *Righteous Persecution: Inquisition, Dominicans, and Christianity in the Middle Ages.* Philadelphia: University of Pennsylvania Press, 1998.

Aprile, Pino. *Terroni.* Milano: Piemme, 2010.

Arielli, Nir. *Fascist Italy and the Middle East, 1933–40.* London: Palgrave Macmillan, 2010.

Attanasio, Sandro. *Gli anni della rabbia: Sicilia 1943–47.* Milano: Mursia, 1984.

Avicenna. *A Compendium on the Soul*, trans. Edward Abbott Van Dyck. Verona: N. Paderno, 1906.

Balestrini, Nanni and Primo Moroni. *L'orda d'oro. 1968–1977: la grande ondata rivoluzionaria e creativa, politica ed esistenziale.* Milano: Feltrinelli, 2015.

Banu (Sons of) Musa Bin Shakir. *The Book of Ingenious Devices*, trans. Donald R. Hill. Dordrecht: D. Reidel, 1979.

Barbagallo, Francesco. *Lavoro ed esodo nel sud 1861–1971.* Napoli: Guida Editori, 1973.

Barbera, Gioacchino, Luisa Martorelli, Fernando Mazzocca, Antonella Purpure, Carlo Sisi, ed. *Francesco Lojacono.* Milano: Silvana Editoriale, 2005.

Barbera, Paola. *Architettura in Sicilia tra le due guerre.* Palermo: Sellerio, 2002.

Bartelletti, Sapio. *La Cucina Siciliana: Nobile e Popolare.* Milano: FrancoAngeli, 1980.

Baudelaire, Charles. *Paris Spleen and La Fanfarlo*, trans. Raymond N. Mackenzie. Indianapolis: Hackett Publishing, 2008.

Bennici, Giuseppe. *L'ultimo dei trovatori arabi in Sicilia, versione da antico manoscritto.* Palermo: Luigi Pedone Lauriel Editore, 1874.

Benso, Camillo (Cavour) and Costantino Nigra. *Il carteggio Cavour-Nigra dal 1858 al 1861.* Bologna: Nicola Zanichelli, 1926.

Berezin, Mabel. *Making the Fascist Self: The Political Culture of Interwar Italy.* New York: Cornell University Press, 1997.

Bianco, Annibale. *Il Fascismo in Sicilia*. Catania: Vincenzo Muglia, 1923.

Blunt, Anthony. *Barocco Siciliano*, trans. Bruno Maffi. Milano: Edizioni il Polifilo, 1968.

Boardman, John. *The Cambridge Ancient History*, vol. III. *The Expansion of the Greek World: Eighth to Sixth Centuries B.C.* Cambridge: Cambridge University Press, 1982.

Bonanno, Giovanni. *Novecento in Sicilia*. Palermo: Serpotta, 1990.

Bonomo, Giuseppe. *Pitrè la Sicilia e i siciliani*. Palermo: Sellerio, 1989.

Bosher, Kathryn, ed. *Theater outside Athens: Drama in Greek Sicily and South Italy*. Cambridge: Cambridge University Press, 2012.

Botta, Carmelo and Francesca Lo Nigro. *Il sogno negate della libertà: I Fasci siciliani e l'emancipazione dei lavoratori*. Palermo: Navarra, 2015.

Brancati, Vitaliano. *L'amico del vincitore*. Milano: Casa Editrice Ceschina, 1932.

Braudel, Fernand. *The Mediterranean in the Ancient World*. London: Penguin, 2002.

Brydone, Patrick. *Travels in Sicily and Malta*. Aberdeen: George Clark and Son, 1848.

Bufalino, Gesualdo. *Diceria dell'untore*. Palermo: Sellerio, 2009.

———. *The Plague Sower*, trans. Stephen Sartarelli. Colorado: Eridanos, 1988.

Burckhardt, Jacob. *The State as a Work of Art*. London: Penguin, 2010.

Burton, R. W. B. *Pindar's Pythian Odes*. London: Oxford University Press, 1962.

Buttitta, Ignazio. *Il poeta in piazza*. Milano: Feltrinelli, 1974.

———. 'Lu fascista' in *Prime e nuovissime*, ed. Marta Puglisi. Torino: Gruppo Editoriale Forma, 1983.

Calaciura, Giosuè. *Malacarne*. Milano: Baldini & Castoldi, 1998.

Camilleri, Andrea. *Il cane di terracotta*. Palermo: Sellerio, 1996.

———. *Il ladro di merendine*. Palermo: Sellerio, 1997.

————. *La forma dell'acqua*. Palermo: Sellerio, 1994.

Canosa, Romano. *L'ultima eresia: quietisti e inquisizione in Sicilia tra Seicento e Settecento*. Palermo: Sellerio, 1986.

Capuana, Luigi. *Giacinta. Secondo la prima edizione del 1879*. Milano: Mondadori, 1988.

Carbone, Salvatore and Laura Grimaldi. *Il popolo al confino. La persecuzione fascista in Sicilia*. Roma: Archivi di Stato, 1989.

Caridi, Francesco D. *Wops. La radici di 'Cosa Nostra' negli Stati Uniti d'America*. Napoli: Il Cappio, 2004.

Carocci, Giampiero. *Storia dell'Italia moderna dal 1861 ai nostri giorni*. Roma: Newton Compton, 1995.

Castiglione, Pietro. *Novecento siciliano: da Garibaldi a Mussolini, 1860–1943*. Catania: Edizioni del Prisma, 2008.

Christa Canitz, A. E. and Gernot R. Weiland, eds. *From Arabye to Engelond: Medieval Studies in Honour of Mahmoud Manzalaoui*. Ottawa: University of Ottawa Press, 1999.

Cicero. *Select Orations*, trans. C. D. Yonge. New York: Harper & Brothers, 1877.

————. *Tusculan Disputations* vol. V, trans. A. E. Douglas. Warminster: Aris & Phillips, 1990.

Ciurcina, Paolo. *Tirannide e Democrazia a Siracusa, da Dionisio il Grande a Berlusconi attraverso Voltaire*. Siracusa: Lombardi, 2003.

Cogni, Giulio. *Il Razzismo*. Milano: Fratelli Bocca, 1937.

Coluccia, Rosario. *Storia, lingua e filologia della poesia antica. Scuola siciliana, Dante e altro*. Firenze: Franco Cesati, 2016.

Corrao, Francesca Maria. *Poeti arabi di Sicilia*. Messina: Mesogea, 2005.

Correnti, Santi. *Il futurismo in Sicilia e la poetessa catanese Adele Gloria*. Catania: CUECM, 1990.

————. *Storia di Sicilia come storia del popolo siciliano*. Milano: Longanesi, 1982.

————. *Storia e folklore di Sicilia*. Milano: Mursia, 1975.

Cowell, Alan. 'Italy Dispatches 7000 Anti-Mob Troops to Sicily'. *The New York Times*, 26 July 1992.

Crispi, Francesco. *Carteggi politici inediti di Francesco Crispi (1860–1900)*. Roma: L'Universelle, 1912.

Cruciani, Sante, Maria Paola Del Rossi, Manuela Claudiani, eds. *Portella della Ginestra e il processo di Viterbo: Politica, memoria e uso pubblico della storia (1947–2012)*. Roma: Ediesse, 2014.

Cusumano, Nicola. *Libri e culture in Sicilia nel settecento*. Palermo: New Digital Press, 2016.

D'Addio, Mario. 'La giustizia dopo L'unità' in *Amministrazione della giustizia e poteri di polizia dagli stati preunitari alla caduta della destra. Atti di congresso di storia del risorgimento italiano. Pescara 7'10 novembre 1984*. Roma: Istituto per la storia del Risorgimento italiano, 1986.

Dall'Osso, Claudia. *Voglio d'America: Il mito americano in Italia tra Otto e Novecento*. Firenze: Donzelli, 2007.

Dandelet, Thomas James. *Spain in Italy: Politics, Society, and Religion 1500–1700*. Leiden: Brill, 2006.

D'Angio, Anteo. 'La Situazione Finanziaria Italiana dal 1796 al 1870' in *Storia d'Italia* vol. II. Torino: De Agostini, 1973.

Davidson, James. *Courtesans and Fishcakes: The Consuming Passions of Classical Athens*. London: HarperCollins, 1997.

De Felice, Renzo. *Mussolini il Duce. Lo Stato totalitario 1936–1940*. Milano: Einaudi, 1997.

De Martino, Ernesto. *Sud e Magia*. Milano: Feltrinelli, 2016.

De Roberto, Federico. *The Viceroys: A Novel*, trans. Archibald Colquhoun. London and New York: Verso, 2016 (Kindle edition).

Dickie, John. *Blood Brotherhoods: The Rise of the Italian Mafias*. London: Sceptre, 2012.

———. *Cosa Nostra: A History of the Sicilian Mafia*. New York: Palgrave Macmillan, 2004.

———. *Mafia Republic, Cosa Nostra, 'Ndrangheta and Camorra from 1946 to the Present*. London: Sceptre, 2013.

Di Brolo, Lancia and Domenico Gaspare. *Storia della Chiesa in Sicilia*. Palermo: Lao, 1880.

Di Gesù, Matteo. *La tradizione del postmoderno*. Milano: Francoangeli, 2003.

————. *L'invenzione della Sicilia: Letteratura, mafia, modernità*. Roma: Carocci, 2015.

Di Leo, Maria Adele. *Feste Patronali di Sicilia: culti, tradizioni, rituali e folclore della devozione popolare*. Roma: Tascabili Economici Newton, 1997.

Di Matteo, Nino. *Il patto sporco: Il processo Stato-Mafia nel racconto di un suo protagonista*. Milano: Chiarelettere, 2018.

Di Torrearsa, Vincenzo Fardella. *Ricordi su la Rivoluzione siciliana degli anni 1848 e 1849*. Palermo: Sellerio, 1988.

Djebbar, Ahmed. 'Philosophy and Science in Islam: A Fruitful Cohabitation' in *Arab Muslim Civilization in the Mirror of the Universal*. Paris: UNESCO, 2010.

Dolci, Danilo. *Inventare il futuro*. Bari: Laterza, 1968.

DuBois, Page. *Sappho*. London and New York: I. B. Tauris, 2015.

Dufour, Liliane and Henri Raymond. *Dalle baracche al Barocco: la ricostruzione di Noto*. Siracusa: A. Lombardi, 1990.

Duggan, Christopher. *Fascist Voices: An Intimate History of Mussolini's Italy*. London: Vintage, 2013.

Dumas, Alexandre. *The Sicilian Bandit*, trans. Jose Maria de Pereda. Auckland: The Floating Press, 2015.

Dummett, Jeremy. *Syracuse: City of Legends*. London: I. B. Tauris, 2010.

Dunbabin, Katherine M. D. *Mosaics of the Greek and Roman World*. Cambridge: Cambridge University Press, 2006.

Eco, Umberto. *Il superuomo di massa. Retorica e ideologia nel romanzo popolare*. Milano: Bompiani, 1998.

Einashe, Ismail. 'How 10 Asian Shopkeepers Took on the Sicilian Mafia in Palermo and Rebuilt Their Neighbourhood'. *South China Morning Post*, 2 January 2019.

————. 'The Bangladeshi Shopkeepers Who Took on Sicily's Cosa Nostra Mafia'. *The Sunday Times*, 1 December 2019.

Elsie, Robert, ed. and trans. *An Elusive Eagle Soars, Anthology of Modern Albanian Poetry*. London and Boston: Forest Books, 1993.

Erdkamp, Paul. *The Grain Market in the Roman Empire: A Social, Political and Economic Study*. Cambridge: Cambridge University Press, 2005.

Fava, Ferdinando. *Lo Zen di Palermo: Antropologia dell'esclusione*. Milano: FrancoAngeli, 2008.

Favarò, Sara. *Giufà il semplice*. Palermo: Euno, 2015.

Fedele, Santi. *I Fasci siciliani dei lavoratori: 1891–1894*. Cosenza: Rubbettino, 1994.

Federico II. *De arte venandi cum avibus. Testo latino a fronte*, ed. A. L. Trombetti Budriesi. Bari: Laterza, 2007.

Fernandez, Dominique and Leonardo Sciascia. *I Siciliani*. Milano: Einaudi, 1977.

Ferrara, Francesco. *Memorie su la rivoluzione siciliana del 1847 e 1848: Brani di una lettera da Palermo sul movimento avvenuto in quella citta nella fine di novembre 1847*. Roma: Tip. di L. Tonna, 1847.

————. 'Sul giusto modo d'intendere l'annessione della Sicilia all'Italia', in *Opere complete* vol. VIII, ed. Riccardo Faucci. Roma: Assobanca, 1976.

Ferreiro, Alberto, ed. *The Devil Heresy and Witchcraft in the Middle Ages*. Boston: Brill, 1998.

Finkelstein, Monte. *Separatism, the Allies and the Mafia: The Struggle for Sicilian Independence*. Pennsylvania: Lehigh University Press, 1998.

Fiume, Giovanna. 'Soundless Screams: Graffiti and Drawings in the Prisons of the Holy Office in Palermo' in *Journal of Early Modern History* 21, no. 3, June 2017.

Flaubert, Gustave. *Madame Bovary*, trans. Geoffrey Wall. London: Penguin, 2003.

Fotia, Carmine. 'Palermo, capitale dell'accoglienza: la grande lezione della Sicilia a tutta l'Italia' in *L'Espresso*, 2 January 2019.

Franchina, Nino. *Antologia*. Palermo: Sellerio, 1997.

Freeman, Kathleen. *Ancilla to the Pre-Socratic Philosophers: A Complete Translation of the Fragments in Diels*. Cambridge: Harvard University Press, 1996.

Gabrielli, Francesco. 'Arabic Poetry in Sicily' in *East and West* 2, no. 1, April 1951, pp. 13–16.

Galasso, Giuseppe. *Il Mezzogiorno: da 'questione' a 'problema aperto'*. Manduria: Lacaita, 2005.

Gallo, Cinzia. *Il verismo minore in Sicilia*. Roma: Bonanno, 1999.

Ganci, Salvatore, ed. *La Sicilia e l'unità d'Italia: atti del Congresso internazionale di studi storici sul Risorgimento italiano. Palermo 15–20 aprile 1961*. Milano: Feltrinelli, 1962.

Gentile, Giovanni. *Che cos'è il fascismo?* Firenze: Vallecchi, 1925.

———. *Il Pensiero Italiano Del Rinascimento*. Firenze: Sansoni, 1939.

———. *Il tramonto della cultura siciliana*. Firenze: Le Lettere, 2003.

Giarrizzo, Giuseppe. *Cultura e Economia nella Sicilia del '700*. Caltanissetta and Roma: Salvatore Sciascia, 1992.

Gillette, Aaron. *Racial Theories in Fascist Italy*. London: Routledge, 2014.

Ginsborg, Paul. *A History of Contemporary Italy 1943–1980*. London: Penguin, 1990.

Giordano, Francesco. *Domenico Tempio, cantore della Libertà*. Catania: Akkuaria, 2011.

Giuffrida, Romualdo. 'Introduzione' in *Esposizione nazionale Palermo 1891–1892. Catalogo Generale*. Palermo: Accademia Nazionale di Scienze, Lettere e Arti, 1991.

Goethe, Johann Wolfgang. *Goethe's Travels in Italy*, trans. Charles Nisbeth. London: Bell & Sons, 1885.

Gorgias. *Encomium of Helen*, trans. D. M. MacDowell. Bristol: Bristol Classical Press, 1991.

Gramsci, Antonio. 'Some Aspects of the Southern Question' in *Selections from Political Writings 1921–26*, trans. Quintin Hoare. London: Lawrence and Wishart, 1978.

Guggino, Elsa. *La magia in Sicilia*. Palermo: Sellerio, 1978.

Hamdis, Ibn. 'Earthly Pleasure' in *Moorish Poetry*, trans. A. J. Arberry. London and New York: Routledge Curzon, 2001.

Henze, Paul B. *Layers of Time: A History of Ethiopia*. Basingstoke: Palgrave Macmillan, 2000.

Hesiod. *Theogony and Works and Days*, trans. M. L. West. New York: Oxford University Press, 1988.

Hobsbawm, Eric. *Primitive Rebels*. Manchester: University of Manchester Press, 1963.

Homer. *The Odyssey*, trans. A. T. Murray. London: Heinemann, 1919.

Houben, Hubert. *Roger II of Sicily: A Ruler between East and West*, trans. Graham A. Loud and Diane Milburn. Cambridge: Cambridge University Press, 2002.

Ibn Jubayr, Muhammed Ibn Ahmad. *The Travels of Ibn Jubayr*, trans. R. J. C. Broadhurst. London: Jonathan Cape, 1952.

Ibn Qalāqis. *Splendori e misteri di Sicilia*, trans. Adalgisa De Simone. Messina: Rubbettino, 1996.

Impastato, Peppino. *Lunga è la notte: poesie, scritti, documenti*, ed. Umberto Santino. Palermo: Centro siciliano di documentazione, 2002.

Janelli, Guglielmo. *Utilizziamo il teatro greco di Siracusa. Manifesto dei futuristi siciliani*. Messina: Edizioni della Balza Futurista, 1924.

Johns, Jeremy. *Arabic Administration in Norman Sicily*. Cambridge: Cambridge University Press, 2002.

Jones, William. *The History of the Christian Church from the Birth of Christ to the XVIII Century*. Dover: Trustees of the Freewill Baptist Connection, 1837.

Justus, Friedrich Carl. *The Black Death in the Fourteenth Century*. London: A. Schloss, 1833.

Kantorowicz, Ernst. *Frederick the Second 1194–1250*, trans. E. O. Lorimer. New York: Frederick Ungar, 1957.

Karagoz, Claudia and Giovanna Summerfield, eds. *Sicily and the Mediterranean: Migration, Exchange, Reinvention*. New York: Palgrave Macmillan, 2015.

Kassabova, Kapka. *Border: A Journey to the Centre of Europe*. London: Granta, 2017.

Kreutz, Barbara M. *Before the Normans: Southern Italy in the Ninth and Tenth Centuries*. Philadelphia: University of Pennsylvania Press, 1996.

Kwakkeland, Erik and Rodney Thomson, eds. *The European Book in the Twelfth Century*. Cambridge: Cambridge University Press, 2018.

Labanca, Nicola. *Oltremare: storia dell'espansione coloniale italiana*. Bologna: Il Mulino, 2002.

La Lumia, Isidoro. *Gli Ebrei Siciliani*. Palermo: Sellerio, 1984.

Lampedusa, Tomasi di. *The Leopard*, trans. Guido Waldman. London: Vintage, 2007.

La Villa, Pina and Sergio Failla. *I sessantotto di Sicilia*. Roma: Zero-Book, 2016.

Lea, Henry Charles. *The Inquisition in the Spanish Dependencies*. New York and London: Macmillan, 1922.

Leanti, Giuseppe. *La satira contro il settecento galante in Sicilia*. Palermo: Bruno Leopardi Editore, 1999.

Lentini, Giacomo da. *The Complete Poetry*, trans. Richard Lansing. Toronto, Buffalo and London: University of Toronto Press, 2018.

Leone, Nicola Giuliano, ed. *Edoardo Caracciolo. Urbanistica, architettura, storia*. Milano: FrancoAngeli, 2015.

Ligt de Luuk and Laurens E. Tacoma. *Migration and Mobility in the Early Roman Empire*. Boston: Brill, 2016.

Littell, Eliakim and Robert S. Littell. 'Sicily as It Is and Was' in *Living Age*. Third Series Volume X. Boston: Little, Son, and Company, 1860.

Lotringer, Sylvere and Christian Marazzi, eds. *Autonomia: Post-Political Politics*. Los Angeles: Semiotext(e), 2007.

Mack Smith, Denis. *The Making of Italy, 1796–1866*. London: Palgrave, 1988.

Marinetti, Filippo Tommaso. 'The Founding and Manifesto of Futurism'. *Le Figaro*, 20 February 1909 in Lawrence Rainey, Christine Poggi and Laura Wittman, eds. *Futurism: An Anthology*. New Haven and London: Yale University Press, 2009.

Marrone, Salvatore. *Giufà e G. Pitrè. Cultura e ironia*. Roma: Aletti, 2016.

Marx, Karl. 'Sicily and the Sicilians'. *New York Daily Tribune*, 17 May 1860.

Maupassant, Guy de. *La Sicilia*. Palermo: Sellerio, 1990.

Maxwell, Gavin. *God Protect Me from My Friends*. London: Pan Books, 1972.

Melati, Piero and Giorgio di Noto. 'Dal Belice ad Amatrice sprechi e corruzione restano i protagonisti del post-sisma' in *L'Espresso*, 15 January 2018.

Mendola, Louis. *Frederick, Conrad and Manfred of Hohenstaufen, Kings of Sicily: The Chronicle of Nicholas of Jamsilla 1210–1258*. New York: Trinacria, 2016.

———. *The Kingdom of Sicily 1130–1860*. New York: Trinacria, 2015.

Menighetti, Romolo Franco Nicastro. *Storia dell'autonomia siciliana dal fascismo allo Statuto*. Torino: Ediprint, 1987.

Messana, Maria Sofia. *Inquisitori, negromanti e streghe nella Sicilia moderna*. Palermo: Sellerio, 2007.

Messana, Vincenzo and Salvatore Pricoco. *Il Cristianesimo in Sicilia: dalle origini a Gregorio Magno*. Caltanissetta: Seminario, 1985.

Monastra, Rosa Maria. *L'isola e l'immaginario. Sicilie e siciliani del novecento*. Soveria Mannelli: Rubbettino, 1998.

Munro, Dana C. '"Letters of the Crusaders", Translations and Reprints from the Original Sources of European History', vol. I, no. 4. Philadelphia: University of Pennsylvania, 1896.

Mussolini, Benito. 'Aqua e strade per la Sicilia' in *Corriere di Alessandria*, 15, no. 83, 24 August 1937.

Natoli, Luigi. *I Beati Paoli*. Palermo: Flaccovio, 1971.

Neff, Anliese, ed. *A Companion to Medieval Palermo. The History of a Mediterranean City from 600 to 1500*. Leiden and Boston: Brill, 2013.

Nicolosi, Salvatore. *Apocalisse in Sicilia, Il terremoto del 1693*. Catania: Tringale, 1982.

Nietzsche, Friedrich. *Beyond Good and Evil*, trans. Walter Kaufmann. New York: Vintage, 1966.

———. 'Ecce Homo: How to Become What You Are', trans. Judith Norman, in Aaron Ridley and Judith Norman, eds, *The Anti-Christ, Ecce Homo, Twilight of the Idols and Other Writings*. Cambridge: Cambridge University Press, 2005, p. 127.

Nocifora, Enzo. *La città inesistente. Seconda abitazione e abusivismo edilizio in Sicilia*. Milano: FrancoAngeli, 1994.

Nohl, Johannes. *The Black Death. A Chronicle of the Plague*, trans. C. H. Clarke. Pennsylvania: Westholme Publishing, 2006.

Norwich, John Julius. *Sicily: An Island at the Crossroads of History*. New York: Penguin, 2015 (Kindle edition).

———. *The Normans in Sicily: The Normans in the South 1016–1130 and the Kingdom in the Sun 1130–1194*. London: Penguin, 2004.

Ovid. *Ovid's Erotic Poems: 'Amores' and 'Ars Amatoria'*, trans. Len Krisak. Philadelphia: University of Pennsylvania Press, 2014.

———. *The Metamorphoses*, trans. Horace Gregory. New York: The Viking Press, 1958.

Panarese, Angelo. *Le 'due Italie': Liberalismo e socialismo. La questione meridionale da Croce e Gramsci ai giorni nostri*. Napoli: Guida Editori, 2017.

Panvini, Bruno. *Poeti Italiani della corte di Federico II*. Catania: CUECM, 1989.

Patera, Benedetto. *Il Rinascimento in Sicilia: da Antonello da Messina ad Antonello Gagini*. Palermo: Kalós, 2008.

Pavone, Vincenzo. *Storia di Catania: dalle origini alla fine del secolo XIX*. Catania: SSC, 1969.

Perriera, Michele. *Delirium cordis*. Palermo: Sellerio, 1995.

Perrotta, Leandro. '14 milioni per i borghi fascisti. Lo storico: "Creati per isolare"'. *Focus Sicilia*, 16 September 2019.

Petriaggi, Roberto. *Il Satiro danzante da Mazara del Vallo. Il restauro e l'immagine*. Napoli: Electa Napoli, 2005.

Pindar. *Olympian Odes, Pythian Odes*, trans. William H. Race. Cambridge: Harvard University Press, 1997.

Pirandello, Luigi. *I vecchi e i giovani*. Milano: Rizzoli, 2011.

————. *Sei personaggi in cerca d'autore & Enrico IV*. Milano: Mondadori, 1990.

————. *Uno, nessuno e centomila*. Milano: Einaudi, 2014.

Pitrè, Giuseppe. *Fiabe, novelle e racconti siciliani*, ed. Jack Zipes. Firenze: Donzelli, 2013.

————. *Usi e costumi, credenze e pregiudizi del popolo Siciliano*, vol. III. Firenze: G. Barbera,1952.

Pitrè, Giuseppe and Leonardo Sciascia. *Urla senza suono. Graffiti e disegni dei prigionieri dell'Inquisizione*. Palermo: Sellerio, 1999.

Plastino, Goffredo. *Cosa Nostra Social Club. Mafia, malavita e musica in Italia*. Milano: Il Saggiatore, 2014.

Plato. *Gorgias*, trans. Terence Irwin. Oxford: Oxford University Press, 1979.

————. *The Platonic Epistles*, trans. J. Harward. Cambridge: Cambridge University Press, 1932.

————. *The Republic*, trans. Desmond Lee. London: Penguin, 2013.

Plutarch. *Lives*, vol. VI, trans. Bernadotte Perrin. Cambridge: Harvard University Press, 1954.

Polybius. *The Histories*, trans. Robin Waterfield. New York: Oxford University Press, 2010.

Powell, James M., ed. and trans. *The Liber Augustalis or Constitutions of Melfi Promulgated by the Emperor Frederick II for the Kingdom of Sicily in 1231.* New York: Syracuse University Press, 1971.

Procida, John of. *Sicily's Rebellion against King Charles*, trans. Louis Mendola. New York: Trinacria, 2015, p. 117.

Ptolemy. *Ptolemy's Almagest*, ed. and trans. G. J. Toomer. New Jersey: Princeton University Press, 1998.

Quartarone, Carla. *Sicilia Romana e Bizantina.* Palermo: Grafill, 2006.

Quasimodo, Salvatore. *La vita non è sogno.* Milano: Mondadori, 1949.

————. *The Selected Writings of Salvatore Quasimodo*, trans. Allen Mandelbaum. Toronto: Mondadori, 1960.

Quatriglio, Giuseppe. *A Thousand Years in Sicily: From the Arabs to Bourbons.* Ottawa: Legas, 1985.

Reale, Claudio. 'Diciotti, Miccichè contro Salvini: "Sei uno str...".' Cancelleri all'attacco: "Fi supera il Pd a sinistra"'. *La Repubblica*, 24 August 2018.

Renda, Francesco. *I Beati Paoli: storia, letteratura e leggenda.* Palermo: Sellerio, 1988.

————. *I fasci siciliani: 1892–94.* Torino: Einaudi, 1977.

————. *L'emigrazione in Sicilia 1652–1961.* Caltanissetta and Roma: Salvatore Sciascia Editore, 1989.

————. *L'Inquisizione in Sicilia: i fatti, le persone.* Palermo: Sellerio, 1997.

————. *Movimento di massa e democrazie: nella Sicilia del dopoguerra.* Bari: De Donato, 1979.

————. *Storia della Sicilia* vol. II. *Da Federico III a Garibaldi.* Palermo: Sellerio, 2007.

————. *Storia della Sicilia dal 1860 al 1970* vols. I–III. Palermo: Selleri, 1999.

Resnick, Irven M. *Writings against the Saracens: Peter the Venerable.* Washington, DC: Catholic University of America Press, 2016.

Riall, Lucy. *La rivolta, Bronte 1860*, trans. David Scaffei. Roma and Bari: Laterza, 2012.

———. *La Sicilia e l'unificazione italiana: politica liberale e potere locale*. Milano: Einaudi, 1998, p. 249.

———. *Under the Volcano: Revolution in a Sicilian Town*. New York: Oxford University Press, 2013.

Rossi, Adolfo. *L'agitazione in Sicilia. A proposito delle ultime condanne*. Milano: Max Kantorowicz, 1894.

———. 'La Situazione in Sicilia: Le notizie giunte finora sull' organizzazione dei Fasci. Le donne'. *La Tribuna*, 8 October 1893.

Runciman, Steven. *I vespri siciliani*. Milano: Rizzoli, 1976.

Ruskin, John. *The Complete Works* vol. 21, 'The Pleasures of England'. New York: The Kelmscott Society, 1885.

Ruta, Anna Maria. *Il futurismo in Sicilia: per una storia dell'avanguardia letteraria*. Gioiosa Marea: Pungitopo, 1991.

Ruta, Anna Maria and Ettore Sessa. *I caffe' storici di Palermo: dalle origini agli anni settanta*. Palermo: Dario Flaccovio Editore, 2003.

Sanfilippo, Matteo. *Emigrazione e storia d'Italia*. Cosenza: Luigi Pellegrini, 2003, pp. 157–8.

Sanguineti, Edoardo, ed. *Sonetti della scuola siciliana*. Milano: Einaudi, 1965.

Santangelo, Giorgio. *Letteratura in Sicilia da Federico II a Pirandello*. Palermo: S. F. Flaccovio Editore, 1976.

Santino, Umberto. *La democrazia bloccata: La strage di Portella della Ginestra e l'emarginazione delle sinistre*. Soveria Mannelli: Rubbettino, 1997.

Savatteri, Gaetano. *I siciliani*. Bari: Laterza, 2017.

———. *Non c'è più la Sicilia di una volta*. Bari: Laterza, 2017.

Scianna, Ferdinando. *Altre forme del chaos*. Roma: Contrasto, 2000.

Sciascia, Leonardo. *A ciascuno il suo*. Milano: Adelphi, 2002.

———. *Candido ovvero un sogno fatto in Sicilia*. Milano: Adelphi, 1990.

————. *Gli ʒii di Sicilia*. Milano: Adelphi, 2013.

————. *Il giorno della civetta*. Milano: Adelphi, 2002.

————. *Il mare colore del vino*. Milano: Adelphi, 1996.

————. 'I professionisti dell'antimafia'. *Corriere della Sera*, 10 January 1987.

————. *La corda paʒʒa: Scrittori e cose della Sicilia*. Milano: Adelphi, 2007.

————. *La Sicilia come metafora*. Milano: Mondadori, 1989.

————, ed. *La noia e l'offesa: il fascismo e gli scrittori siciliani*. Palermo: Sellerio, 1991.

————. *Nero su Nero*. Milano: Adelphi, 1991.

Scolè, Pierluigi. 'I morti' in *Diʒionario Storico della Prima Guerra Mondiale*, ed. Nicola Labanca. Bari: Laterza, 2014.

Scott, Susan and Christopher J. Duncan. *Biology of Plagues: Evidence from Historical Populations*. Cambridge: Cambridge University Press, 2001.

Sgalambro, Manlio and Franco Battiato. *Il cavaliere dell'intelletto. Libretto dell'Opera in due atti*. Milano: Sonzogno, 1994.

Shaw, Brent D. *Spartacus and the Slave Wars*. London and New York: Palgrave Macmillan, 2001.

Shringarpure, Bhakti, Michael Busch, Michael Bronner, Veruska Cantelli, Melissa Smyth, Jessica Rohan, Gareth Davies, Jason Huettner, Noam Scheindlin, eds. *Mediterranean: Warscapes*. 2017.

Siculo, Diodoro. *La rivolta degli schiavi in Sicilia*. Palermo: Sellerio, 1999.

Soraci, Cristina. *Sicilia frumentaria: contributi allo studio della Sicilia in epoca repubblicana*. Catania: Libreria Culc, 2003.

Spica, Giusi. 'Forconi, blocchi vietati. "Ci faremo arrestare" Trovato un volantino shock: "Viva la mafia"'. *La Repubblica*, 7 December 2013.

Stagni, Virginia. 'Cultura e valorizzazione in Sicilia. Intervista al Presidente Rosario Crocetta'. *La Stampa*, 20 August 2015.

Stewart, Edmund. *Greek Tragedy on the Move: The Birth of a Panhellenic Art Form c. 500–300 BC*. New York: Oxford University Press, 2017.

Strabo. *Geography*, trans. Horace L. Jones. Cambridge: Harvard University Press, 1924.

Sucato, Ignazio. *La Lingua Siciliana: origine e storia*. Palermo: La Via, 1975.

Tarozzi, Giuseppe. *Made in Italy. Storia della mafia in America*. Milano: Bompiani, 1973.

Tedesco, Natale. *Viaggi in Sicilia: arte, cinema, teatro*. Roma: Bonanno, 2005.

Tempio, Domenico. *La Carestia: Poema epico*, trans. Francesco Belfiore. Canterano: Aracne, 2017.

Terranova, Nadia. *Gli anni al contrario*. Milano: Einaudi, 2016.

Testa, Tiziana. 'I sindaci contro il dl sicurezza. Orlando e De Magistris: "Non lo applichiamo". Salvini: "Ne risponderanno legalmente"'. *La Repubblica*, 2 January 2019.

Theocritus. *The Idylls*, vol. 16, trans. Robert Wells. Manchester: Carcanet Press, 1988.

Thonemann, Peter. *The Hellenistic Age*. Oxford: Oxford University Press, 2016.

Thucydides. *The Peloponnesian War*, trans. Martin Hammond. New York: Oxford University Press, 2009.

Tilbury, Gervase of. *Otia Imperialia. Recreation of an Emperor*, ed. and trans. S. E. Banks and J. W. Binns. New York: Oxford University Press, 2002.

Titone, Virgilio. *Sicilia e Spagna*. Palermo: Novecento, 1998.

Tocco, Elio. *Guida alla Sicilia che scompare*. Milano: Sugar, 1969.

Tocco, Francesco Paolo. *Il regno di Sicilia tra Angionini e Aragonesi*. Milano: Monduzzi, 2008.

Tondo, Lorenzo. '"They are our salvation": the Sicilian town revived by refugees'. *The Guardian*, 19 March 2018.

Tramontana, Salvatore. *L'isola di Allah*. Milano: Einaudi, 2014.

Trilling, Daniel. *Lights in the Distance: Exile and Refuge at the Borders of Europe*. London: Picador, 2018.

————. 'Five Myths about the refugee crisis'. *The Guardian*, 5 June 2018.

Valera, Paolo. *L'assassinio Notarbartolo, o, Le gesta della mafia*. San Cesario di Lecce: Manni, 2006.

Vasari, Giorgio. *The Lives of the Artists*, trans. Julia Bondanella and Peter Bondanella. New York: Oxford University Press, 1991.

————. *Vite de'più eccellenti pittori, scultori e architetti*, vol. 11. Siena: Pazzini Carli e Compagno, 1794.

————. *Il tempo materiale*. Roma: minimum fax, 2010.

Vaughan, Richard. *Matthew Paris*. Cambridge: Cambridge University Press, 1979.

Verga, Giovanni. *I Malavoglia*. Firenze: Giunti, 2012.

————. *Little Novels of Sicily*, trans. D. H. Lawrence. New York: Thomas Seltzer, 1925.

————. *Tutte le novelle*. Milano: Rizzoli (Collana Radici BUR), 2008.

Wærn, Cecilia. *Mediæval Sicily, Aspects of Life and Art in the Middle Ages*. London: Duckworth and Co., 1910.

Wardy, Robert. *The Birth of Rhetoric. Gorgias, Plato and Their Successors*. London and New York: Routledge, 1996.

Willan, Philip. 'Mafia supergrass fingers Berlusconi'. *The Guardian*, 12 January 2003.

Yehoshua, Abraham B. 'Può nascere in Sicilia la comunità del Mediterraneo'. *La Stampa*, 21 July 2017.

Zeldes, Nadia. 'Auto de Fe in Palermo, 1511. The First Executions of Judaizers in Sicily' in *Revue de l'histoire des religions* 219, no. 2, 2002, pp. 193–226.

Zipes, Jack. *Catarina the Wise and Other Wondrous Sicilian Folk and Fairy Tales*. Chicago and London: Chicago University Press, 2017.

Films

Belluscone una storia siciliana. Directed by Franco Maresco. Ila Palma, Dream Film, Sicilia Consulenza, Frenesy Film Company, Avventurosa, Lemur Films, 2014.

Cinema Paradiso. Directed by Giuseppe Tornatore. Cristaldifilm, Les Films Ariane, Rai 3, TF1 Films Production, Forum Picture, 1988.

Cinico TV. Directed by Daniele Ciprì and Franco Maresco. Rai 3, 1992–96.

Clouds Over Sidra. Directed by Directed by Gabo Arora and Barry Pousman. VRSE.works, 2015.

I cavalieri dalle maschere nere (I beati paoli). Directed by Pino Mercanti. O.F.S., 1947.

I cento Passi. Directed by Marco Tullio Giordana. Rai Cinema, Tele+, Titti Film, Ministero per i Beni e le Attività Culturali, 2000.

Il gattopardo. Directed by Luchino Visconti. Titanus, Société Nouvelle Pathé Cinéma, Société Générale de Cinématographie, 1963.

Kaos. Directed by Paolo and Vittorio Taviani. Filmtre, Rai 1, 1984.

The Godfather. Directed by Francis Ford Coppola. Paramount Pictures, Alfran Productions, 1972.

The Sicilian. Directed by Michael Cimino. Gladden Entertainment, 1987.

Totò che visse due volte. Directed by Daniele Ciprì and Franco Maresco. Tea Nova, Lucky Red, Istituto Luce, 1998.

Videocracy. Directed by Erik Gandini. Atmo Media Network, Zentropa Entertainments, Sveriges Television, BBC Storyville, Danmarks Radio, YLE Co-Productions, Swedish Film Institute, Det Danske Filminstitut, Nordisk Film- & TV-Fond, MEDIA Programme of the European Union, 2009.

Newspaper Editorials

'Aquarius, da Napoli a Palermo i sindaci contro Salvini: "I nostri porti sono aperti. È senza cuore e viola le norme"'. *Il fatto quotidiano*, 10 June 2010.

'Come si diventa milionari negli Stati Uniti'. *La Domenica del Corriere*, 20 July 1902.

'Editorial'. *Corriere della Sera*, 9–10 January 1900.

'Editorial'. *The Times* of London, 17 January 1928.

'Editorial'. *Time*, 17 July 1950.

'La motivazione ufficiale: blasfemo e sacrilego'. *La Repubblica*, 4 March 1998.

'Executioner'. *Time*, 30 April 1951.

La difesa della razza 1, no. 1, 1938.

'Le miserie dell'emigrazione. Gli italiani a New York'. *La Domenica del Corriere*, 29 January 1905.

'On the Sulphur Trade of Sicily, and the Commercial Relations between that Country and Great Britain' in *Journal of the Statistical Society of London* 2, no. 6, January 1840.

Terrore mafioso: Palermo come Beirut'. *L'Unità*, 30 July 1983.

Archive Materials

Archivio Centrale dello Stato, *'L'inchiesta sulle condizioni sociali ed economiche della Sicilia 1875–1876'* vol. II, eds S. Carbone and R. Crispo, Bologna: 1969.

Document 4, *Prefettura Gabinetto, b.77. c.1672*, Archivio di Stato di Catania (ADSDC).

Emerico Amari's speech in *Atti di Parlamento italiano, Discussioni della Camera dei Deputati 5 aprile 1861*, p. 419.

Le compagne I compagni: il movimento del'77 a Palermo. Palermo: Cooperative editorial centofiori, 1988.

'Partito Socialista Siciliano. Comitato Centrale. Lavoratori della Sicilia!' in *Lotta di Classe*, 13–14 January 1894, no. 2.

Presidenza della Regione Siciliana, Elezioni in Sicilia: Dati e grafici dal 1946 al 1956. Milan: A. Giuffre, 1956.

'Rapporto Sangiorgi' in Archivio Centrale dello Stato, DGPS aa.gg, Atti speciali 1898–1940, b. 1, f. 1.

The Athenæum, Journal of Literature, Science, and the Fine Arts, no. 979. London: Holmes, 1846.

Digital Sources

Archivio degli Iblei. 'Il grande terremoto del 1693'. Grazia Ruffino in conversation with Marcella Burderi, archiviodegliible.it.

Caccia, Giuseppe. 'From the Centre of the Mediterranean: "Freedom of Movement as a Human Right"', PoliticalCritique.org, 9 June 2017.

Crispi, Francesco. 'A' suoi amici di Sicilia Francesco Crispi già deputato al Parlamento'. Digitised by Google Play Books.

Dipartimento per gli Affari Interni e Territoriali. Risultati Referendum, 2 June 1946, elezionistorico.interno.gov.it.

Eurostat. 'Unemployment in the EU Regions in 2017', ec.europa.eu.

Federico, Giovanni, Alessandro Nuvolari and Michelangelo Vasta. 'The Origins of the Italian Regional Divide: Evidence from Real Wages, 1861–1913'. Conference paper, EH-TUNE Economic History Workshop, Siena, 2016. Digitised September 2017. siecon.org/sites/siecon.org/files/oldfiles/uploads/2017/04/Vasta.pdf

Il Sole 24. 'Andrea Camilleri', ilsole24ore.it.

International Organization on Migration. 'IOM Applauds Italy's Life-Saving Mare Nostrum Operation: "Not a Migrant Pull Factor"'. IOM.int press release, 31 October 2014.

Istituto Nazionale di Geofisica e Vulcanologia, emidius.mi.ingv.it/CPTI15-DBMI15/query_eq/

Istituto Nazionale di Statistica. 'Povertà in Italia, 2018, istat.it/it/files//2018/06/La-povert%C3%A0-in-Italia-2017.pdf

Magnum Photos. Ferdinando Scianna – Dutch model, MARPESSA, photographed for Dolce & Gabbana, 1987, Promagnumphotos.com.

Manifesta12 curatorial concept. 'The Planetary Garden. Cultivating Coexistence'. Bregtje van der Haak, Andrés Jaque, Ippolito Pestellini Laparelli and Mirjam Varadinis, M12.manifesta.org.

'Movimento dei Forconi lancia la protesta siciliana: bloccheremo la Sicilia'. YouTube, 16 January 2012.

Muhammad al-Idrisi, the Kitab Rudjdjar. Digitised by the Bibliothèque nationale de France, gallica.bnf.fr.

Municipality of Palermo. 'Carta di Palermo 2015'. Comune.palermo.it.

————. 'Verde e Vivibilità Urbana – Giardini pubblici e spazi verdi', Comune.palermo.it.

Pietropaolo, Damiano. 'The Wonder of the World: Frederick II, Part 1'. CBC.ca podcast, 13 July 2015.

'Soldier's Guide to Sicily'. Digitised by museosicilia1943.it. museosicilia1943.it/site/wp-content/uploads/2014/06/SOLDERS-GUIDE-to-SICILY1.pdf

SOS Impresa. 'Le mani della criminalità sulle imprese'. sosimpresa. it/userFiles/File/Documenti%201/Microsoft_Word_-_Progress _2007_Lino_Bus_.pdf

The Assizes of King Roger (Cod. Vat. Lat. 8782). Digitised by Leeds University. www2.hawaii.edu/~kjolly/Assizes%20of%20King%20 Roger.htm

The Sicilian Constitution of 1812. Digitised by Harvard University. babel.hathitrust.org/cgi/pt?id=hvd.hnpmlt;view=1up;seq=9

University of Catania. 'La nostra storia', Unict.it.

Index

INVENTION OF SICILY